AMERICAN
FOREIGN POLICY

AMERICAN FOREIGN POLICY

ASSUMPTIONS, PROCESSES, AND PROJECTIONS

Ronald J. Stupak

Miami University at Oxford, Ohio
and the Federal Executive Institute

Harper & Row, Publishers
New York,   Evanston,   San Francisco,   London

To Dolores and Valeska

. . . I love them both so very much.

Sponsoring Editor: Ronald K. Taylor
Project Editor: Holly Detgen
Designer: Andrea Clark
Production Supervisor: Will C. Jomarrón
Compositor: Bi-Comp, Inc.
Printer and Binder: The Murray Printing Company

AMERICAN FOREIGN POLICY: Assumptions, Processes, and Projections

Library of Congress Cataloging in Publication Data
Stupak, Ronald J   1934–
    American foreign policy—assumptions, processes, and projections.

    Bibliography: p.
    Includes index.
    1.   United States—Foreign relations—1945–
I.   Title.
JX1417.S7   327.73   75-14137
ISBN 0-06-046501-8

CONTENTS

The Religion of Realism and the Truman Administration: An Analysis of the "Creation Years" of Contemporary American Foreign Policy   71

The United States and Its "World Policeman" Period: Superactivism and the Use of American Combat Troops   121

VII The Bankruptcy of Superactivism and the Resurgence of Diplomacy and the Department of State: An Interpretive Projection   162

Appendixes

PREFACE

There could probably be no more propitious time to be writing a book on U.S. foreign policy; at the same time, paradoxically, it is also one of the most vulnerable times for the scholar to attempt to explain how foreign policy is made in the United States.

A fundamental reevaluation seems to be taking place in the American political community concerning the philosophical bases of the nation's involvement in the international system, as to the constitutional dimensions of who makes (or controls) foreign policy and the role of the United States in terms of its leadership "obligations" in the post-Vietnam environment. And because, ultimately, a conviction is emerging among a growing portion of academics and policymakers that the Cold War is being phased out and that the old "East-West" bipolarism of the post-World War II period is dead. In addition, an environment of policymaking ambiguity is being encountered as Watergate and its fallout are muddying the waters of presidential power, diplomatic consistency, and the linkages between the foreign and domestic policymaking processes.

On a more theoretical level, there is a growing methodological sophistication surfacing in the study of foreign policymaking. From James Rosenau's "linkages concept"[1] and David Wilkinson's comparative foreign policy framework[2] to the research efforts of such groups as the foreign policy events data scholars at Ohio State and the CARE

---

[1] James N. Rosenau, ed., *Linkage Politics* (New York: Free Press, 1969).
[2] David O. Wilkinson, *Comparative Foreign Relations: Framework and Methods* (Belmont, Calif.: Dickenson, 1969).

events data analysis of Lincoln Bloomfield and his M.I.T. associates,[3] there are increasingly sophisticated attempts to analyze the foreign policy process empirically and scientifically. For despite the well-established history of scholarship in foreign policy, it still remains a field in its infancy with respect to scientific methods of inquiry—in part because of the lack of attention to the development of behavioral measures with more empirical and theoretical import.[4] And yet, even though these efforts are in their embryonic stages, they nonetheless demonstrate that the discipline may be on the threshold of some major methodological revolutions. Hence, any attempt from the traditional textbook format simply becomes more grist for the mills of those of us who are looking for different and more effective techniques by which to analyze foreign policy in the United States and elsewhere.

Essentially, on both a practical, substantive level and on an abstract theoretical level, the foreign policymaking arena is in flux. The hard-and-fast rules of bipolarism, East-West analysis, and the Cold War framework no longer hold the magic they once held in the pre-Vietnam period. At the same time the Morgenthau "realist concept,"[5] the Snyder et al. "decision-making approach,"[6] and the "Cold War Historian" analyses[7] no longer need to be rigidly adhered to. With policymakers and ivory-tower academics alike having second thoughts about their respective frameworks of analysis, it is a challenge and source of enjoyment to write a book that attempts to describe, analyze, and project U.S. foreign policy because with any luck one might add something novel—maybe even suggest something important and innovative for foreign policy analysis at this crucial junction in American history.

Put simply, it is an exciting and critical period for American foreign policy as we move beyond Vietnam into the current period of SALT agreements and the Nixon Doctrine toward internal and external political readjustments exemplified by the emergence of the People's

---

[3] For an example of these approaches, see *Leads and Lags*, the newsletter of the International Studies Association Study Group on Foreign Policy and International Events.

[4] Charles F. Hermann, "Some Conceptualizations of Foreign Behavior Compatible with Events Data," *Leads and Lags* (March 1974), p. 13.

[5] Hans J. Morgenthau, *Politics Among Nations*, 4th ed. (New York: Knopf, 1967).

[6] Richard C. Snyder, H. W. Bruck, and Burton Sapin, eds., *Foreign Policy Decision-Making* (New York: Free Press, 1962).

[7] For an example, see Norman A. Graebner, *Cold War Diplomacy: American Foreign Policy, 1945–1960* (New York: Van Nostrand Reinhold, 1962).

Republic of China and the glimmering of an evolving multipolar international environment. Thus, I welcome the opportunity which this book affords to comment upon U.S. foreign policy in this time of transition and readjustment, using essentially an eclectic approach based on power and strategic dimensions, rather than the more traditional "balanced descriptive-theoretical" textbook approach. This is done consciously in order to immerse the beginning foreign policy student in the real-world dimensions of American foreign policy and in order to raise classroom interest and controversy within a "teaching-stimulating" framework. In other words, the foreign policy environment will be analyzed through the lenses of a scholar who has certain personal, substantive, and methodological interpretations of what happened, is happening, and will happen in American foreign policy. The hope is that this book will add something different and useful to the academic study of foreign policy while at the same time stimulating controversy and opinions which will make it a catalyst for classroom discussions on college and university campuses across the nation. In effect, selective perceptions, rather than encyclopedic renditions, govern the analysis of the issues, problems, institutions, and situations covered within the framework of this book.

Sincere thanks to Dolores Stupak, William Quigley, David McLellan, Walter Busse, Terry Busch, Holly Duncan, Richard Herrmann, Jeff Krans, Haider Mehdi, Otteno Okelo, Robert Parrish, and Milton Potten, Jr., for their assistance in the writing of this book. A special thanks to the publishers of *Foreign Affairs, Social Science,* and *United Asia* and to the Bobbs-Merrill Company, Inc. and the Odyssey Press for allowing me to use materials that were first published in somewhat different form in their pages. And finally, my sincere appreciation to Liz Pantle, Karen Muth, and Jean West for their secretarial assistance. All these people, along with "my buddy," Patty Wallendjack, made this an easier venture than I ever thought it could possibly be. I owe them, Miami University, and the Federal Executive Institute so very much; but, of course, I alone take full responsibility for the text.

INTRODUCTION

No nation lives unto itself, except in fancy. No nation is without neighbors, however isolated its geographic position might be. For better or for worse, every nation is obliged to discover ways to get along with those on the other side of its borders. Thus, every nation has a foreign policy. To create and manage such a policy is essential to its existence as an independent state in an international system dominated by the power, prestige, and influence of nation-states with different cultural experiences, historical traditions, institutional structures, national goals, and political aspirations. As long as there is no universal agreement as to the moral, ethical, and legal codes which might govern the behavior of nation-states toward one another, tensions will persist, conflicts of interest will arise which will have to be tolerated, accommodated, and resolved. Hence, a nation's reactions to other nations will continue to dominate the abstract analyses of academics and the operational policies of decision makers, even in this 1970s world of growing interdependence and transnational linkages. This means that nation-states and their foreign policy will continue to be explained in the continuing and interlocking tensions of domestic and foreign realities. For, clearly, the internal conditions of a nation will always affect its external relations, and vice versa. Of course, the emphasis placed on internal vis-à-vis external factors (and vice versa) will color the thrust of any analysis. And yet, it is the internal decision-making dimensions that are essential to the understanding of how foreign policy is made in the United States.

The interaction of the external factors cannot be overlooked, but for the goals of this book, the major emphasis is given to the internal policymaking dimensions of the American political system as it pursues its objectives, strategies, and tactics in the international system. That is to say, in effect, that this book places as much emphasis upon intranational factors as it does upon the more traditional external foreign relations factors in explaining U.S. behavior in the international system. What the United States did, is doing, or will do is largely understood as the result of bargaining among internal policy actors positioned institutionally and hierarchically, formally and informally, in the federal governmental structure. And these institutional policy actors must be cognizant of the extrainstitutional factors such as pressure groups, the mass media, national and multinational corporations, ethnic groups, and ideological movements. Foreign policy is better understood through this two-level framework, rather than through the more traditional approach of looking at a nation-state as a monolithic actor making autonomous rational decisions in an international system of other rational autonomous nation-state actors.

It is therefore essential that we recognize that the people who make decisions and determine policy for nation-states do not respond necessarily to the objective facts of a situation and the international environment. It is what a nation's decision makers think the world is like, not what it is really like, that determines their behavior and essentially the output of the policy process which becomes identified as a nation's foreign policy.[1] It will help us to remember throughout the analysis in this book that no one factor alone is responsible for structuring the foreign policy of a nation: therefore, fundamental national values, strategic debates, role definitions, bureaucratic conflicts, and the variables of the American civic culture intersect and conflict in the foreign policy arena before final policy output is established. In sum, foreign policy is not the outcome of a rational, calculating policy machine; rather, it is the end result of a tough, competitive battle in both an internal national political process and an external international political arena.

In essence, then, the groundwork for an understanding of U.S. foreign policy must be laid by: (1) describing the historical precedents and philosophical roots at the base of the American political system; (2) analyzing the nature of the constitutional and institutional

---

[1] Kenneth E. Boulding, "National Images and International Systems," in James N. Rosenau, ed., *International Politics and Foreign Policy* (New York: Free Press, 1961), p. 391.

structures which are the action channels and set the rule parameters within which foreign policy is formally made; and (3) explaining the tremendous impacts of external forces on the American foreign policy process in the post-World War II international environment of the nuclear age.

Foreign policymaking in the American political system can only be conceptually understood and substantively analyzed once the philosophical guidelines, legal parameters, bureaucratic interests, and personal actors are investigated and described in a broad historical contextual framework.

THE AMERICAN HERITAGE IN FOREIGN AFFAIRS
National Style in the Philosophical Context

Reduced to its most fundamental ingredients, foreign policy consists of two elements: first, national objectives to be achieved; and second, the means of achieving them. Hence, it is essential to have an understanding of the culture of the American political system because it is from this culture in terms of customs, historical experiences, and philosophical beliefs that the short-term, and especially the long-term, objectives of American foreign policy are forged. And even though situations and circumstances may change, there tends to be a thread of durability and persistence in the ideas and ideals that shape any nation's desires and actions. In addition, the concept of national style is an essential framework from which policymakers offer generalizations about the actions of their internal audience as well as their external friends and adversaries. Hence, an analysis of the American heritage in foreign affairs is vital to an understanding of the strengths and weaknesses as well as the protean and confining dimensions of the American foreign policy environment.

Furthermore, an understanding of the cultural environment allows one to see the gaps between declarative statements and the operational actions of American foreign policymakers in the contemporary period of national disillusionment and international transformation. In essence, even though noble objectives are not always helpful guides to policy, it is essential to understand the perceptual lenses through which American policymakers view the world in terms of philosophical beliefs, as well as understanding the multiple psychological and sociological determinants of the American foreign policymakers and their domestic constituents.

The net consequences of the interaction of the most diverse psychological, sociological, and cultural inputs is the existence of recognizable value systems—genetically derivative from the total cultural context, and of inestimable significance for the operational setting in which hard decisions are made. The value systems: (1) determine the relevance of the various elements of the practical environment; (2) assist in the formation of the psychological one; (3) form what could be called the vision of the good life; (4) determine the principles of behavior in terms of objectives, goals, and ends of foreign policy; and (5) structure the guidelines within which the means and instrumentalities in terms of institutions and tactics are chosen.

The uniqueness of the American experience, its geographic isolation, its humanitarianism, and its basic moralism all have combined to frame the national style of American foreign policy.

ISOLATIONISM: THE NEW WORLD

Traditionally, American foreign policy was supported by geographic isolation. Away from the Old World and separated by a vast ocean, the Americans laid the foundations of a new nation. They visioned a new world and dreamed of a new society. To the new immigrants, the old world of Europe was full of turmoil, hopelessness, and bigotry. They wanted to bury it forever, with one objective in mind: to find a new birth, as it were, in a faroff continent.[1]

Not only was it the physical distance that was creating a new world and a new society in America. Emotionally and mentally the Americans divorced all links with Europe. In their vision of new life and of new birth was emerging a theme of cultural separation that pervaded American literature during the nineteenth century.

[1] For a detailed discussion, see Arthur A. Ekirch, Jr., *Ideas, Ideals, and American Diplomacy: A History of Their Growth and Interaction* (New York: Appleton, 1966), pp. 22–39. It should be noted that many of the general assumptions undergirding this chapter are based on the following books: Robert H. Ferrell, *American Diplomacy* (New York: Norton, 1959); Samuel Flagg Bemis, *The Diplomacy of the American Revolution* (Bloomington, Ind.: Indiana University Press, 1957); Joyce and Gabriel Kolko, *The Limits of Power* (New York: Harper & Row, 1972); and Thomas A. Bailey, *A Diplomatic History of the American People* (New York: Appleton, 1955).

James Russell Lowell wrote in "A Fable for Critics":

> Forget Europe wholly,
> your veins throb with blood,
> To which the dull current
> in hers is but mud; . . .
> O my friends, thank you God
> if you have one, that he
> Twixt the Old World and you
> Sets a gulf of a sea; . . .
> To your own New World instincts
> contrive to be true. . . .[2]

This type of thought had deep psychological effects on the American outlook of life. Filled up to the brim like a cup of wine, the Americans sipped the joy and pleasure of constructing a new society. For them it was their only chance and they were inspired, they had broken the old chains and the sun was rising on new horizons—the land was plenty and zeal for betterment and success overwhelming. They had escaped the political intrigues and conflicts witnessed on the continent of Europe and it was a time and place of peace, prosperity, and creativity. Americans diverted all their energies, thoughts, and ambitions inward. Americans devoted themselves passionately to the theory of progress that "civilization has moved, is moving, and will move in a desirable direction."[3] The idea of progress settled deep in American thought and they blended this concept with pragmatism. Human solutions were applied to human problems and out of this conception developed the concepts of individualism, freedom, free enterprise, and liberty. Thus, the American mind rejected the idea of political and ecclesiastical authoritarianism, predicted a great leap ahead for mankind in America, and saw the key to progress in science and its applications to human problems. Americans were feverishly creating out of their seemingly unlimited resources vast wealth and expanding opportunities for all. They were solving the age-old problems of unemployment, unequal distribution of land, religious liberty, illiteracy, political oppression, inequitable distribution of wealth, and hereditary rights.

"Isolationism thus derived as much from the dominant concern of the American society with domestic affairs as it did from a deliber-

---

[2] Russel B. Nye, *This Almost Chosen People* (East Lansing, Mich.: Michigan State University Press, 1966), p. 184, quoting James Russell Lowell.
[3] Ibid., p. 1.

ate rejection of foreign entanglements,"[4] The achievement of virtually every goal associated with the American dream demanded that internal interests receive primary attention. This fact prompted one of the nation's leading modern historians, Charles A. Beard, to prefer the term "continentalism," rather than isolationism, to characterize the nation's historic orientation in foreign policy.[5] The contemporary American observer Max Lerner elaborated on Beard's idea: "It was not so much a question of cutting America off from the world as it was of rounding out and fully exploiting the part of the world that was America."[6]

Isolationism, therefore, was not merely the desire to avoid foreign entanglement. It was a much deeper phenomenon which reflected above all a habit of mind, a cluster of national attitudes, a feeling of spiritual separation from other countries, especially Europe, with roots penetrating deeply into the nation's heritage and experience. Isolationism reflected the American cultural experience, its philosophy, and what may be called more generally "the American way of life."[7]

Isolationist thinking produced a culture tremendously nationalistic in character. It mixed the romanticism of nationalism with a philosophy of life and gave it a uniquely American flavor and touch. Walt Whitman, America's outstanding poet, wrote a song entitled "I Hear American Singing."

> Thou, too, sail on, O Ship of State!
> Sail on, O Union, strong and great!
> Humanity with all its fears,
> With all the hopes of future years,
> Is hanging breathless on thy fate![8]

Whitman was essentially sharing the same pervasive nationalistic feelings of his fellow Americans. Hans Kohn called the United States the "Universal Nation" in two senses: "First, American institutions, philosophies, and accomplishments have mirrored the hopes of mankind. Second, for over a century, American doors were open to receive anyone and provide all the opportunities to flourish in the best possible conditions of life."[9] Thomas Jefferson expressed this idea when

[4] Cecil V. Crabb, Jr., *American Foreign Policy in the Nuclear Age*, 3rd ed. (New York: Harper & Row, 1972), p. 37.

[5] Ibid., quoting Charles A. Beard.

[6] Max Lerner, *America as a Civilization* (New York: Simon & Schuster, 1957), p. 888, quoted in Crabb, op. cit., p. 37.

[7] Crabb, op. cit., p. 36.

[8] Ibid., p. 37, quoting Walt Whitman.

[9] Ibid., p. 38, quoting Hans Kohn.

he wrote that the American mission was:

> to consecrate a sanctuary for those whom the
> misrule of Europe may compel to seek happiness
> in other climes. This refuge once known will
> produce reaction on the happiness even of those
> who remain there, by warning their taskmasters
> that when the evils of Egyptian oppression become
> heavier than those of the abandonment of country,
> another Canaan is open where their subjects will
> be received as brothers. . . .[10]

Ralph Waldo Emerson was convinced that "Our whole history appears like a last effort of the Divine Providence in behalf of the human race.[11] And in 1839, John Louis O'Sullivan wrote:

> Our national birth was the beginning of a new history, the formation and progress of an untried political system, which separates us from the past and connects us with the future only; so far as regards the entire development of the rights of man, in morals, political and national life, we may confidently assume that our country is destined to be the great nation of futurity.[12]

The historical experience, the theme of building a great society within America, and the emphasis on preserving freedom of action at home all called for an isolationist foreign policy. America demanded that the Old World keep out of the New and, in turn, the United States would forego intervention in the affairs of other regions. Americans remembered George Washington's farewell address, which included a solemn warning against unnecessary alliances. Later, the Monroe Doctrine was proclaimed and Americans adopted isolationism as a philosophy of national character.

The isolationist philosophy, the theory of progress, mounting success, and strong nationalist feelings created in the American mind a sense of pride and superiority. Here was a people blessed by the Almighty. They were the chosen people, entrusted with a mission to lead the world. They were to provide a model and guidance; they had the torch of enlightenment. Dignity, faith, honor, prosperity, and enlightenment were bestowed on them by the will of God and the American mission was to reform the world, to remodel it into their pattern. The salvation of the world was to adopt the "American way of life." Americans believed they were the source of "goodness." One

[10] Ibid., quoting Thomas Jefferson.
[11] Ibid., quoting Ralph Waldo Emerson.
[12] Ibid., quoting John Lewis O'Sullivan.

can appreciate that a perfectly understandable set of circumstances provided the impulse to create a sense of moralistic mission in the American outlook.

THE AMERICAN MISSION

The sense of mission was also the outcome of the search by Americans for a precise definition of their national purpose and the development of an American ideology. After all, this was a young country full of nationalistic enthusiasm and it was felt that the development of a conviction of national purpose was an historical necessity. In the first place, it provided a basis for continuity for a new nation which had no developed historic past.[13] Second, it established a concept in which the American could define the meaning of his life and his institutions, and set goals for his purpose and destination.

This conviction of mission also provided grounds to incorporate religion into the new American ideology. This combination supported the basic American concept of liberty and freedom in all spheres of life. Religious tolerance was being assimilated in a new political environment and it was the beginning of a new pluralistic democratic society.

Strong religious convictions and a sense of mission developed a deep belief that the American people were divinely designed for certain great achievements. Herman Melville wrote: "And we Americans are peculiar, chosen people, the Israel of our times; we bear the ark of the liberties of the world."[14] Edward Johnson in 1630 saw the new country as "the place where the Lord will create a new Heaven, and a new Earth, new churches, and a new commonwealth together."[15] Jedidiah Morse, the scientist and historian, wrote in 1789:

> Here [America] the sciences and the arts of civilized life are to receive their highest improvement. Here civil and religious liberty are to flourish, unchecked by the cruel hand of civil or ecclesiastical tyranny.

[13] For a detailed discussion see Nye, op. cit., pp. 1–40; also Stow Person, *American Minds: A History of Ideas* (New York: Holt, Rinehart & Winston, 1958); Ralph H. Gabriel, *The Course of American Democratic Thought* (New York, Ronald, 1940); Morris Ginsberg, *The Idea of Progress* (Westport, Conn.: Greenwood, 1972).

[14] Nye, op. cit., p. 164, quoting Herman Melville.

[15] Ibid., p. 165, quoting Edward Johnson.

Here genius, aided by all the improvements of former ages, is to be exerted in humanizing mankind . . . in expanding and enriching their minds with religious and philosophical knowledge, and in planning and executing a form of government, with as few of their defects as is consistent with the imperfection of human affairs, and which shall be calculated to protect and unite, in a manner consistent with the natural rights of mankind, the largest empire that ever existed.[16]

The mission of America, according to Albert Gallatin was:

to be a model for all other governments and for all other less favoured nations, to adhere to the most elevated principles of political morality . . . , and by [your] example to exert a moral influence most beneficial to mankind.[17]

George Baneroff believed that the United States would eventually "allure the world to freedom by the beauty of its illustration."[18] The Reverend Timothy Dwight believed the United States to be "by Heaven designed, th' example bright, to renovate mankind."[19] Alexander Hamilton believed that the American Revolution set a precedent that would force Europe to "inquiries which may shake it to its deepest foundations."[20] And Jefferson called the American experiment "the last best hope of mankind," and "a barrier against the returns of ignorance and barbarism."[21]

Obviously, the idea of a unique American mission flourishing under such tremendously favorable psychological and political orientations has had an important impact on United States foreign policy. Already blessed by the natural support of the environment of the New World and the automatic security of geographical distance, more credentials were added to the doctrine of a unique American mission by the political and social contributions of the American Revolution. The success of the revolution made the new nation conscious of its unique position as a republic in a world of monarchies. Psychologically, the Americans were well prepared and even anxious to proclaim their political and social concepts to the rest of the world. They were developing liberal political and social institutions and "naturally" were constructing their government with respect for the natural rights of man. In spite of their isolationist inclinations, most Americans felt

[16] Ibid., p. 166, quoting Jedidiah Morse.
[17] Ibid., p. 168, quoting Albert Gallatin.
[18] Ibid., p. 169, quoting George Baneroff.
[19] Ibid., quoting Timothy Dwight.
[20] Ibid., p. 170, quoting Alexander Hamilton.
[21] Ibid., quoting Thomas Jefferson.

a concern and sympathy for foreign people who still suffered under tyrannical governments. In 1782 Benjamin Franklin predicted:

> Establishing the liberties of America will not only make that people happy, but will have some effect in diminishing the misery of those, who in other parts of the world groan under despotism, by rendering it more circumspect, and inducing it to govern with a lighter hand.[22]

John Adams predicted in 1785 that the United States was "destined beyond a doubt to be the greatest power on earth, and that within the life of man."[23]

Thus, the Americans started the formulation of their ideas in foreign relations under the impact of the political notion of a mission. Reformation of less fortunate people was to be at the forefront of this mission of America.

The climax of the Age of Enlightenment coincided with the American Revolution, and liberals across the Atlantic, such as Condorcet, paid glowing tributes to the new republic. This French liberal philosopher said America was living proof of the universal truth of the principles of the Enlightenment, on which human progress depended. He wrote: "it is not enough that the rights of man be written in the books of philosophers and inscribed in the hearts of virtuous men; the weak and ignorant must be able to read them in the example of a great nation. America has given us this example."

Therefore, the outbreak of the French Revolution was seen by Americans in the image of their own glorious revolution. It was the American revolutionary mission that was taking France in its grip and freeing the French people from the yoke of monarchy and setting them on to the path to democracy.

Tom Paine was a militant opponent of tyranny and joined the revolutionary struggle in France. He advocated that the revolution was the logical continuation of the struggle for the rights of man which had been inaugurated in the thirteen colonies. Paine wrote:

> I see in America the generality of people living in a style of plenty unknown in monarchical countries; and I see that the principle of its government, which is that of the equal rights of man, is making rapid progress in the world. . . .[24]

---

[22] A. H. Smyth, ed., *Writings of Benjamin Franklin* (New York, 1905–1907), VIII, 416, cited by Ekirch, op. cit., p. 25.

[23] Ibid., p. 25, quoting John Adams.

[24] Ibid., p. 28, quoting Thomas Paine.

Paine linked the continuity of revolution to the American spirit of liberty and freedom and maintained that America would be the scene of coming reformation of the world. He concluded:

> From the rapid progress which America makes in every species of movement, it is rational to conclude that, if the governments of Asia, Africa, and Europe had begun on a principle similar to that of America, or had not been very early corrupted, therefrom, those countries must by this time have been in a far superior condition to what they are.[25]

Replacement of monarchy by a constitutional regime was regarded as the embodiment of the American spirit and the fulfillment of its liberal teachings.[26]

With the passage of time and the rising tide of liberal trends in Europe, the Americans' faith in their sense of mission was further strengthened. American public opinion swept in favor of the revolt of the Greeks against their Turkish rulers in 1821. American statesmen, including President Monroe, became warm advocates of the Greek cause. Elsewhere in Europe the mass uprisings for national self-determination and political and economic reforms aroused popular feelings and sympathy in the United States. But in the wake of the momentary failure of these revolutionary movements, the American liberals were forced to believe that their mission to advance the cause of world liberty would have to be confined to perfecting the democratic model at home.

However, the doctrine of an American mission continued to have an indirect connection with United States foreign policy. Scientific and technological breakthroughs provided new inputs to the American sense of pride and confidence and enhanced its prestige abroad. The dynamic progress made in the fields of science and industry was having important international significance and adding tremendously to the prestige of America. America was breaking all political, social, economic, and technological barriers to human progress and for more and more people it became the land of promise and opportunity. Perhaps, American techniques of invention and mass production and the increasing reputation of its literature abroad did more to spread American institutions and ideas than any explicit interventionist policy could ever have achieved.

---

[25] Ibid., quoting Thomas Paine.
[26] For more on this, see Louis Hartz, *The Liberal Tradition in America* (New York: Harcourt Brace Jovanovitch, 1955), passim.

MANIFEST DESTINY

Americans believed in the uniqueness of their country and its institutions, and to them the mission was the reflection of this uniqueness. Naturally, psychological implications led to the excessive moralizing of this doctrine; the political consequences were justification of means for ends. It was the impact of moral superiority and the constant evocation of uniqueness that led the American people and especially its leaders to embrace the doctrine of "manifest destiny." Territorial expansion became accepted as part of the faith that America's multiplying missions were manifestly destined to spread their republican institutions into the contiguous areas of Mexico and maybe even Canada.

According to historian Thomas A. Bailey:

> Many factors contributed to the acceptance and implementation of the notion of manifest destiny. Successful experimentation in electricity and telegraph and developing railroad lines made it possible to integrate the Pacific Coast with the rest of America. Secondly, more lands were required for the American pioneers and planters. Thirdly, Texas and Oregon were considered to be rewarding as a fresh start on the way to wealth. Fourthly, [communications improvements] and mass media found a very receptive audience for the expansionist themes and appeal of new democracy. American people believed in the reality of material progress and embraced all opportunities for any such advancement. And above all the notion of manifest destiny found overwhelming thrust in the political personality of Andrew Jackson, who in his own person and career glamorized the spirit of manifest destiny.[27]

The notion of manifest destiny proved a popular and useful phrase for justification and rationalization of the expansionist course of American foreign policy in the 1840s. It reinforced the belief that Americans were a people chosen to spread across the continent. Consequently, manifest destiny conveyed a strong impression that American expansionism was inevitable and providential. A second interpretation linked the idea of progress to the specific terms of a law of natural territorial growth. Third, now under the guiding hand of manifest destiny, new dynamism was added to the doctrines of the American expansionist mission and "holier-than-thou" isolationism. Fourth, by expansionism the American mission to spread democracy was translated into actuality.

[27] For detailed discussion, see Thomas A. Bailey, *The Man in the Street* (New York: Macmillan, 1948), pp. 270–279.

In fact, the idea of manifest destiny was an expression of exaggerated nationalism in American foreign policy. The doctrine not only implied inevitability but placed no barriers of time or place on the process of expansion. Eventually, the concept of manifest destiny was identified with the search for foreign markets and the latent and potential desire to exercise a dominating military and ideological influence in world affairs. Thus, the general philosophy and outlook of manifest destiny became one of the major controlling assumptions underlying American foreign policy in both the nineteenth and twentieth centuries—as the proponents of explicit American involvement in the world continually reared their self-righteous heads.

Americans decided quite early that their country had been blessed with all the attributes needed to make it the final scene in the unfolding drama of a free mankind. So, as the turn of the twentieth century changed the international environment, another major shift took place in the American outlook and the conduct of the foreign policy. This was a time when the major powers seemed to have achieved in large measure a form of international concert or balance. The prospects for peace seemed brighter than ever before. The two Hague Conferences created a sense of confidence in the possibility of world peace despite the continued imperialism, militarism, and navalism of the great nations. European countries were coming more and more into the grip of progressive and democratic movements. Therefore, ideals of peace, formerly linked with isolationism in the United States, now became an intergral part of an expanded concept of American diplomacy. Moreover, the increasingly interventionist cast of United States foreign policy, reminiscent of the old mission idea, illustrated anew the determination of many Americans to encourage the worldwide spread of democracy. Thus, the goals of peace and democracy, which had never been absent from American foreign policy, became in the twentieth century even more important components of that declarative policy.[28]

THE MORAL EXPLANATIONS FOR
INTERNATIONAL INTERVENTIONS

Americans began to search for some moral principles and justification for their increasingly interventionist conduct of international affairs. Psychologically, it was impossible for them to perceive a role

[28] Ekirch, op. cit., p. 102.

without "good" aims and ideals. Politically, the stage had already been reached in which America was involved in international affairs simply because of the reality of its increasing power politics base and expanding economic system. Subsequently, the net effect of Theodore Roosevelt's interventionist and aggressive diplomacy around the world was the maintenance of a strong United States position in Latin America and its monitoring of the continuance of the precarious balance of power among the nations in the Far East and Europe. But Americans maintained that all such foreign policies were conducted in the cause of peace and democracy.[29]

The rapid changes in the international environment, however, presented a paradox. Along with the pursuit of ideals of peace and democracy, for example, went peripheral involvement in war and power politics and the paradox of a growing peace movement in the midst of mounting appropriations for armaments and battleships. For virtually the first time in its history, except in war, the United States began to take very seriously the establishment of a strong military force.[30]

But the moral rhetoric of American foreign policy continued to be the underlying basis of its aims. Exercising its new-found powers, America moved toward world leadership, intervening in the cause of peace and democracy and urging the view that peace must be enforced, if necessary—through what was certainly the ultimate paradox—by war. In this fashion, in a period of only some twenty years, a foreign policy that had been formulated to free Cuba was transfigured, via the Philippines and the Far East and then World War I, into a holy crusade which overwhelmingly began to be seen as a mission to make the world safe for peace and democracy. For such a task the American people felt themselves equipped not only by history but also by the aggressively jingoistic foreign policies asserted in the era from William McKinley to Woodrow Wilson.[31]

IMPERIALISTIC TENDENCIES

Thus, in the period from the turn of the century to America's entrance into World War I, there began to be seen the beginnings of a major shift in the thinking about American foreign policy. "With-

[29] Ibid., p. 102.
[30] Ibid., p. 103.
[31] Ibid.

out yielding their faith in the goals of peace and democracy as main-springs of that policy, the American people became more willing to accept new means to accomplish these ends. The methods of peace through power, and of democracy by intervention and force rather than by example, though not without precedent in American history, came to achieve nevertheless a new degree of official sanction and popular support."[32] Imperialistic ambitions and the passing of a century of relative security meant that military considerations would have to play an increasingly important part in foreign affairs. And, involvement in world politics now also entailed sending American soldiers and sailors as well as missionaries and traders to the far corners of the world.

This moral imperative of U.S. foreign policy found its strongest expression in Wilsonian internationalism. Wilson's ideals were in fact a projection of American nationality into universal terms. To Wilson, American ideals were in perfect harmony with the principles of liberated mankind and were applicable to any society at any time. Americanization of the world appeared to be the ultimate ideal of Wilson's vision. Therefore, even entry into World War I was voiced in strident moral, eithical, and holy terms. In Wilson's concern with the internal stability of nations along with their international harmony, he adhered to his belief that the foreign and domestic policies of a country could not be separated. Therefore, in his mind, peace and democracy were linked as related goals in American foreign policy—and the hint of America's need to intervene in the internal affairs of other nations became a latent tenet of U.S foreign policy.

THE PUBLIC AND FOREIGN POLICY

One thing more needs to be said. American foreign policy historically (and even today) has always been formulated by an elite group.[33] Nevertheless, the American public from time to time has been passionately involved in foreign policy issues. But their involvement has usually been based on emotional feelings. Thomas Bailey, discussing American attitudes toward foreign affairs, had much to say about the sectionalism, Anglophobia, suspicion of foreigners, and

[32] Ibid., p. 105.

[33] For detailed discussion, see Norman L. Hill, *The New Democracy in Foreign Policy Making* (Lincoln, Neb.: University of Nebraska Press, 1970), passim; and Gabriel A. Almond, *The American People and Foreign Policy* (New York: Praeger, 1960), pp. 136–157.

other emotionalized attitudes behind early American behavior. Slogans such as "atrocities," "holy war," "Huns," and "Hang the Kaiser" moved the American public; and the notions of manifest destiny, isolationism, American mission, and the Monroe Doctrine fed mostly on the people's emotions.

Americans have always been able to find a glow of ethics in their foreign policy. Their actual influence on foreign policy questions, however, has never been too deep. On the whole they have been rather consistently indifferent to the questions of foreign policy. Gabriel Almond has called this attitude a "mood" which is the outcome of America's material culture. To Americans internal prosperity and personal success are the immediate questions and challenges to which one looks and which shape one's world. Americans are in a constant race with time and self-recognition of their respective achievements by the society. Thus, the American's outlook and outward orientation is limited; he is more "inward" and is apt to be unconcerned with the larger questions of foreign policymaking. He gets involved only when his personal interests are threatened. At other times, his deeply nationalistic attitudes command and motivate his inclinations on foreign policy questions.[34]

Americans have created an artificial paradise of their own—a world full of material prosperity and the race to continually accumulate more and more of it. Therefore, outlook on foreign policy is based on some sort of "balance sheet" concept—an estimate of profit and loss calculations. Nevertheless, it is not an "amoral" attitude. It has its own philosophy, historical justification, and creative forces. On the positive side, it has produced interesting and valuable changes in consciousness and released the forces of pragmatism to "march forward" ahead of everyone. This consciousness has given birth to a society which is "self-centered" and progressive within its own definition of a self-created paradise: nothing succeeds more than success—it is the never ending force wrapped around people, moving them at a very fast pace within their own cycles and generating more and more wealth, more and more prosperity, and more and more conformity to their already well-established norms, values, attitudes and ideas. Obviously, the American public happily shares the views of the media and its opinion leaders on international questions and they seek guidance from the political elite and especially the president on foreign policy issues.

[34] John Spanier and Eric M. Uslander, *How American Foreign Policy Is Made* (New York: Praeger, 1974), pp. 93–102.

This process of dependence on the "political elite" in the arena of world politics has minimized the effects of public opinion on foreign policymaking. No doubt rising public resentment against the Vietnam War had some impact on President Johnson's decision not to seek reelection in 1968. On the other hand, the American public had supported Wilson's moralisms leading to the interventions in Latin America; gave moral consent to support Western governments to consolidate power in China at the beginning of this century and felt justified in suppressing the Boxer Rebellion; accepted in principle the "immoralism" of communism; felt morally obliged to support the Truman Doctrine; wholeheartedly stood behind the rhetorical preachings of John Foster Dulles; felt spiritually elevated in fighting the war of "free people" and "freedom" in Korea; hated "Castro" in Cuba; rejoiced in Kennedy's hour of glory in the Cuban Missile Crisis; feared the Soviet plans to spread "communist sin" in Europe and in Southeast Asia; generously contributed taxes to build up heavy defense against communist "nuisance"; mourned the "loss" of China; welcomed Madam Chiang Kai-shek to American and spread the "red carpet" for her. And yet, strangely, in the final analysis the American public has accepted the restraints and limitations of the Nixon Doctrine. Painlessly, they have listened to changing tunes on old issues, thereby almost effortlessly changing their moods at the whims of presidential changes in perception. Amicably they have accepted the new realities of China in the 1970s and with a broad spreading smile have supported friendly gestures to the Soviet Union. The old concepts are drowned in old memories, it is continually a new age. For Americans in general it is easy to accept "coexistence" with the Soviet Union and friendship with China—changes which might ensure world peace and prosperity. Old enemies become new friends; old fears vanish into new romantic feelings; the American public historically and even today accepts the guidance of the political elite in the foreign policy process on the questions of world politics—of course, not without any reservations, but certainly without much sophisticated questioning.

THE POLITICAL SYSTEM: THE GLORY OF
THE AMERICAN DEMOCRATIC EXPERIMENT

Not least important is the reality of the political structure and the American system of government which necessitates the creation of a "nucleus" around which runs the total show of foreign policy formation. America with its expanding political and economic influence requires an "expertise" knowledge to deal with foreign relations. This has naturally made the president more powerful and centered in him essentially all powers to cope with foreign issues and crisis situations. Throughout American history these have tended to accentuate his predominance even more. Naturally, under these circumstances, the political leaders project their views on foreign issues and help develop (or manipulate) images in the public mind. This process by no means developed any sophisticated philosophy of international politics among the people, and even ideological matters remain blurred in their minds. Norman L. Hill has noted:

> The people are handicapped in their thinking on world problems not so much by a lack of information on current issues—although they are handicapped in this respect—but rather by their lack of a well-considered philosophy of international politics. They read the papers without the ideological tenets, background knowledge, and assumptions necessary to transform facts, rumors, events, and allegations into tenable opinions on policy problems. Without a guiding philosophy, the thinking of the people tends to be shallow.[35]

Yet, set into a cultural pattern that is intoxicated with speed, and necessitated by a political system which thinks of itself as the historical "number one nation," the ideal choice for the American public has always been the acceptance of elite guidance on international politics. The question of the guiding philosophy does not pose any problem. After all, the ideas and ideals of moralism, manifest destiny, democracy, the Monroe Doctrine, and the isolationist tradition do provide a rich heritage to depend on and give real and fairly substantial meaning to a concept which is more forceful and has deep links with the past. No nation grows without links to its past; and the future is very much a reflection of past history. Past history binds the glory of a nation with the future accomplishments of its people; it is a relationship of soul with life; one ends, the other ends. And America has grown within its bondage to the past; the American people have never found any reasons to regret their historical accomplishments—and there are enough reasons to justify their philosophy of life. So far their outlook has helped America flourish and there lies all the reason and logic and morality and ethics to believe in what has been believed so far.

The American public's contentment with material progress in

---

[35] Hill, op. cit., p. 77.

their society has made and added to the blend of spiritual happiness in the form of a vague but reassuring belief system toward the world. Moralism has been the guiding principle and ethics have been the underlying concern—liberty, peace, and democracy have been the ultimate ends of American foreign policy. Could the world ask for more? Thus, American foreign policy hinged both in rhetoric and in practice upon ethnocentric moralistic grounds. To Americans foreign policy was thought to be the cosmic struggle between right and wrong; the perpetual repulsion of tyranny; the true belief in individual liberty, freedom, and equality; total dedication to the rule of law; and peaceful settlement of disputes with an ethical, democratic missionary zeal undergirded with intense moral idealism. This attitude produced a false antithesis in the American mind between morality and power politics; in effect, arrogating to the United States all the moral values and placing the stigma of immorality on the corrupting theory and practice of power politics pursued by other nations.[36]

As Orestes Brownson noted in an essay entitled "The American Republic":

> Each people had a mission selected by God, . . . some great, some small. Of these entrusted with great duties, the Jews were to establish worship of a single God, and belief in the Messiah. The Greeks were chosen to develop beauty in art and truth in philosophy. The Romans to develop law, order, political systems. The United States has divine orders to continue these, and to contribute its own, that is, its mission is to bring out in life the dialectic union of authority and liberty, of the natural rights of man and society.[37]

There is an unbroken chain of continuity of thought deeply rooted in the American spirit of missionary zeal. The hope for the world has always been closely linked with American ideals. Thus, a Massachusetts orator told his Fourth of July audience in 1827: "The spark kindled in America, shall spread and spread, until all the earth shall be illuminated with its light."[38] Theodore Roosevelt reaffirmed the faith in American mission and wrote in 1901: "We people of the United States, as to whether or not we shall play a great part in the world, that has been determined for us by fate, . . ."[39] Adlai Stevenson, speaking in 1952 during the Korean conflict, phrased his

[36] George F. Kennan, *American Diplomacy, 1900–1950* (Chicago: University of Chicago Press, 1951), passim.
[37] Nye, op. cit., p. 173, quoting Orestes Brownson.
[38] Ibid., p. 174.
[39] Ibid., p. 176, quoting Theodore Roosevelt.

message in a biblical spirit:

> God has set for us an awesome mission: Nothing less than the leadership of the free world. Because He asks nothing of His servants beyond their strength, He has given to us vast power and vast opportunity. And like that servant of Biblical times who received the talents, we shall be held to strict account for what we do with them.[40]

Earlier Woodrow Wilson, taking America into World War I, told Congress that the nation was entering war with a mission:

> for democracy, for the right of those who submit to authority to have a voice in their own governments, for the rights and liberties of small nations, for a universal dominion of right by such a concert of free peoples as shall bring peace and safety to all nations and make the world itself at last free.[41]

Even John F. Kennedy, in 1963, touted the American concept of national mission as a great personal dedication. He stated:

> The iron of the new world being forged today is now ready to be molded. Our job is to shape it, so far as we can, into a world we want for ourselves and our children and for all men.[42]

The faith in the idea of mission has understandably created the will and desire for world leadership in the American mind. In 1900, Senator Albert Beveridge said:

> American law, American order, American civilization, and the American flag [were] agencies of God [intended by Him to make] shores hitherto bloody and benighted . . . henceforth beautiful and bright.[43]

He further affirmed:

> God has made us the master organizers of the world to establish a system where chaos reigns. . . . He has marked the American people as his chosen nation to finally lead in this regeneration of the world. This is the divine mission of America and it holds for us all the profit, all the glory, all the happiness possible to man.[44]

And the contents of the President's Commission on National Goals in 1960 reaffirms the old goals of American foreign policy. The American aim, the report states, is not only "to preserve and enlarge our own liberties," but equally "to extend the area of freedom throughout

---

[40] Ibid., p. 177, quoting Adlai Stevenson.
[41] Ibid., p. 176, quoting Woodrow Wilson.
[42] Ibid., p. 177, quoting John F. Kennedy.
[43] Ibid., p. 199, quoting Albert Beveridge.
[44] Ibid.

the world." The report continues:

> Our enduring aim is to build a nation and help build a world in
> which every human being shall be free to develop his capacities to
> the fullest. We must rededicate ourselves to this prinicple and thereby
> strengthen its appeal to a world in political, social, economic and
> technological revolution. . . . Our goals abroad are inseparable from
> our goals at home.[45]

THE SYNDROME OF ASSURED CONFIDENCE

The American way of life has laid special stress on the concept
of assurance in every endeavor. Expectancy is the mark of the American temper, which has found its classic expression in the quest, the
mission, the journey toward destiny. The confidence of national purpose was going to be fulfilled in a world remade by others following
the example of the ultimate progress of mankind—namely, the United
States.

The combination of moralism, expectancy, confidence, assurance,
and the idea of destiny has generated a kind of "faith" in the American
style of handling international politics and foreign relations. This concept of faith derives its sanctions from spiritual as well as material
culture. Faith united the goals of American material prosperity with
its aims of ultimate good in mankind. Within this definition of faith
Americans combined the emotional element of ecstatic openness toward the spiritual presence in the conduct of human affairs and gave
full expression to the reality and usefulness of their material culture.
Therefore, there is no essential contradiction and confusion in the
American mind between seeking goals of national self-interest and
international betterment. Every war becomes a holy war—until Vietnam—and idealism and moralism gave American foreign policy an
extremely ethnocentric and potentially aggressive character. As George
F. Kennan has pointed out, this spirit of moralism identified with
the Manifest Destiny of American democracy led to the fervent involvement of the United States in such crusades as the Spanish-Ameri-
can War and World War I—which were supposed to be the wars
to end all wars.[46] And surely this faith in American national purpose
was the motivating force behind the frontier spirit—that physical
and psychological belief that the American could and should extend

[45] Ibid., pp. 178–179.
[46] Kennan, op. cit., passim.

his abilities and influence into every nook and cranny of the continent. In fact, many cherished the notion that once the continent was explored, American psychological and entrepreneurial energies would be obliged to discover new frontiers in which to find expression, new opportunities to expand and grow. Of course, this frontier spirit, based on the acceptance of the idea of faith in national purpose, foreshadowed many of the latter-day manifestations of American capitalism, dollar diplomacy, manifest destiny, and cultural imperialism in the twentieth century. Indeed, overtones of the idea that there is some overriding psychological necessity for a locale for the expression of the energies of the frontier spirit have led to the externalization of the frontier so that the present generation explores space and initially welcomed the thrust into Vietnam.

THE TENSIONS OF ISOLATIONISM AND INTERVENTIONISM

In sum, American culture sets the framework of ideas, ideals, and objectives within which foreign policymakers operate. The tensions between recurring patterns of isolationism and aggressive interventionism—for whatever purposes—expand and contract the intangible guidelines within which decisions are made. Surely there were and there will continue to be periods of intense American involvement in world affairs. Yet is seems certain that the traditions of isolationism and domestic concerns will continue to be the dominant tendencies of American character—the ones which United States foreign policymakers have struggled against and come to terms with—all the way from the "no entangling alliances" of our first president to the defeat of Wilson's glorious dream of American involvement in a League of Nations; from Franklin Roosevelt's neutrality acts to the current enchantment with international disengagement so clearly exposed in the language of the Nixon Doctrine.

THE CONSTITUTIONAL FRAMEWORK OF THE AMERICAN FOREIGN POLICY PROCESS
National Style in the Institutional Context

The American democratic system is governed by a network of legal, governmental, and organizational rules. At the very beginning of American independence a constitutional formula was established for the construction of a governmental system which would, through such means as the separation of powers, checks and balances, and federalism, avert tyranny and guarantee the dignity and rights of the individual. In essence, the action channels for American foreign policy were constrained by a conscious effort on the part of the Founding Fathers to fragment governmental power territorially, institutionally, and legally. The elements of bargaining within a governmental and democratic framework of consensus and conflict were built into the foreign policy process right from the beginning. Hence, special attention must be given to a description of the formal patterns of authority and the distribution of power as it is structured in the foreign policymaking process. Formal authority and actual power realities do not, of course, always coincide. However, in a democratic environment, the legal, constitutional framework sets the rules by which decision makers interpret the setting in which they must act. The rhetoric that must be used to justify (legitimate) their decisions to the domestic constituents and the action channels that can be used to implement policies must be consistent with the principle of democratic control of foreign policy.[1]

[1] Michael H. Armacost, *The Foreign Relations of the United States* (Belmont, Calif.: Dickenson, 1969), chaps. 3 and 5.

In addition, formal organization, which depends upon a constitution, legal custom, and administrative precedent, establishes a framework which directly affects the more abstract and informal aspects of philosophical thought, personal style, role perception, force of circumstance, interpersonal relations, interinstitutional conflicts, and even crisis decision making. The formal organization of American foreign policymaking allows a fairly relaxed system of day-to-day accountability, if one compares this organization to any domestic policymaking organization, but the prerequisites of democratic control are clearly present in every aspect—legally, philosophically, and politically. A short description of institutional developments over the course of American history will explain this aspect of the foreign policy environment.

THE INSTITUTIONAL CONTEXT OF
AMERICAN FOREIGN POLICY

The initial heritage and national style of American foreign policy was born with the birth of this nation in 1776. Under the Articles of Confederation, the administration of foreign policy was managed by congressional committee and a secretary of foreign affairs chosen by Congress. The Constitution, on the other hand, provided a strong executive branch, and it was explicitly the aim of those who wrote the constitution that the president was to exercise control over the management of international relations. However, though the president is charged with responsibility for the conduct of foreign affairs, constitutional provision and political problems both demand that he coordinate his programs in collaboration with the Congress. For example, the Founding Fathers provided in the Constitution that the president must consult and must get the approval of two-thirds of the Senate on all treaties.

The policy style—the policy of isolationism—of pre-World War II (1774–1940) can be categorized in the following institutional timeframes regarding institutional characters, fundamental concepts, terminology, and dilemmas of antiquity. First, during the Continental Congress and the Articles of Confederation period (c. 1774–1789), the adminstration of American foreign policy exhibited the following dichotomous salient traits: (1) It was whollistically congressional (i.e., Congress administered foreign policy and delegated the rest of the executive functions through subordinating committees or units);

and (2) vagueness surrounded the domestic administration of international enterprise, which resulted from the definitional deficiency of functions and its distribution among the units of the Second Continental Congress.

The latter trait manifested itself in duplications, overlappings, and often counterproductive efforts. During this time-frame (1781) of foreign affairs evolution, a Department of Foreign Affairs was set up to coordinate the management of foreign policy. The department operated under the strict scrutiny of the committee-dominated Congress which in itself was a weak and ineffective body incapable of managing the new nation.

The second category of institutional time-frame in the development of American foreign policy spans 1790–1860, during the continental expansion. The adoption of the Constitution during this period generated a new sense of direction in this arena; that is, it marked an executive-congressional cosharing of foreign relations which prevailed until the twentieth century. Presidential foreign affairs leadership initiative was carefully examined and subject to congressional consultation. The institution of foreign affairs, first known as the Department of Foreign Affairs, and later as the Department of State, was founded in 1789. Its name change was due to the fact that certain functions of domestic dimensions and types were allocated to it.

The third category of institutional time-frame in the evolution of American foreign affairs directives could be categorized as having taken place sometime between 1860 and 1895. Throughout the period of American isolationism and particularly during this third institutional time-frame, the problem of the spoils system became dominant and highly visible in the already existent institutions of foreign affairs. In this respect, Congress passed an act in 1856 which was the first legislative step in an attempt to evolve a career consular service. It also for the first time raised criticism about the incapability of those involved in the administration of American foreign affairs; furthermore, the act disclosed a weak assault on conflict of interests within foreign affairs functions.

The fourth and last institutional time-frame in the periodization of systematic isolationist continuity in the development of the American foreign policymaking arena preceeding World War I could be categorized as falling between 1895 and 1914.

At this time, it seemed that the range and significance of American foreign affairs development during the period of isolationism required both a permanent center and concomitant institutional mechanisms for consensus formation to support the foreign policy decisionmaking center. This period was marked by an increasing effort at reorganization of foreign affairs areas by successive American presidents. The various presidential-congressional reorganization programs grew out of numerous consultations and communications which encouraged, maintained, and institutionalized them. For instance, a reorganization of 1909 created four geographic divisions, replacing the old diplomatic bureaus; that is, a division of information, a division of trade relations, a division of citizenship, and a division of indexes. The executive's role in foreign affairs as a continuum of concern and particularly during this time-frame continued to expand because complex decisions had to be made quite frequently and more urgently since Congress was only to be consulted about the most vital affairs. President William Howard Taft, for example, extended the merit system of promotion to the diplomatic service, established a board of examiners, and prescribed written and oral tests for diplomatic secretaries.

The linkage period in the American policy of isolationism and post-World War II foreign policy of vigorous involvement occurred perhaps between 1914 and 1939. The pre-1914 years of American foreign policy could probably be best described as a period of institutional growth and the simultaneous conceptual embodiment of a belief value system of isolationism. The subsequent linkage period (1914–1939) marked diversification of foreign interests and involvements. The period also saw the vitality of foreign affairs roles by executive departments besides the Department of State. The division of roles occurred perhaps because of the increasing scope of foreign matters which interpenetrated domestic concerns; furthermore, perhaps because their evolving vitality aroused bureaucratic rivalry and competition. American foreign policy during the linkage period demonstrated a back and forth movement between the extreme of an indiscriminate isolationism and an unequal but increasingly stronger internationalism of unilateral self-righteousness.

The conflict management resolutions of World War II and its consequences transformed the United States from a predominantly isolationist nation concerned mainly with its internal economy to the most powerful and deeply engaged nation in the universe of international politics. Hans J. Morgenthau put it in the following context: "American foreign policy has tended, in this century, to move back and forth between the extremes of an indiscriminate isolationism and an equally indiscriminate internationalism or globalism."[2] But regard-

---

[2] Hans J. Morgenthau, *A New Foreign Policy for the United States* (New York: Praeger, 1970), p. 13.

less of philosophical direction, the institutions involved within the policymaking process have diversified and grown in number. This development places constraints of accountability on the policymaker, whether he is held responsible to Congress or to other executive departments. The parameters of his decisions are set by formal constitutional and procedural restraints. Formal organization governs the inputs, and in turn, helps to determine the product.[3]

THE PRESIDENT AND FOREIGN POLICYMAKING

By law, custom, and tradition, the president is the central figure in the conduct of foreign policy. In fact, the making of foreign policy in the twentieth century has been predominantly presidential policy. And, in the post-World War II nuclear age which produced a massive increase of U.S. involvement in foreign affairs, the powers of the president have been magnified even more relative to other institutions, roles, and personalities in the foreign policymaking arena.

The president has a vast array of constitutional powers to support his leadership in foreign policy. He holds the initiative in treaty-making situations. With executive agreements[4] he can reach understandings with the heads of other states, thereby bypassing Congress. Article 2, Section 2, gives him authority over the military establishment in his role as commander in chief. He can commit American troops to other nations without prior congressional approval to rescue American nationals in other lands and to protect American national security (e.g., Korea, Dominican Republic, and Vietnam in the post-World War II era) And finally, the president plays the central role in the maintenance of diplomatic relations with other governments. Addition-

---

[3] For the development of this section the following books were consulted: Richard Johnson, *The Administration of United States Foreign Policy* (Austin, Tex.: University of Texas Press, 1971); Ernest W. Lefever, *Ethics and United States Foreign Policy* (New York: Meridian, 1957); and John W. Spanier, *American Foreign Policy Since World War II* (New York: Praeger, 1968).

[4] An executive agreement is an international agreement, reached by the president with leaders of other nations, that does not require Senate approval. Such agreements are concluded under the president's constitutional power as commander in chief and his general authority in foreign relations, or under power granted to him by Congress. In 1930, the president concluded 11 executive agreements; in 1958, the president concluded 182 executive agreements.

ally, he uses such elements as diplomatic appointments and summit diplomacy to retain a tight control of the information channels in the arena of foreign affairs and international relations.[5]

The president also has an array of techniques garnered from historical and traditional patterns of presidential leadership on which he can draw. First, the president has tremendous control over information. He has the machinery of the executive departments, the expertise of the civil service supergrades, personal White House appointees, and a special staff of personal advisers which keeps his information sources continuous and up-to-date. Furthermore, all flows of information move toward him; even information hidden in the system eventually moves toward him. The essential communications flows tend to intersect, for all kinds of reasons, only in his office. Finally, it is generally accepted by commentators and practitioners alike that foreign policy is the major area of small group control of national policy.[6] And with the constant recurrence of crisis decision making in post-World War II America, foreign policymaking has become even more select and elite. Therefore, the president, as "decider-in-chief," has been able to use the powers of secrecy, ad hoc appointments of decisional units, and the pressures of crises to accentuate his power and control over information even more clearly in the period of rapid change and instant communications of the post-World War II technological age.

Second, the president, as the only nationally elected figure, has great powers available to him in the area of public opinion. He can command the use of the electronics media through major presidential addresses on key foreign policy issues. Press conferences and intentional leaks can center the attention of the American public on presidential concerns. Diplomatic meetings, summit conferences, and vice-presidential errands for the president all place the massive instruments of the news media at the fingertips of the chief executive in his foreign policymaking efforts. No individual organization or office can challenge the central and salient role of the president in his ability to take his case to the American public in foreign policy matters.

The twentieth century acceptance of the president as the chief legislator in the American political process has strengthened the posi-

[5] An excellent discussion on the president and foreign policy is contained in Cecil V. Crabb, Jr., *American Foreign Policy in the Nuclear Age* (New York, Harper & Row, 1960), chap. 3.

[6] For example, see Arnold Rose, *The Power Structure: Political Process in American Society* (New York: Oxford University Press, 1967), p. 488.

tion of the president in the foreign policymaking arena. He has an increased initiative factor, which further makes foreign policymaking emanate from his choices. Foreign policy is placed into his overall administrative program package, and Congress can only criticize, question, or approve; it cannot take away the initiative from the man who formulates the overall program. Emphasis and direction are set at the presidential level and passed down from there.

In addition, the concept of central clearance associated with the Office of Management and Budget (OMB) has placed much of the coordination power and monetary direction in presidential hands. What are these clearance operations? Essentially, they amount to central coordination and review of stands taken by various federal agencies at three successive stages of the legislative process.

1. Departmental drafts officially en route to Congress first have to clear OMB for interagency coordination and approval on the president's behalf.
2. Once bills are introduced, regardless of source—congressional committees solicit views, etc.—agency responses are cleared through OMB for coordination and advice on each bill's relation to the president's program.
3. When enrolled enactments come from Congress for the president's signature or veto, the OMB obtains, coordinates, and summarizes agency opinions on the merits of preparing in each case a presidential dossier complete with covering recommendation.

The president is a political animal. He is leader of a major political party and has the power to appeal for support from his fellow party members. The myth that politics stops at the water's edge is shattered during the presidential election campaigns every four years. In fact, foreign policy issues and their differences have been important factors in all presidential campaigns of the post-World War II era: 1948–Cold War; 1952–Korea; 1956–Hungary and Suez; 1960–Cuba, Quemoy-Matsu; 1964–Vietnam; 1968—Vietnam; and 1972—detente. The political content of presidential leadership is used to presidential advantage in the foreign policymaking process to quiet and pressure other segments of the government that challenge him. In addition, the rhetoric of bipartisanship has always been used by the president to condemn and chastise dissenters who question the foreign policy of his administration. When the president zeros in on dissenters with the charge of playing politics with United States foreign policy and

American lives, he has a powerful instrument of political persuasion in his arsenal as foreign policy leader.

The post-World War II nuclear age has magnified the power of the president in the foreign policymaking process in several other very important ways: First, because of the rapid responses needed to react in a possible nuclear exchange, the president realistically has the ability to launch the United States into a war without congressional approval. Second, the Cold War framework placed a premium on secrecy and intelligence in a tightly controlled national security syndrome; hence much information has been classified because of the fear of leaks and espionage. Third, the treadmill of crisis situations has led to the need for rapid decisions in small compacted time segments giving rise to presidential decisions; in fact, only after the crisis decision is made are there discussions (e.g., Korea, the Bay of Pigs, and the Cuban Missile Crisis). Fourth, the bipolar framework of world affairs after World War II made the president extremely visible as the leader and spokesman for the entire non-Communist world; and this visibility gave him tremendous power to commit the nation to directions and situations with an international audience which sometimes intimidated domestic organizations, institutions, and individuals who should have questioned specific decisions more carefully and systematically. Fifth and finally, with the growing linkages between foreign and domestic policies in the shrinking world of the technological age, the president has been able to control much of domestic politics because of his role as chief legislator and, equally, because of his power to ridicule and isolate those who would challenge the post-World War II equation which placed emphasis on foreign policy to stem the Communist threat which was thought to be real. But whatever the definition of the threat, the foreign policy domination by American resources in the post-World War II years gave the president tremendous power over all aspects of the decision-making process, far beyond what the Founding Fathers or historical custom has dictated or desired.

Furthermore, the office of the president has developed during the last century into the institution of the presidency. The presidency as an institution has centralized much of the policymaking process in a White House staff of scientific, economic, political, strategic, and military special assistants and crisis managers who act as the collators and coordinators of information which flows toward the president. These special assistants—whether known as New Frontiersmen, strategic intellectuals, or brain trusters—sit in close proximity to the locus of power and, at times, override the more traditional action channels of the foreign policymaking process—all the way from the State Department to Congress.

In effect, with the growth of the presidency as an institution there has developed a corresponding centralization of policymaking powers into the hands of the president and his hand-picked special entourage in the White House. Whether it be a Clark Clifford for Harry Truman, or a Sherman Adams for Dwight Eisenhower, or more recently, a Henry Kissinger for Richard Nixon, the fact of the matter is that the White House has developed staffs and experts who are closer to the apex of the information inputs and closer to the president who personally appointed them. Hence the presidency has become somewhat of a self-contained unit staffed by trusted individuals who are able to shortcircuit the more cumbersome and traditional channels of constitutional and institutional policymaking patterns which existed in the pre-World War II days. Hence, regardless of whom one reads on United States foreign policy there is no doubt whatsoever of the dominance of the president in the American foreign policy process.[7]

THE OTHER INSTITUTIONS IN
THE FOREIGN POLICY PROCESS

The Department of State. This is the one agency specifically charged with foreign relations. It is responsible for the routine management of external affairs. It provides the general guidance and coordination of all foreign policy activities through its geographical and functional bureaus. And even though the preeminent position of the State Department has diminished within the last century, the secretary of state and his department retain the formal designation for the institutional and constitutional responsibility for the foreign relations of the United States.

The rest of the organizations of the foreign policy arena can be broken down into five subcategories:[8]

The Military Arm. This includes all the institutions involved in the "managing of violence" for the security dimensions of American foreign policy. The Department of Defense and the Joint Chiefs of

---

[7] For example, see D. L. Robinson, "Presidential Autocracy and the Rule of Law," *Worldview* (March 1973), pp. 5–12.

[8] The subcategories are patterned after those cited in Charles O. Lerche, Jr., *America in World Affairs* (New York: McGraw-Hill, 1967), chap. 4.

Staff are the key elements in the foreign policy decisions that require military advice. And, of course, the separate service departments are essential in offering differing military viewpoints on foreign policy matters.

The Economic Arm. This includes the multifarious organizations which advise the president in areas of foreign aid, international economic policy, and foreign trade. The number of organizations involved in this area is legion: The Treasury Department, the Agency for International Development, the Department of Commerce, the Department of Agriculture, etc. This is an area of growing importance, and some major reorganizations in terms of a supercoordinating agency are sure to appear in the 1970s as we move beyond the Cold War period.

The Image Arm. The State Department used to take care of this need in the pre-World War II period. But with the tremendous psychological aspect of Cold War propaganda and the ideological competition between the United States and the USSR, a special foreign policymaking propaganda or image-building organization was developed in the post-World War II period. The United States Information Agency (USIA) is responsible for developing and executing a great variety of informational programs to project and protect the American image throughout the world. In this context the unique propaganda operations of Radio Liberty and Radio Free Europe need to be mentioned. They have played important psychological roles in setting the relationships in terms of mind sets in the European and the Cold War environments.

Technological Arm. There are special agencies which have been essential in the foreign policy process in the post-World War II period of the Cold War. For example, the Central Intelligence Agency (CIA) and the National Security Agency (NSA) coordinate and evaluate intelligence information—and, of course, the CIA also conducts intelligence activities in other nations. The National Aeronautics and Space Agency (NASA) has played an essential role in the competition in space. And there are other agencies which play important roles in foreign policy, such as the Federal Bureau of Investigation (FBI), the Atomic Energy Commission (AEC), and the Arms Control and Disarmament Agency (ACDA). All of these are products of the intersecting of the Cold War and the implosion of technology on the traditional power patterns of international relations which have dominated the contemporary historical era.

The Legislative Arm. Traditionally Congress has mostly played a secondary role in the American foreign policymaking process. It has played a role through the formal powers of ratification (or rejection) of treaties, confirmation of presidential appointees, control over appropriations, power to declare war, and the power to legislate. In addition, it has informal capabilities such as investigatory, electoral, forensic, and the passing of resolutions to augment its constitutional powers. However, the president has consistently been able to subordinate Congress to a passive and reactive position in the foreign policymaking process. And even though there has been an expanded involvement ·of Congress in virtually all phases of external affairs in the post-World War II period, the reactive and secondary nature of Congress has become even more marked in this age of recurrent crises, nuclear deterrence, and bureaucratic expertise. Hence, the legislative arm has been overwhelmed in the essential direction of foreign policy by a presidential domination that has grown to tremendous proportions. There are, of course, "great debates" arising in regard to the presidential-congressional imbalance in the current "post-Vietnam" readjustment period—and yet, it appears clear that Congress will remain at a fundamental disadvantage in relation to the president and the growing bureaucratic institutions which will not be overcome by prosaic rhetoric or second-rate staffing readjustments. In effect, even those who are most anxious for a reassertion of congressional power in the foreign policy process are dismayed by the inability of Congress to match its post-Vietnam rhetoric with operational adjustments and/or institutional solidarity.[9]

THE POWERS OF THE PRESIDENCY: INSTITUTIONAL EXPANSION AND PERSONAL STYLE

In order to clearly understand the circumstantial aspects of presidential dominance of foreign affairs, one must first realize that part of this authority of gradual dominance is vested either directly and/or indirectly in the president by legislative power as well as the concept of exclusive power of the president as the protoplasm or nucleus organ of the national government in the area of international affairs. The concept of the exclusive power of the president does not demand as a rationale the dictates of Congress but, as any other federal bu-

[9] Taylor Branch, "Profiles in Caution," *Harper's* (July 1973), pp. 63–72.

reaucratic power, is subject to practice within the framework of the U.S. Constitution. Robert S. Hirschfield, commenting on the power of the presidency, notes the following: "Thus the crucial issue of executive authority to determine America's position in world affairs—an issue of the most far-reaching importance for our own time—was raised at the inception of the presidency. It was then resolved in favor of the Washington-Hamilton concept attributing broad and independent power to the President as the nation's sole organ of foreign relations."[10]

But the controversy has continued and the arguments of Hamilton and Madison were heard again in the 1960s when President Johnson's secretary of state, Dean Rusk, and Senator J. William Fulbright clashed at the Foreign Relation's Committee's hearings on the Gulf of Tonkin Resolution and the president's authority to conduct war in Vietnam.[11]

Apart from the constitutional provisions in Article II, Sections 2 and 3 relating to the presidential power as "by and with the advice and consent of the Senate to make treaties" and to nominate ambassadors, ministers, and consuls and the power to receive ambassadors and other public ministers, no reference is established by the Constitution to particular presidential power in the international role. In this respect, as already elaborated so far, one would be more appropriately inclined to see that the basic origin of the president's powers lies in the general provisions of Article II vesting the executive power in the president, making him the commander in chief of the army and navy, commissioning him to demand written views from primary administrators of the executive divisions, and commissioning him that the laws be justly executed. In other words, at the apex of this array of constitutional power possibilities, the president has been able to seize the initiative in national crises under the banner of the "emergency powers of the president" derived from the so-called "war powers" in Article II, Section 2 ("commander in chief") and Article II, Section 3 (to "take care that the laws be faithfully executed"). In effect, these constitutional sources have led to a tremendous historical expansion of executive power as the president has taken the lead in defining as well as in dealing with national emergencies. The actions of Lincoln, Wilson, and Franklin Roosevelt in periods of national

[10] Robert S. Hirschfield, ed., *The Power of the Presidency: Concepts and Controversy* (New York: Atherton, 1968), p. 44.

[11] Ibid. In addition, see Ronald J. Stupak, "Dean Rusk on International Relations: An Analysis of His Philosophical Perceptions," *Australian Outlook* (April 1971), pp. 13–28.

crises have led to the dynamic growth and public acceptance of presidential powers during periods of intense internal and external systemic threat. And with the gradual movement of the United States during the twentieth century more and more into the international arena, the president increasingly evoked the emergency powers in an area of politics that seemed to demand quick executive action in order to protect the national security of the American homeland against foreign enemies.

Operationally, it has been frequently evident that the president undoubtedly draws some of his international authority by the rationale of differentiation between the powers of the federal government and the respective states with regard to international role and internal role. In international relations the individual states never had powers of external sovereignty. It is perhaps somewhat clear by now that the Constitution excluded a diverse area of undelegated power in which some structure or figure would be needed if the international functions of the states were to be fulfilled. As Robert Hirschfield notes, "Wilson's World War I regime provided a full-dress preview of that office, but it was not until the current era of continuing crisis that the powerful Presidency concept became institutionalized."[12]

The gradual growth of the institutionalization of the presidency's dominance in international affairs has been historically supported by sophisticated infrastructures that stand behind the president's international leadership. All of these infrastructures have come to participate actively in support of a presidential foreign affairs type of leadership. The notion that the Department of State and the military units play partial roles in the making and execution of foreign affairs is an accepted fact, and the notion that all aspects of domestic affairs in the United States have a direct or indirect consequence on the American international position is becoming an extension of that fact. In a more precise theoretical model, the post-World War II American president must develop and maintain a consciousness of the new and predominant evidence that the dichotomy between foreign and domestic policy has been all but relinquished.

The paradox of presidential power in a simple theoretical model could perhaps best be stated thus: that the Constitution and the coercion of custom have transformed the chief executive into the most powerful individual domestically, and, consequently, the status of the nation in respect to the rest of the world has made him addition-

---

[12] Ibid., p. 46.

ally the most persuasive person in the field of international relations. The postwar era of American foreign policy practices has demonstrated that the decision-making processes have further been complicated by immense institutionalization and by the institutional apparatus developed by Congress to aid the president in the global discipline. The vital status of such substructures as the Council of Economic Advisers, the Joint Chiefs of Staff, the Central Intelligence Agency, the National Security Council, the Atomic Energy Commission, and six or so other agencies inclusive of those previously mentioned in this chapter, do not detract from the president's preeminent position, but it does present a premium on his ability to generate flexible formulae and to persist in command of the affairs of state. While the Constitution of the United States provides for three equal and coordinate branches (executive, judiciary, and legislative), it remains for the president to take the initiative (i.e., to acquire the initiative capability) in evolving new frontiers in both domestic and foreign affairs in order to weaken or relinquish traditions that might not accommodate growth. In this regard, Clinton Rossiter classifies the president's leadership roles into seven categories: that is, the President is leader of (1) the Executive branch, (2) forces of peace and war, (3) Congress, (4) his party, (5) public opinion, (6) rituals of American democracy, (7) "free nations."[13]

From this classification it is clearly easy to see that the president's identitive power in the leadership role is dominant—identitive power is defined as a trait of a branch or branches that could be used to develop, maintain, and traditionalize leadership roles. Amitai Etzioni treats identitive power as a mechanism that "serves to build up and maintain the legitimization of the union and unification efforts."[14]

Clinton Rossiter in his analysis of the status of presidents in the field of foreign affairs notes the following:

> Although authority in the field of foreign relations is shared constitutionally among three organs—President, Congress, and, for two special purposes, the Senate—his position is paramount, if not indeed dominant. Constitution, laws, customs, the practice of other nations and the logic of history have combined to place the President in a dominant position. Secrecy, dispatch, unity, continuity, and access to informa-

[13] Clinton Rossiter, "The Presidency—Focus of Leadership," in Donald B. Johnson and Jack L. Walker, eds., *The Dynamics of the American Presidency* (New York: Wiley, 1964), p. 12.

[14] Amitai Etzioni, *Political Unification* (New York: Holt, Rinehart & Winston, 1964), p. 71.

tion—the ingredients of successful diplomacy—are properties of his office, and Congress, needless to add, possesses none of them. Leadership in foreign affairs flows today from the President—or it does not flow at all.[15]

Perhaps it is worth noting here that many aspects of the American life-style, due to technological advancement, world complexity, and world interdependency, have become dependent upon the status of international polycentrism. For instance, gross national product, international trade balance, full employment, education, and other disciplines, some of which at one time were purely a matter of local concern, are now all directly affecting the position of the United States in the international field and basically have become very much the President's affair. Another good example of this is stated by Warner R. Schilling:

> Indicative of new relationships between science and war, figures and graphs comparing Great Powers with regard to numbers of scientists and engineers have become as familiar as those in the 1930s which compared the Powers with regard to their output of steel, coal, and oil. Nor is it only in the military field that science and technology have become vital to the course of foreign policy. Similarly, the major activities of the Foreign Policy Panel of the President's Science Advisory Committee (PSAC) and the office of the Science Adviser to the Secretary of State have been in connection with the Science Attache program, the facilitation of international scientific programs and conferences, and the exchange of scientists with the Soviet Union.[16]

Hand in hand with the greater involvement of the traditional departments in providing assistance to the president in his new role as preeminent leader in foreign policy, efforts have been made to modify institutions in the more immediate presidential environment to the vital demands for advice and the coordination of policymaking and implementation. Despite the fact that some of these institutions, such as the Council of Economic Advisers and OMB, were created by Congress to deal predominantly with internal problems or activities, they have essentially felt the weight of the presidential international commitment. The other categories of the institutions around the presidency were established particularly to assist the president in managing the international concern. Some of these, such as the Atomic Energy Commission, the Office of Defense Mobilization, the National Security

[15] Rossiter, op. cit., p. 12.
[16] Warner R. Schilling, "Scientists, Foreign Policy, and Politics," in William R. Nelson, ed., *The Politics of Science* (New York: Oxford University Press, 1968), pp. 36–37.

Council, the Central Intelligence Agency, and the Joint Chiefs of Staff, have been on the scene since 1947. In addition, the scope and magnitude of foreign affairs at times has necessitated the sudden growth of many other commissions, offices, and ad hoc individual assignments which come on the scene and then dismantle, depending on the extent of presidential need—but always leading to another accretion of executive dominance in the foreign policy process as well as increasing the number of people reporting to him. How these departments, units, and staffs are utilized, or if they are utilized at all, depends on external world conditions and the administrative priorities of the president and his supportive institutions. In effect there has been no predetermined, appropriate way to structurally arrange the institutional support for presidential global leadership.

There are informal axioms stressing the need for coordination of the global effort, that is, the organizational demand for explicit lines of responsibility and action and the parallel requirement that enough information reaches the president. However, there is no historical pattern that legally or formally sets the operational framework to shape the institutions to fit his personal work-day syndrome and interpersonal style. For example, Richard Johnson notes that "The Kennedy and Johnson administrations reduced the number of committees appreciably, made far greater use of task forces, and gave broader decision-making powers to chairmen, usually to the State Department representative."[17] This trend was continued and achieved its highest level around 1966, when President Lyndon Johnson directed the secretary of state to assume authority for the entire direction, coordination, and surveillance of interunit activities of the United States government overseas. In other words, Johnson charged the Department of State with the administration of international concerns during his administration.

But in no time at all, President Nixon reversed the Johnson institutional, directional approach. He restored substantial authority to the National Security Council and increased the institutionalized role of his special assistant for national security affairs. The National Security Council when established in 1947 as a presidential advisory institution was to have two purposes. The first initial objective was to promote unification of the armed forces; secondly, the council was to have the responsibility of advising the president on high policy decisions regarding the status of national security. However, these two purposes

[17] Johnson, op. cit., p. 190.

have been interpreted and the NSC has been interjected into the policy process in different ways by various presidents. In effect, the personal style of the president continues to be the major determiner of how the mechanisms of the United States policymaking process are used and/or abused within the overall rule parameters of our constitutional democracy.

SUMMARY

The Constitution is substantially imprecise in reference to the distribution of responsibilities between the president and Congress for the making of international policy. Its most distinct expression is restricted and structured around the methods of diplomatic management (Article II, Sections 2 and 3). For example, the president's power to recognize the independence of nations, even though not expressly delegated by the Constitution, is implied by the expressed authority commissioning the establishment of diplomatic relations with foreign countries through the treaty-making and diplomatic exchange mechanisms. The deficiency of definitiveness or lack of certainty of the president and Congress about their legitimate powers has precipitated an ongoing endeavor for domination since independence but is exceptionally visible today in the post-Vietnam era. Explicit separations of authority between the two organs of government have been sequentially structured by sketching the processes of competition. In this respect, it has been demonstrated that the presidency has been able to acquire the dominant responsibility in the foreign affairs environment. Patterns of presidential behavior and practices in regard to foreign affairs have often found legal justification in the executive emergency and war power clause. In other words, any powers which were not expressly delegated to any of the three branches of government are left to claim by the broad, conceptual themes of interpretation in the executive power clause.

From this and the preceeding chapter it is crystal clear that the conduct of foreign policy is predominantly presidential despite the fact that there are many ways of structuring it—through efforts of the supportive institutions. Certain presidents participate so dominantly in foreign policy administration that they become, in effect, their own secretaries of state; conversely, others divide foreign affairs more or less as they choose, that is, they have used supportive traditional institutions, set up new ones, or carried out foreign policy as they wanted to. Presidential constitutional power in foreign affairs (i.e., those powers explicitly delegated to him by the U.S. Constitution), his powers resulting from various constitutional interpretations and implication, his capability to have control over information, his capacity to influence public opinion, his capability as a political leader, and many other situational factors linked with the concept of the presidency have elevated him to a position of dominance in foreign policy matters. Thus, the president's powers in global affairs can be analyzed in the following trichotomous manner:

1. Those clearly expressed in the U.S. Constitution;
2. Those which have developed as a result of customary usage and tradition;
3. Those embodied in his war or emergency powers.

In sum, the president has dominated the American foreign policy process from the very beginning of the Republic, and it is historically correct to say that this power of control in the foreign policymaking process has continued to expand to the present, when presidential domination of the foreign policymaking process has evoked fears from liberals and conservatives, from academics and operational policymakers who are convinced that too much power has gravitated toward the presidency in a political system which calls itself democratic, and which prides itself on such concepts as separation of power, checks and balances, and federalism. However, to fully understand the expanded powers, as well as the institutional and political limitations of the president in the contemporary environment, an analysis needs to be undertaken of the revolutionary transformation that occurred in the American foreign policy process in the post-World War II years.

IV

THE FOREIGN POLICY PROCESS IN THE UNITED STATES SINCE WORLD WAR II

Crisis Environment, Entangling Commitments, and Administrative Transformations

There was a tremendous expansion of problems along with a dramatic increase of complexities interjected into the world and correspondingly into the foreign policy process in the United States after World War II. These reverberations within the international and the domestic policymaking systems were the products of: (1) the transformed nature of the United States' world commitments due to the bipolar balance between Russia and America; (2) the policy precedents formulated by the Truman administration during this period of bipolar confrontation; (3) the technological revolutions in the communication, transportation, and military fields; (4) the organizational and structural transfigurations in the international diplomatic process; (5) the inordinate growth in the size, sophistication, and power of bureaucracies in the foreign policymaking process; and, finally, (6) the dynamic nature of the decision-making process itself in producing change while it dealt with international issues. Not only did these interrelated factors of the postwar international environment shatter traditional American attitudes toward foreign affairs; they produced a series of adjustments, readjustments, and transformations within the policymaking arena of the United States government.

THE EXTERNAL ENVIRONMENT

The post-World War II American generation confronted a most novel experience, especially in the period from 1945 to 1960. Although the nation enjoyed comparative peace, never had it been so freely engaged in world affairs! A major reason for the magnitude of American involvement was the abrupt recognition and essential belief in American leadership circles that the USSR harbored aggressive expansionary designs—and only the United States was in a position to offer any significant obstacle to their realization. Peace, thus, for Americans became a relative phenomenon after the war; in other words, a period of peace in the Cold War context became a peace that constantly had to be worked at. Therefore, the United States-Soviet Union confrontation and its impacts on the American foreign policy process have to be examined first, since it is the foundation upon which the other factors overlapped and interrelated to produce a profoundly different environment in which the American foreign policy machine was forced to operate.

THE CONTENDING INTERPRETATIONS

It must be made clear that a series of different and contending interpretations were advanced by various segments in the American policymaking environment concerning the nature of the Soviet Union, and America's obligations in the world scene; and this cacophony of voices set the framework for a growing visibility of and interest in the foreign policy perspective. Therefore, a sample analysis of these alternative suggestions is in order so that the major options which were available to American policymakers can be understood. First, there were those like Vice-President Henry Wallace who wanted the United States to accept friendship and mutual cooperation with the Soviet Union in building a new world environment under the banner of the grand coalition that had won World War II against dictatorial fascism.[1] Therefore, the bipolar world had to be dealt with within the context of cooperative solutions to world problems, rather than in a competitive environment marked by threats and confrontations.

Secondly, there were those who were convinced that the Soviet Union, under Stalin, was a totalitarian, revolutionary, political unit which would wage a communist onslaught against its non-Communist

---

[1] Alexander DeConde, *A History of American Foreign Policy* (New York: Scribner, 1963), pp. 677, 682, 684. For more detail, see Karl M. Schmidt, *Henry A. Wallace: Quixotic Crusade, 1948* (Syracuse, N.Y.: Syracuse University Press, 1960).

neighbors, unless the United States took the lead to confront it. In other words, this group viewed the Soviet Union as the vanguard of an evil revolutionary force which would not rest until it had submerged the entire world under its collectivistic banner of "godless" conformity. Therefore, the United States had a moral obligation to wage a struggle against this evil in order to save the "free world," and ultimately in order to defeat communism. This ideological perspective meant a total, active, and persistent involvement of the United States in international affairs—in fact, it seemed to augur our eternal involvement until the death of either "us" or "them."[2]

Thirdly, a group of idealistic universalists in the American policy-making process were convinced that the United States had an obligation to make the United Nations work; and, therefore, America should take the lead to deal with the problems of the post-World War II environment within the confines of this new and promising international organization. Since the United States was the "democratic example" for the world, it was only proper that it should lead in structuring a world of cooperation in the new organization of peace. In addition, it was historically correct that the United States should make the United Nations work since it was thought to be the United States' absence from the League of Nations that caused the League's ineffectiveness and ultimately its demise in the rubble of World War II. Hence, for idealistic and historical reasons the United States was encouraged to take the initiative to work out its problems with the Soviet Union and the rest of the world within the context of the new international systemic framework of the U.N.[3]

Fourthly, there were those like Senator Robert Taft of Ohio who were apprehensive of America becoming overly committed to the world. Though they did not believe that the United States could return to the cocoon of pre-World War II isolationism, they did believe that it should be careful and selective in how it became involved in the affairs of the world. They demanded that the United States not become involved in excessive commitments to alliances, regional organizations, or peripheral situations. In fact, though they wanted America to be strong and vigilant toward the Soviet Union, they

---

[2] See Robert Strausz-Hupé, et al., *Protracted Conflict* (New York: Harper & Row, 1959), passim.

[3] This perspective was identified with certain types of people in the Department of State (e.g., Cordell Hull) and with the general optimistic hopes of the American populace immediately after the war.

wanted this to be done within the strategic framework of a "Fortress America," and within the psychological context of capability restraint and discriminate involvement.[4]

Fifthly, the Cold War revisionist historians (e.g., William Appleton Williams, Gar Alperovitz, etc.) contend that the American policymakers at this time, especially Truman and the savants identified with the Council on Foreign Relations, aggressively and consciously wanted to pursue an American power position of military, economic, and political superiority in the world at the expense of both allies and protagonists. Therefore, the United States with its nuclear superiority and economic strength intruded itself into the international system in order to create an American Age of Imperialism. This thrust was championed by those in authoritative power positions who saw the vacuum of power at the end of World War II as an opportunity to increase and ultimately expand American culture and capitalism into a world system of control.[5]

Finally, there was the group of self-styled realists who were convinced that the United States had to adopt a "get tough" policy vis-à-vis the Soviet Union. This group of policymakers, led mostly by the likes of Dean Acheson, saw international relations within the framework of a perpetual struggle among nation-states. A never-ending effort thus was needed to maintain an equilibrium of tolerance among states in order to make certain that no one nation-state became so powerful that it could impress its particular way of life upon others. Hence, the elements of force, power, conflict, and war were seen as "real" facts of international relations, which this group contended could not be wished away or moralized away. Therefore, after 1945, when Russian pressures on Western Europe seemed to be upsetting the balance of the world power equilibrium, Acheson and others demanded that the United States take the lead in building a powerful counterbalancing system against Soviet encroachments. The United States had the power and it had to accept the responsibility of stopping the Soviet Union, because no "balancing system" was possible without active American participation in post-World War II international politics. In essence, both for the sake of international balance

---

[4] See the comments by Senator Robert Taft during the debates concerning the commitment of American troops to NATO, U.S. Senate, *Assignment of Ground Forces of the United States to Duty in the European Area* (Washington, D.C.: GPO, 1951), passim.

[5] See, for example, William A. Williams, *The Tragedy of American Diplomacy* (New York: Dell, 1959), passim.

and for basic national self-interest the United States had to become the container of Soviet expansionist desires.[6]

These contending perceptions of how the United States should or could operate in the context of the bipolar world had to take into consideration the vast number of qualitative and quantitative changes that became evident in the growing interdependent international system of the postwar years. And, finally, it was in 1947, with the enunciation of the Truman Doctrine, that this debate was settled with the realists as the winners and ultimately the shapers of American foreign policy.[7]

THE BIPOLAR FRAMEWORK

Regardless of which interpretation was to predominate, however, the historical reality of the breakdown of the grand coalition that existed during World War II between the Soviet Union and the Western allies ushered in the beginning of the postwar bipolar world. Many differences among the allies had been subordinated during the war, but once the common enemy was defeated, the problems of peace brought to the surface differing conceptions of what paths the world should follow. At the same time, the decline and, in some cases, the disappearance of the great empires of Western Europe, as well as the demise of the Japanese empire, brought the United States and the Soviet Union to the preeminence of world power. The destruction of the military power of Germany and Japan removed the historic counterweights which for many years balanced Russia and retained its historical expansive potential. In addition, the American power, which had been instrumental in this destruction, underwent immediate rapid reduction since once the hostilities were over, Americans were spontaneous and headlong in their eagerness to return to civilian life. Hence, as the war ended, the United States policymakers were faced with: (1) the disintegration of Europe as a protected security barrier; (2) the military and political pressure by the USSR from Berlin to Vienna to the Adriatic; and (3) the domestic pressures for a massive policy of demobilization.

It was with the adoption of the Truman Doctrine in 1947 (see Appendix A for the full text of the doctrine) that the official policy-

[6] U.S. Department of State, *Strengthening the Forces of Freedom* (Washington, D.C.: GPO, 1950), pp. 15, 50, 77.
[7] See Chapter V.

makers in the United States government consciously undertook to contain what they perceived as Soviet power thrusts throughout the world—with this particular decision, the Truman administration effected a major turning point in American foreign relations and in the history of the world.[8] With the Truman Doctrine, the objective of the United States became the conscious, sustained containment of Russian power by the restoration of a balance of power in both Europe and Asia. The Truman Doctrine was an open-ended commitment on behalf of the United States to contain the Soviet Union and communist totalitarian expansionism around the world. It was stated in stark, security-military oriented terms, and it announced to the Soviet leaders and to other nations around the world that the United States was going to take an active, interventionist role in postwar world international politics in order to stem what it perceived to be Soviet national and ideological aggressiveness. In essence, the Cold War as a comprehensive "constant of conflict" between the United States and the USSR was launched for the United States (and probably the world) with the adoption of the Truman Doctrine.

Taking on active leadership of the Western world through such policy initiatives as the Truman Doctrine, the Marshall Plan (the economic assistance program to help the Western Europeans toward economic stability), and the North Atlantic Treaty (the defense commitment by the United States to the European continent) brought about a tremendous impact on the internal foreign policy processes in the United States. The sustained leadership and effort which has been put forth by the government and people of the United States in the years after 1947 represented a revolution in American foreign policy and the assumption of burdens and responsibilities wholly new to the American people. Never before, short of all-out hostilities, had the international energies and potentials of the United States been so mobilized and so committed to a struggle during a period of relative peace. The dimensions of this bipolar conflict with Russia and communism were no less than dramatic in their effects on the foreign relations of the United States—it meant that the country had to become involved in entangling and sustained interrelationships in the international environment. It led to such foreign policy innovations and complications as large military budgets, a powerful military force-in-being, a continuous and expansive research and development complex, foreign aid programs, military assistance programs, alliance

[8] Joseph M. Jones, *The Fifteen Weeks* (New York: Viking, 1955), pp. vii, 12.

agreements, and limited warfare. In effect, this bipolar confrontation created a forced interlocking of the political, economic, propaganda, educational, and military aspects of United States foreign policy. And, at the same time, it led to the growth of numerous bureaucracies in the increasingly institutionalized foreign policy process which developed in order to handle the multifarious aspects of the Cold War environment.

THE ALLIANCE FRAMEWORK

The need for the United States in the Cold War environment to blend its policies more closely with those of allied nations in such organizations as the Southeast Asian Treaty Organization (SEATO), the North Atlantic Treaty Organization (NATO), and the Organization of American States (OAS) magnified the many complications which were inherent in coalition diplomacy. The United States had to pursue its own national interests with consistency and determination, yet it had to allow itself a degree of flexibility within which it was able to incorporate, or at least take account of, the desires of its allies. This led to the interjection of both a foreign and historical dimension to the formulation of American foreign policies. In effect, foreign policy decisions made by the United States since World War II had to weigh not only the effects that these policies would have on the Soviet Union but it had to sound out its allies.[9] In other words, American policies came to influence the course of events not only for the United States, but for many nations throughout the world. Thus, the magnitude of American foreign policies themselves added greatly to the pressures on the internal American foreign policy process and on individual policymakers within that process. A parallel aspect of this alliance environment was the fact that the United States became increasingly involved in the internal affairs of many nation-states. The intrusion of American presence into these countries through foreign aid missions, military advisory groups, and intelligence organizations (e.g., the CIA) led the United States into a quagmire of involvement that demanded numerous operational specialists, with a concomitant growth of bureaucratic organizations. In addition, it created tensions between the United States and some of its allies

---

[9] Dean G. Acheson, "How Are We Doing?," *Vital Speeches* (January 15, 1952), p. 194.

because of alledged American manipulation and/or imperialistic activities in the domestic political affairs of other nations.

THE NEW STATES

The sudden and dramatic emergence of new states, particularly in Africa, South Asia, and Southeast Asia infused with a sense of nationalism, economic expectations, and social equality, produced major international complications for the United States. The multiplication of small states and their drives toward neutralism and self-sufficiency brought forth such foreign policy innovations as foreign aid, military aid, counterinsurgency theories, and the increased use of multilateral diplomacy within the regional and international organizational context. In addition, the relative weakness of these new states, coupled with perceived Russian and Chinese expansionist desires, pushed the Cold War competition directly into the underdeveloped areas. President Truman vividly explained the importance of the peaceful development of these new nations to American national security and to international stability when he remarked that "the development of those areas had become one of the major elements of our foreign policy."[10]

The fact that most of these new nations were "nonwhite" nations had an additional impact on the United States—the domestic problems of race suddenly became international problems of image, self-esteem, and Cold War manipulation. The tightening of the foreign-domestic linkage was accelerated by the multiplication of these new states in their quest for human rights for themselves and for all their brothers.

NUCLEAR ENERGY

The discovery and development of nuclear weapons as an instrument of unlimited violence reduced the geographical security of the United States, exposed the homeland of the United States to the immediacy of possible devastation, transformed the nature of modern warfare, exacerbated civil-military relations, magnified the role of

[10] Harry S Truman, *Memoirs: Pears of Trial and Hope*, vol. II (Garden City, N.Y.: Doubleday, 1956), p. 233.

the military in the policymaking process, and ushered in a new scientific era in man's understanding of nature's forces. The impact that nuclear power was to have on international relations in general and on the American foreign policy process in particular clearly was seen in the development of new strategic doctrines, the revolution in military weapon systems, and the massive power placed in the hands of strategic intellectuals such as Herman Kahn and military ideologues such as General Edwin Walker in the foreign policymaking process. The expenditures involved in the "research and development" of the technology of nuclear weapon systems and the costs associated with the search for strategic doctrines in order to use and/or control nuclear deterrence created a monetary strain and a psychological screen that had tremendous impacts on the foreign policy process and the American mentality. Force in being, a massive military establishment, and astronomic defense budgets became a constant of the American post-World War II political system.

THE SHRINKING WORLD

The shrinkage of the world in terms of the contacts among states and between any given state and its official representatives abroad produced an immediacy in foreign affairs never known before. The demands for speed in decision making generated a paradox for American policymakers in that, on the one hand, the need for quick action caused many decisions to be made with insufficient information, while on the other hand, due to the increase of communicative interaction between states and between the home offices and the field offices, there arose the problem of too much information, too much uncoordinated "noise" within the policymaking process. Furthermore, these technological and communicative improvements in a growing electronic age produced a vast increase in the amount of paperwork within the process along with a parallel increase in the personnel and computer hardware needed to analyze this tremendous influx of information. In other words, the impact of the communications revolution produced a need for speed in decision making and a quantitative increase in the number of decisions to be made, which constituted a wholly new experience to American foreign policymakers. This generated the search for more efficient and more coordinated information-gathering procedures within the American foreign policy process, along with a parallel search for a more favorable balance between centralized and decentralized decision-making patterns. In effect, this fed the power of executive organizations and positions at the expense of the more leisurely programed legislative branch of government. And, at the same time, it led to a proliferation of bureaucratic institutions and coordinating committees in an attempt to find an efficient and effective way of dealing with this massive amount of contacts and information generated by the technological revolutionary postwar world.

The Image Dimension. With the rise of new states and closed societies in the Cold War environment of the postwar world, there arose the perceived need to deal with people as well as with their governments. A great deal more attention had to be paid to the many forces, factions, and interests which existed within the domestic political systems of these states. Consequently, this intensified the search for more productive and manipulative educational, cultural, and propaganda procedures. The use of these new communicative and propaganda tools became essential in projecting a favorable image of the United States to the peoples of the world. In addition, there developed with the forceful advent of these new instrumentalities the need to coordinate more closely a nation's actions with its words. Thus, such problems as informal penetration,[11] managed news, open diplomacy, credibility gaps, and imagery projection became recurring elements in the foreign policy process, and they had to be integrated into the policy formulation and execution phases of the process with skill in order to achieve beneficial payoffs.

Postwar Diplomacy. The widespread appearance of international and regional groupings in such forms as the United Nations, defense alliances, and economic unions after World War II led to what many experts called the "new diplomacy," challenging such long accepted, traditional diplomatic methods as secret diplomacy and bilateral negotiations. This, in effect, caused diplomatic negotiations to be conducted more and more under the kleig lights of world opinion and, at the same time, in a continuous sustained fashion never before attempted by American statesmen.

In summary, then, it can be observed that the interacting transfor-

---

[11] In the Cold War technological environment, formal government-to-government relations have been increasingly supplemented by informal relations (e.g., CIA agents and surveillance satellites), in which the agents of one country are able to reach inside the borders of another, without the knowledge and/or approval of the government of the second country. See Andrew M. Scott, *The Revolution in Statecraft: Informal Penetration* (New York: Random House, 1965).

mations analyzed above had a tremendous impact on the external and internal dimensions of the American foreign policy process. On the one hand, the traditional international boundaries between foreign and domestic affairs, between peace and war, and between public and private concerns were obliterated in the Cold War atmosphere which fused all aspects of international and domestic relations for the United States into a crucible of conflict, action, and concern. At the same time, the boundaries existing within the American foreign policy process itself, between legislative and executive affairs, between civilian and military concerns, and between policy formulation and policy execution became correspondingly vague. This dual process created a fluid and complicated environment in which to formulate foreign policy. Alternately, acute frustrations and satisfactory compromises permeated the policy process at different times, as a search was undertaken to improve and expand both the machinery and the personnel within that process.

Domestic Adjustments. The external systemic changes in the international arena produced dramatic reverberations within the American foreign policy process after World War II. These overlapping and interrelated internal changes included: (1) the heightened awareness of both public opinion and Congress of foreign policy issues, (2) the increased tensions in civil-military relations, (3) institutional-bureaucratic proliferation, (4) the tremendous growth of the presidency, (5) problems within the Department of State, and (6) the changing nature of diplomacy.

PUBLIC OPINION

The profound intrusion of the problems of foreign affairs into the lives of the American people, coupled with the uncertainty inherent in the solving of problems in the "external realm," created difficult situations for American foreign policymakers in their relations with both the American public and the Congress. For suddenly in this transformed world environment, foreign policy, instead of remaining the esoteric province of a few professionals, became a part of everyday life for the American people as television brought events instantaneously into the homes of millions of Americans. The state of the world became a personal inconvenience for the average citizen in the postwar days of rapid communications as critical events led to the preempting of prime-time television programs and the telecasting in their stead of the actions of the U.N. Security Council, some news account from a distant place, or some speech by the president.

Immediately after World War II, most Americans were not ready or willing to accept the new demands which were being made on them and on American resources. Therefore, many turned against the foreign policymakers with a vengeance. The secretary of state, for instance, quickly became the official scapegoat for many American people who resented the sacrifices of two world wars and the frustration of their idealistic hopes which had carried them to victory. The Truman administration's inability to establish an absolute basis for peace exacerbated these feelings of disillusionment. Many Americans had not foreseen the difficulties which were inherent in the problems of the international arena and the inability of statesmen to produce final solutions to these problems. In fact, in 1946, Dean Acheson warned both the American people and their statesmen about the need to change their traditional and historical perceptions on the nature of the problems inherent in the area of foreign relations:

> it [involvement in foreign affairs] is a long and tough job and one for which we as a people are not particularly suited. We believe that any problem can be solved with a little ingenuity and without inconvenience to the folks at large. We have trouble-shooters to do this. And our name for problems is significant. We call them headaches. You take a powder and they are gone. These pains about which we have been talking are not like that. They are like the pain of earning a living. They will stay with us until death.[12]

The American public had to be educated to or manipulated into the burdens and responsibilities of sustained involvement in foreign affairs. The need to withstand the pressures from without and to adjust to the changes from within necessitated a yet unfinished effort even in the 1970s to cultivate a more informed public opinion so that consistency and maturity could be the foundations on which the American commitments throughout the world were built.

Congress. The president and his secretaries of state found after World War II that they could not shoulder their foreign affairs task without the constant support of Congress. Congress, in turn, found that most of its legislative acts affected some aspect of foreign policy. In other words, foreign and domestic policies were seen more and more as two sides of a single coin. Therefore, the separation of power

---

[12] Dean G. Acheson, " 'Random Harvest': The Perverted Ingenuity of Propaganda," *Vital Speeches* (August 1, 1946), p. 635.

concept had to be altered in the foreign relations field—the president became the chief legislator, while Congress became more and more subservient to executive undertakings in foreign affairs.

But since it became next to impossible to discuss domestic problems coherently without having them become inextricably entangled in foreign affairs, the president became increasingly adept at cultivating and/or manipulating the congressional consensus needed to prosecute effectively foreign policy programs in the tense Cold War environment. At the same time, many in the Congress became increasingly disillusioned with their inferiority relative to the presidency. And some congressmen and senators even became suspect of the president and his men as they seemed to pull more and more information and policymaking out from the channels of legislative involvement and public oversight. In effect, speed, secrecy, and threat seemed to be short-circuiting the traditional democratic processes, as national security and foreign policymaking in the Cold War environment clearly relegated Congress to a minor place in the policymaking process. The president and his appointed advisers overwhelmingly came to dominate the elected officials on "the Hill" in all aspects of the foreign policy process.

NATIONAL SECURITY

With the increasing importance of nuclear weapons and military strength in the mutual deterrence balance between the United States and the Soviet Union, the president had to give extensive attention to strategic policies and military requirements. For example, Samuel P. Huntington has written:

> The drastic changes in the external environment following World War II made national security policy the overriding goal of the nation's foreign policy. . . . . Security was no longer the gift of nature—the starting point of policy. Instead, it now had to be the product of conscious and sustained effort—the end result of policy. It became the dominant goal of foreign policy, with foreign policy itself often defined as a branch of national security policy.[13]

In effect, the adequate framework for policy had to go far beyond military means. It had to embrace the whole range of the interlocked purposes and instruments involved in the foreign policy process. As

[13] Samuel P. Huntington, *The Common Defense* (New York: Columbia University Press, 1961), p. 426.

military strength succeeded in deterring aggression, it merely bought time and opportunity to readjust military strategy and tactics to the changing nature of modern warfare, as direct major-power conflicts were replaced by indirect aggression, limited warfare, and guerrilla warfare. In truth, with the confluence of the war and peace dimensions within the postwar environment, the need to integrate military and nonmilitary instruments within the foreign policy process was magnified—with the military dimension more and more dominating the mix within the process.

The old division between "political" and "military" became virtually impossible to maintain with the advent of defense alliances, military aid missions, flexible response, and guerrilla warfare. Military force levels and weapons systems became indispensable factors in the diplomatic equations of the postwar international arena. Increasingly, the machinery for the integration of civilian and military viewpoints had to operate smoothly and responsibly, so that the president could control military means for the larger political ends. Accordingly, the continuing reappraisal of political-military relationships became an essential function within the strategic foreign policy framework. The president had to see to the coordinated development of the military instrumentalities and to their judicious use in support of the larger foreign policy objectives. The president in the policy process spent increasing amounts of time and energy in attempting to maintain a proper balance and mix of the military inputs with the other requirements of the foreign policy process. In essence, the role of commander in chief began dangerously to overwhelm the other diverse roles that the president was charged to perform both constitutionally and historically. In fact, as Thomas E. Cronin has noted in this context: "The blunt fact of the contemporary period is that approximately two-thirds of Presidential time has been spent on national security and foreign policy considerations."[14]

Bureaucratic Proliferation. The emergence of the United States as one of the two superpowers in the post-World War II environment resulted in a proliferation of bureaucracies within the government interested in foreign policymaking and its implementation, and forced significant readjustments upon the foreign policy mechanism.

---

[14] Thomas E. Cronin, " 'Everybody Believes in Democracy Until He Gets to the White House . . .' " *Law and Contemporary Problems* (Summer 1970), p. 605.

A United States document on foreign commerce, published in 1960, reported:

> The State Department's ability to coordinate foreign economic policy has declined greatly because of fragmentation, institutional proliferation, differing concepts of goals of economic policy, and a lack of Department of State economic experts.[15]

And former Secretary of Defense Robert A. Lovett, in testifying before the Senate Subcommittee on National Security Machinery on February 23, 1960, clarified what he identified as the bureaucratic "foul-up factor" in the foreign policy process:

> Whether or not this itch to get in the act is a form of status seeking, the idea seems to have got around that just because some decision may affect your activities, you automatically have a right to take part in making it. . . .[16]

Indeed, the interlocking of the military, political, and economic aspects of foreign policy produced such innovative elements as interdepartmental committees, an increase in importance of the Department of Defense, and the employment of such operational concepts as task forces, study groups, and country teams. The "noise" and "static" within the foreign policy process grew both in quality and quantity as bureaucratic organizations started to carve out autonomous spheres of influence—often competing for tasks, resources, and prestige.

The multiplication of departments, agencies, and committees interested in the making of foreign policy tended to force more and more of the burden for final decisions upward to the president himself. Many times the presidency itself seemed to be the only place where departmental lines of decision and action could be integratively converged. In addition, the growth in importance of the nuclear input placed the final decision for its uses in the hands of the president himself. As a result, the president rarely was able to look to one man or one department for advice and assistance on any major matter, and he was thus forced to look for ways in which to more effectively make final policy decisions. This produced three major adjustments in the foreign policymaking process.

---

[15] U.S. Senate, 86th Congress, Second Session, *The Role of the State Department in Coordinating the Reciprocal Trade Agreements Program* (Washington, D.C.: GPO, 1960), pp. 2–4.

[16] Henry M. Jackson, ed., *The Secretary of State and the Ambassador* (New York: Praeger, 1964), p. 5, quoting Robert A. Lovett.

First, since the growing tendency was to coordinate the formulation and operation of national policy at the White House level rather than in the major executive departments, the office of the presidency grew even more in size and importance. Thus, presidential assistants, special advisers, crisis managers, strategic intellectuals, and ad hoc presidential crisis groups came to prominence in the postwar years.

Second, the president had to construct a web of special interdepartmental committees, advisory groups, and ad hoc task forces to deal with specialized and technical problem areas.

Third, since speed was of the essence in the making of crucial decisions within the foreign policy process in the revolutionized postwar world, each president virtually seemed to choose to become his own secretary of state or to depend on special formal and/or informal advisers in the White House itself.

In essence then, the importance of the presidency expanded at the expense of other sectors of the government involved in the foreign policy process and at the expense of such constitutional principles as separation of powers and checks and balances.

The Domestic Setting. No factors had so revolutionary an effect upon the position of traditional diplomatic and policymaking techniques after World War II as did improvements in the art of communications coupled with the vast increase in American commitments throughout the world. Informational, cultural, foreign aid, and similar programs; people-to-people campaigns; good-will visits; grass-roots approaches; unilateral presidential pronouncements and summit diplomacy gestures; news conferences; military aid missions; and the rapid speed of world communications produced a tremendous impact on the diplomatic process. In essence, the traditional role of the nation's diplomacy was challenged by four postwar diplomatic phenomena: crisis diplomacy, open diplomacy, scientific diplomacy, and summit diplomacy.

As noted above, the dominant facts of volume and speed tended to negate the coordination of policy at the lower administrative levels. There was so much to be correlated and so little time to do it that the adverse effects of structural difficulties were multiplied. The rapid succession of problems which demanded action forced the United States after World War II to operate on the treadmill of crisis diplomacy. The demands for rapid decisions had a centralizing effect on the diplomatic process. Accordingly, the president and his advisers, such as the Special Assistant for National Security Affairs, coordinated strategic, diplomatic, and political materials, and made "can do" military-dominated types of decisions because the slower-moving machinery and "wait and see" diplomatic predelictions of the State Department were caught in a policy lag during crisis situations.

The concept of open diplomacy gained overwhelming acceptance in the international community. The political and technological structures of the postwar international arena (e.g., the United Nations) produced built-in prejudices toward open diplomacy. There was an increased feeling among national foreign policymakers that public opinion and mass support were essential in the evolution of a diplomatic policy. So negotiations were increasingly held before the light of world publicity. This tended to produce situations in which the act of negotiating itself became more important to the participants than the agreements to be concluded. In other words, propaganda victories and imagery projection came to challenge substantive agreements as the goal of diplomatic negotiations, often to the dismay of those diplomats who were products of the traditional school of diplomacy which stressed secrecy, compromise, and confidence as the bases of diplomatic endeavors.

The interjection of such scientific techniques as cost accounting and computer analysis, which became associated with the economic, military, and social elements of the new diplomacy, produced a certain amount of pressure for more scientific diplomatic procedures in the modern world environment. The diplomats were counseled to improve their control of the international interaction factors so that a higher degree of predictability could be achieved in diplomatic negotiation. In other words, the increase in the rational control of interrelationships in other problem areas and academic disciplines led some people to believe that more rational procedures were necessary in the diplomatic field, and that such procedures could be found if energetic searches were made. The suggestion caused chagrin among those elements within the diplomatic corps who were inwardly persuaded from vast experience that the variables in the international arena could not be scientifically nor rationally controlled by "can-do Mr. Fix-its."

The bipolar nature of the international environment after World War II generated a belief among many Americans that all the problems between the United States and the Soviet Union could be solved if only the leaders of the two countries could sit down together and talk things over. This belief, interrelated with the other factors mentioned above, helped to bring about an increased application of summit diplomacy in the international arena after World War II. This practice of summit diplomacy tended to undercut the traditional role of the State Department, lessen flexibility, create illusions, place excessive stress on personality factors, produce a "football" atmosphere, and generate a "court of last appeal" effect. In many ways, the reliance upon summit diplomacy obviated the accepted procedures of traditional diplomacy. Indeed, long before he became secretary of state, Dean Rusk warned against the excessive use and/or abuse of this diplomatic technique: "Summit diplomacy is . . . a technique to be employed rarely and under the most exceptional circumstances, with rigorous safeguards against its becoming a debilitating or dangerous habit."[17] And yet, it continued to become more and more used as the tool for presidential dominance of American foreign policy with other nations.

THE MILITARY ESTABLISHMENT: ORGANIZATIONAL SOPHISTICATION AND THE AMERICAN POLITICAL SYSTEM—A CASE STUDY IN BUREAUCRATIC POWER

One of the revolutionary changes in the American political system and in the dimension of the foreign policy process emanating from the Cold War period was the quantitative and qualitative growth of the military establishment.[18] A nation which once prided itself on its control of the military suddenly faced the interjection of a massive military influence in the policymaking process—an intrusion so massive that many analysts are convinced that American foreign policy has become militarized, while the foreign policy process itself has become a tool of the military-industrial complex. Regardless of whether these contentions are true, it surely is correct to cite the military as the most sophisticated of the foreign policy bureaucracies, and as the organizational unit which seems most able to systemically challenge and/or undercut the idea of strict presidential control of the foreign policy process. Thus, a short analysis of the organizational sophistication and adaptability of the military establishment will serve as a microcosm of what bureaucratic power means in the foreign policy process in particular as well as in the American political system in general.

[17] Dean Rusk, "The President," *Foreign Affairs* (April 1960), p. 361.
[18] See Terry J. Busch and Ronald J. Stupak, "The U.S. Military: Patterns of Adaptation for the 1970's," *Orbis* (Winter 1973), pp. 990–1007.

The Growth in Size of the Military Establishment

Even the most cursory glance into the subject of military power and potential in the United States today is bound to be an impressive one. Among the most obvious realities are the direct employment by the military of over four million persons; the indirect employment through defense related industries of several million more; the management of roughly half the federal budget, and approximately 7 to 10 percent of the Gross National Product (GNP); and the maintenance of a nuclear capability which affects not only the security but the very survival of our twentieth-century society. More sophisticated research also reveals that large areas of manufacturing, employment, and economic stability in the United States now largely depend upon defense contracts; and that the Defense Department today is the largest single managerial and educational complex in history. From a sociopsychological standpoint, the U.S. military has been so pervasive and influential that it has created a "Nation of Veterans," in which even those without direct military training understand the importance of patriotism, national security, and various aspects of aggressive national and ideological communism.

Since the full range and strength of the United States military goes far beyond what might be adequately covered in a short analysis, a brief and general investigation of the trends and basic causes by which the military has gained its present position will be of significant advantage in understanding the growing influence of the military establishment and other bureaucratic structures within the American political system.

The acquisition of this general understanding of the total picture of military power and potential must serve as a necessary prerequisite to any further in-depth analysis of this subject's individual parts. For it is clear that there are few specific answers to be uncovered about the strengths, responsibilities, and actions of the U.S. military by investigating any of its component parts in isolation, since it only the sum of these parts, their interactions and interdependencies, and their continual development and improvement which shed some clarity on the subject of the range and strength which the U.S. military holds in today's technological environment—only through a complex, holistic investigation can the nature of bureaucratic power be understood.

This analysis will thus point to and briefly discuss several of the avenues by which the military has come to assume its role as an active political organization in the American governmental system. For the purpose of organization, we will subdivide our discussion into two parts. First we will discuss the use of modernization techniques by the military in achieving its accumulation of power, and second we will attempt an extrapolation concerning its direction and future. It is essential for us to understand the internal ramifications of the national security syndrome in order to understand the power of internal bureaucratic needs to dictate external foreign policy positions, alternatives, and interpretations.

Modernization Techniques and the Military

In order to understand the importance of the military or any other modern institution, one must first understand that the evolution of society depends upon what we will call "modernization." This involves a worldwide cultural shift away from small, personal, homogeneous populations with sacred and slowly changing beliefs and low levels of technological advancement. The trend in the technetronic age is toward such features as urbanization, centralization, bureaucratization, scientism, mobility, and adaptability, which we will henceforth call "modernization techniques." This trend becomes highly significant when we discover that those nations or institutions within nations which have best developed these modernization techniques are the most influential and powerful structures in the world. And in many respects American society and its institutions have simply become perfections, or monstrous exaggerations, of these trends toward modernization through the maximization of such characteristics as specialization, specificity, centralization, bureaucratization, technological advance, mobility, and rapidity of change. If, as some imply, the military has gained its present position through a successful utilization of these modernization techniques, this should be substantiated by an investigation of the specific actions and areas of growth of the military in recent years.

For all practical purposes, the logical starting-point for an analysis of the military's growth of influence is at the end of World War II. For it was at this time that the professional military's effort to achieve a recognized place in the policy advisory process was finally successful. In 1947, Truman agreed that, at least in form, the military establishment should have an institutionalized role in advising him on foreign policy. He sponsored a National Security Act which, in addition to making the Air Force a separate service and providing for a Secretary of Defense, set up a statutory National Security Council designed as an inner cabinet to deal with issues of foreign and defense policy. Therefore, our investigation of modernization techniques will start from this point.

The first technique to be investigated in the light of military accomplishments is centralization. This, of course, covers a wide area of concern. The key word in understanding centralization is organization, and organization has always proved a military strength. The structure of the military ranges all the way from the most insignificant enlisted man to the office of the president. Its chain of command is ideal for the passing of orders and information. At the head of the Defense Department sits the secretary of defense, and during his seven years of service Secretary Robert S. McNamara seemed to understand the importance of centralization in the management of the mammoth military institution. Through the use of such programs as Planning Program Budgeting Systems (PPBS), flexible response, and cost-effectiveness, McNamara sought to strengthen the organizational, managerial, and efficiency capabilities of the military establishment.

In addition, the military has its own bureaucracy, probably the largest in the nation, which greatly enhances the military's lobbying interests, its ability to acquire funds, and its opportunity to influence decision making. Because such decision makers as the president must, by necessity, rely on military advisers for varying types of information, this influence has been substantial.

The Defense Department is also the world's largest educator of highly skilled men and it possesses its own system of rules, courts, and punishments. Outside of U.S. boundaries, we find ourselves tied militarily to numerous other countries through mutual defense treaties such as NATO, SEATO, and ANZUS. And coupled with this we find extensive influence of the U.S. military in other countries through Military Assistance Advisory Groups (MAAG), civic action programs, and its educational programs for foreign military officers. Therefore, when we consider all of this, as well as the overwhelming economic dependency of various types of U.S. industry upon military contracts, it becomes clear that the organizational extensions of the Department of Defense are both highly developed and widespread.

A second modernization technique is the use of a "secular approach" to problem solving and decision making. The key concepts in this secular approach are efficiency, convenience, and getting the job done, and it represents a socioevolutionary shift away from the use of sacred, proper, and traditional approaches to problems.

Once again, the nature of the military seems to be well suited for this modernization technique. Granted, the military has numerous traditions and values which it holds to be sacred, among which are the West Point motto of duty, honor, and country and the various other loyalties of military professionalism. But these do not hamper modern military efficiency. Instead they enhance it. The military's "can do" philosophy, coupled with its very tangible strength in terms of men, weaponry, and sheer massive power give this institution a psychological advantage over such agencies as the State Department, which operate primarily through words and negotiations. Furthermore, the option of utilizing the military's potential for efficient and decisive action in times of crisis often appears more logical than anything the State Department might suggest.

McNamara's PPBS system and the entire concept of adopting managerial techniques within the military establishment shows a willingness on the part of the Defense Department to improve its own efficiency. However, this efficiency is not to be confused with what might be termed a cutback in effectiveness or overall strength. For the Department of Defense has indicated that when the Southeast Asian war effort is "totally" eliminated, the momentum of various weapons systems already approved or in advance planning, plus existing commitments and other rising costs, will largely consume not only savings from the end of hostilities in Vietnam, but many of the increases in the GNP during the coming years.

One final example of military efficiency is the current move toward an all-volunteer military. Once again, the results of this action are not expected to decrease the power and potential of the military, despite the fact that fewer men will be wearing the uniform. For it is projected that improvements in such areas as task, efficiency, technology, discipline, and expertise will improve, rather than decrease, the effectiveness of the military when the all-volunteer system is fully employed.

A third modernization technique, closely related to the use of secularism in the context of decision making, is the growing sophistication of and dependence upon technology. Once again, the consciousness of the military to this modernization technique and the response which has followed is of massive proportions. As has been observed, in the modern age a thriving science and a dynamic technology have become the dominant force in human life. It is primarily technological innovation which makes enterprises, industries, and national economies grow in the modern world. The fact that today the United States has attained such prominence as an industrial and military power is often attributed to its tremendous allocations for technological research and development, which while only $100 million in 1940 are expected to reach nearly $20 billion in the 1970s. Among the institutions being funded are sixteen Federal Contract Research Centers, or "think tanks," which serve as specialized consulting firms in an independent, nonprofit, (but extremely well-paid) capacity for the Department of Defense. When one considers the complex of scientists, technologists, computers, missile delivery systems, and other weapon systems under the employment, control, and maintenance of the United States military, it is easy to realize the high level of technological sophistication which the military establishment has developed. The wedding of such technological sophistication with the secular approach to decision making permits the feasibility of many programs impossible ten years ago. The development of the C5A, the C-141 Strategic Airlift, and the fast deployment logistic ships, for example, make it possible (if necessary) to station the entire troop consignment committed to the defense of Western Europe within the territorial United States.

The final modernization technique we will discuss in this case study involves adaptability. Those who view the military as rigid and inflexible in all of its programs and techniques do not correctly understand the modern military. The programs adopted since World War II show a marked *flexibility* in nature. For example, the current trend towards an all-volunteer military is a response by the military which should not only result in better efficiency but which will also probably quiet and pacify recent public displeasure with the draft. The technological advancements of the past twenty years also show the Defense Department's consciousness of the changing nature and demands of warfare, conflict, and national security. To meet the demands of changing public attitudes, the military recruitment program now "wants to join you," in an appeal to a more individualistic-minded American. This and other military public relations efforts are conveyed to the public by the latest means and uses of the media.

Perhaps the best example of military flexibility, however, is to be found in Robert McNamara's strategic concept of flexible response. For John F. Kennedy and Robert McNamara, the concept of flexible response was simple and straightforward: to provide the United States with what they both were convinced it lacked, namely, a much wider range of options in using its national power. Thus, they sought to give American decision makers alternatives for meeting aggression other than those of resorting to nuclear war or doing nothing at all. McNamara's employment of flexible response, combined with his managerial use of cost-effectiveness, had undeniably significant effects upon his decisions in office concerning weapons systems and general security policies. His decisions and reasoning concerning the "thin" version of the antiballistic-missile system, the TFX issue, the importance of NATO, and the possibilities of limiting strategic weapons, are only a few examples. Another though perhaps less publicized aspect of McNamara's flexible response set the framework for the entry of the military into traditionally nonmilitary areas of concern. According to McNamara, such domestic problems as poverty and social injustice could easily be viewed as a threat to the very essence of our national security. It was thus under this assumption that McNamara led the military into such direct social reform programs as "Open Housing," "Project 100,000," and "Project Transition"; and this, of course, led to a major military emphasis on civic action and domestic assistance in the Nixon years. In essence, this represents not only an extreme version of applied flexible response but also marks a significant extension of the military's base of concern, perception of responsibility, and its increasingly active search for a post-Vietnam role.

At this point, before moving into a discussion of the ramifications of the military's success in utilizing these modernization techniques, it will perhaps be helpful to briefly summarize three essential points which emerge from our discussion thus far.

First, where the military is concerned, all of these modernization techniques have interacted with each other in producing the powerful establishment that exists today. No single modernization technique has alone been solely responsible for this development. For example, the military would never have been able to develop its present expertise in technological weaponry if it hadn't possessed either a strong bureaucracy capable of raising funds and influencing decision makers or the organizational ability started by the managerial genius of Robert McNamara.

Second, as has been argued by James Peacock and Thomas Kirsch, in their book *The Human Direction*,[19] it is those countries or institutions within countries which have best developed these modernization

[19] James Peacock and Thomas Kirsch, *The Human Direction* (New York: Appleton, 1970).

techniques that will enjoy the most power and influence in the technetronic age.

Finally, the military establishment has so successfully employed these techniques that it now enjoys the position of an institution so powerful and so well developed that it is not only a logical and well-prepared instrument for dealing with military oriented problems and crises, but also an institution potentially capable of expanding its capacities and responsibilities into traditionally nonmilitary areas of concern.

The Future: A Blessing or a Monster?

It is now appropriate for us to deal with the more difficult problem of attempting some projections concerning the direction and future of this modernized military establishment. Therefore, let us start by turning our attention toward C. Wright Mills' discussion of the "power elite." According to Mills, the almost continuous military crisis of current times has placed tremendous amounts of power into the hands of the bureaucratized military. From their strategic "command posts," the power elite can make the crucial decisions that determine the direction of American life, and remain uninfluenced by the mass democratic process. Indeed, the democratic games of the masses, such as elections, serve the interests of the power elite: They keep the people at play in the yard while the decisions are made upstairs.[20]

Although according to Mills the dangers of an overly powerful military already exist, the point to be made here is that whether one accepts Mills' proposition as valid or not, a brief study of the Department of Defense's accumulation of power, as outlined at the outset of this discussion, should indicate the clear possibility of such an occurrence.

Keeping in mind this potential, let us next look at the military as a bureaucracy, defining a bureaucracy as an organization which strives to maintain or improve its autonomy, organizational morale, organizational essence, roles and missions, and its budget. America's largest and most influential bureaucracy, the military establishment seems well suited to operationalizing this definition. And consider if you will, the tone of this definition. It implies a kind of individual strength and momentum characteristic of this specific bureaucracy

[20] See C. Wright Mills, *The Power Elite* (New York: Oxford University Press, 1956), chap. 12.

and above and beyond the actual functions for which the bureaucracy was created. This is not atypical of other institutions in the modern age. Indeed, by American law, the corporation is to be regarded as an entity separate from the individuals who own it. It can enter into contracts, can sue or be sued, can own property and contract debts, etc. This concept, in which the bureaucracy may operate on a level of reality distinct in its nature from the biological and psychological level from which it is derived, is known as "superorganic." This concept may be extremely relevant in a discussion of the exercise of power in the modern nation, for the bureaucracy upon reaching a high level of sophistication and complexity may take on an autonomous momentum of its own; then the question arises, are men controlling the bureaucracy or is the bureaucracy controlling the men? To pose the question another way, can the U.S. military bureaucracy, the largest and most developed in the world, take on an autonomous momentum in which it strives to maintain or improve or extend its legitimacy, morale, essences, roles, missions, and budget, above and beyond the best interests of the men who run it? This is indeed a difficult question to deal with. However, we do have a few facts and propositions to draw upon in an attempt to find an answer.

It has already been established that through the aid of its bureaucracy the military controls a substantial share of the federal budget. We also know that the importance of our national security interests has been so overstressed in recent years that an armed conflict in an undeclared war with a small underdeveloped Asian country 8400 miles from U.S. shores was deemed essential. In addition, we find many of the leading decision makers in the American political system convinced that the fabric of world peace is dependent upon the establishment and maintenance of a massive, costly, sophisticated nuclear arms capability, the suicidal use of which might bring about unlimited war, causing unimaginable destruction, the death of literally hundreds of millions, and the possible genetic impairment of a million generations to follow. Also, further consideration reveals that with increasing magnitude, the military is being used as an instrument to deal with traditionally nonmilitary problems. Two of the most obvious examples of this shift involve the areas of education and social work, so prevalent in the growing areas of concern at the John F. Kennedy Institute for Military Assistance at Fort Bragg, North Carolina.

These facts alone may not be enough to positively conclude the existence of an autonomous, self-motivated military bureaucracy.

However, they do raise enough questions to call for further investigation of this subject. Let us consider, at this time, the thoughts of a man once deeply involved in the fundamental workings of the military establishment, Colonel James A. Donovan, U.S. Marine Corps, (Retired):

> Within the Federal government a national security state has evolved since the National Security Act of 1947 created the three separate armed services, the Central Intelligence Agency, the National Security Agency, and the Atomic Energy Commission. These government bodies, which, together with defense industry, academic research groups, and Congressmen with vested interests, bolster each other and receive such a disproportionate amount of the Federal funds that there is no effective counterbalance. . . . There is a growing problem of uncontrolled bureaucratic power. The principal instrument of the power of this bureaucracy is fear, fear of the hazards and disruptions which is claimed will result if the defense establishment is not provided with all that it demands.[21]

The implication of Donovan's message, supported by the preceding facts, should be of concern to all Americans, who have historically shown such an abhorrence to any aspect of foreign domination and who have traditionally looked outside the boundaries of this nation for evidence of threats to their liberties and security. Now the possibility exists that one of the largest threats to their inherent rights may exist *within* the boundaries of this nation. This realization is not altogether removed from the theories ventured by C. Wright Mills in *The Power Elite.*

Through its utilization of the modernization techniques discussed here, the United States military establishment has transformed itself into one of, if not the most, modernized institutions in the world. Its organized centralization effort has extended its influence from mutual defense treaties with foreign nations all the way to the education of underprivileged U.S. citizens. Its efficiency makes it the foremost instrument of power and influence within the United States. Its technological sophistication ranges from the computer to the delivery systems of nuclear warheads; its mobility involves the fastest and most powerful transport systems in existence; and perhaps most important of all, its adaptability could allow it to enter areas of traditionally nonmilitary significance with such a sophistication that there is no indication of a counterbalance or means of checking its momentum and direction. If all of these capabilities will be utilized

[21] James A. Donovan, *Militarism: U.S.A.* (New York: Scribner, 1970), p. 2.

in the honest and sincere interest of the security of the American public, then no foreseeable danger within the discernable future can threaten this nation. On the other hand, if the momentum built up by this massive and sophisticated organization has indeed created a self-motivated, autonomous institution capable of pursuing its own organizational essence, then Americans may be facing a potentially greater threat than any now imagine.

SUMMARY

In summary, then, the foreign policy process of the United States changed dramatically after World War II due to the interaction of the numerous factors discussed above. And at the center of these revolutionary forces, generating this transformation, was the office of the president.[22] The challenges offered to the president in his role as chief policymaker within the foreign policymaking process have always been historically present, but with the changes produced by the post-World War II environment, they became monumental as more was asked of the man who was president. At the same time, the growth of the problems transformed the whole of the foreign policy process into competing and fragmented fiefdoms controlled by powerful bureaucratic units.[23] In essence, there was a revolution of involvement of the United States in the international system and a corresponding and sometimes dichotomous growth of presidential power coupled with fragmented, decentralized bureaucratic bargaining in the domestic foreign policy process. In effect, though presidential power became increasingly visible in the foreign policy process, at the same time, the president had become dependent upon members of the executive bureaucracies for the information upon which to base his decisions. In many ways, therefore, the president became the prisoner of bureaucratic politics and institutional compromises exactly at the time that his leadership at the apex of the foreign policymaking process was being solidified.

In crisis decision-making situations (e.g., Korea, the Cuban missile crisis) the president seemed to control and dominate the foreign

[22] See Spanier and Uslander, op. cit., pp. 28–53, for an excellent position in favor of presidential dominance in the foreign policy process.

[23] On bureaucratic politics, see Morton H. Halperin and Arnold Kanter, eds., *Readings in American Foreign Policy: A Bureaucratic Perspective* (Boston, Mass.: Little, Brown, 1973), pp. 4–16, 80.

policymaking process. But, in the more day-to-day programatic deci-sion-making situations (e.g., defense budgets, foreign country surveil-lance) the bureaucrats and their respective institutional interests seemed to control the elements of power. Hence, the tensions between presidential power and personal style clashing with bureaucratic poli-tics and institutional self-interest became (and remain) a systemic constant in the foreign policy environment of contemporary America.

THE RELIGION OF REALISM
AND THE TRUMAN ADMINISTRATION
An Analysis of the "Creation Years" of Contemporary American Foreign Policy

Having noted the significant modification in the institutional structures responsible for decision making in the foreign policy field, and having noted as well the changed international environment after World War II, plus the impact of such changes upon public opinion in addition to its implications for practitioners of traditional diplomacy, one must focus upon the changes made in the underlying philosophy upon which diplomacy rested. The difficulties surrounding both the substance of, and the processes by which decisions are now made, epitomized by Vietnam, but evident in numerous other instances, result as much from faulty modes of thought as they do from defects of personality, or errors of execution. The makers of post-World War II foreign policy have not always been wise, efficient, and honest, but they have always acted on basic assumptions about the world and on basic principles concerning American purposes, interests, and power. More often than not, they have taken the empirical validity as well as the philosophical and political soundness of these assumptions for granted; unfortunately, the assumptions were on occasion frightfully false and the principles equally dubious.

There are those who feel that application of the principles of realism in the making of foreign policy leads to the most tenable position for the United States internationally. During the Truman administration the theory and practical application of what was to be known as "political realism" came into its own. Terms such as "national interest" and "balance of power" replaced the humanitarian, moralistic shibboleths which propelled the makers of pre-World War II foreign policy (Cordell Hull, Frank Kellogg, Henry L. Stinson, Charles Evans Hughes). The objective of this chapter is to analyze the realism of the policies devised by the Truman administration in response to the challenges of the seven years following the close of World War II.

It is absolutely essential that this be done, because regardless of whether one agrees or even violently disagrees with the policies of the Truman administration, it was Truman and his key advisers who set the foundations of postwar American foreign policy. These self-styled realists operated upon a set of assumptions about the fundamental nature of the international system and the bipolar, postwar world. And it was the philosophical assumptions of realism as enunciated by George Kennan, Dean Acheson, and Harry Truman that set the intangible, but nonetheless understandable, parameters within which the American policymakers viewed the world—and, ultimately, set the framework within which operational policies were made and pursued.

The lessons of Munich, the aggressiveness of Hitler, and the weaknesses of the League of Nations made this group of men "realists" who were determined not to let America make the same mistakes again. Therefore, they acted in a tough, activist, and internationalist framework, which brought about the revolution in American foreign policy.

No one can understand or come to grips with any aspect of contemporary American foreign policy without first confronting the ideas and the actions of the Truman administration. For it set the foundations and the style upon which all succeeding administrations have operated. The incrementalism of the American political system allowed other administrations to nurture, massage, and even somewhat bastardize the realist scheme of the Truman years. But, underneath all the rhetoric of the ensuing presidential administrations, it is our contention that the realism of the Truman years remained the undergirding of American foreign policy.

In an effort to establish a common base for analysis, the philosophy and methods of realism will first be outlined. Then major postwar American policies will be studied and evaluated by comparing the political assumptions, objectives, means, and results in each case against the standards of realistic decision making. Finally, an attempt will be made to gauge the impact of the policies of the Truman era on the realism of American foreign policy in the 1970s. There is no need for any of us to necessarily agree with the tenets of realism, but we all have an obligation to investigate them so that we can understand the perceptual lenses through which the Truman people viewed world politics.

REALISM: THEORY OR METHODOLOGY?

Hans J. Morgenthau, a spokesman for the contemporary school of political realism, has observed that realism in foreign policy is a theoretical construct of a purely rational foreign policy which experience can never completely achieve.[1] Realism, in this, its most abstract interpretation, is based on the assumption that there exists an objective and universally valid truth about matters political. It also assumes that this truth is accessible to human reason. It contends that the world, imperfect as it is from a rational point of view, is a result of forces inherent in human nature; so to improve the world one must work with these forces, not against them. Furthermore, because the world is made up of inherently opposing interests, conflict and a struggle for power are inevitable.[2]

The advent of realism in political theory has shifted the emphasis from domestic to international policymaking under scholars and policymakers such as Hans J. Morgenthau, Dean Acheson, and George Kennan. It can, in theory, be expanded into a conceptual scheme that explains the world in terms that bear practical application to the making of foreign policy. Nevertheless, the abstract theory of realism in foreign policy is not practicable in so far as it attempts to gauge the realism of specific foreign policy programs. The theory in its purest sense assumes complete accuracy and availability of information regarding economic, political, and military capabilities; the internal political climate; and the intentions of the opposition. It does not make allowances for time and personnel factors, nor does it correct itself for errors in the aforementioned calculations.

Realism is not only an approach to the theory of foreign policymaking, but also to the study of the making of foreign policy. It can be an analytical tool for systematically analyzing foreign policy

[1] See Appendix B for the Six Principles of Realism.
[2] Hans J. Morgenthau, *In Defense of the National Interest* (New York: Knopf, 1951), p. 2. This entire discussion of realism is based on Morgenthau, but see also, Ronald J. Stupak, "Dean Acheson's Concept of International Relations," *International Review of History and Political Science* (February 1969), pp. 81–97.

decisions. The key is the result of the policy, not the objectives or the intentions. Alternatives are evaluated according to their projected result. With the advantage of hindsight, the predicted result is confirmed or denied, and the policymaking can be retraced in search of a maximum gain/minimum loss combination. In each case, focus is on what *is* actually to be done, not on what *ought* to be done.

Realism is also a methodology for the making of foreign policy. The decision maker analyzes the individual policy problems, not comparing them to a nebulous ideal, but matching them against alternative courses given specific circumstances, taking into account the imperfect availability of information, time frame, personnel, and capabilities. It does not pretend to provide the right answer so much as it contends that it supplies a methodology through which "realistic" foreign policy decisions can be made. It is the process of officially selecting from a number of possible courses of action, a desired result by applying certain of available means to attain selected ends.[3] It focuses on actions and their consequences, rather than on the intentions which are espoused as justification for these actions. Realistic ends sought through unrealistic means doom a policy to failure. Realism focuses on the intellectual ability of a policy scientist to comprehend the essentials of foreign policy and on the political ability of a decision maker to translate this into successful political action.

Realism makes explicit the values and nature of those applying it. Elements such as humanitarianism and moralism are present only until they conflict with the national interest. Facts are different from opinion, and objective analysis is separate from rationalization. Evidence must be illuminated by reason. Novelty is no virtue and tradition is no defect.

Realism as a method for making foreign policy is founded on certain basic assumptions about the perpetual conflict among nation-states and their national interests, the relative balance of power, and the relationships between intentions and capabilities—the ends and the means—in the making of foreign policy.

A realistic approach to foreign policy as recommended by Morgenthau, Acheson, and Kennan, recognizes that the world is and will in the forseeable future continue to be composed primarily of individual nation-states. These basic units of international relations remain the primary actors in the world arena. Despite competition for loyalties

[3] Edgar S. Furniss, Jr., and Richard C. Snyder, *American Foreign Policy* (New York: Holt, Rinehart & Winston, 1955), p. 94.

from regional alliances and international organizations, nation-states are here to stay.[4]

Each of these nation-states, which is a separate element of the international system, determines its foreign policy objectives in accordance with its own national interest. Each nation has one primary national interest in its relations with other nations—the security of its territory and institutions. Secondary interests for nations of the "free world" include such matters as peace and security elsewhere, the protection and promotion of democratic governments, the containment of aggressive Communist and other expansionist governments, and the relief of poverty. These are not pursued at the expense of the primary interest of national security and can be pursued only within narrow limits of available power.

National security is elastic, never static. Absolute security is impossible. Security lies in accepting moderate risks in order that immoderate ones may be avoided. Defense, military and economic aid, propaganda, military alliances, collaboration with allies, are all means to preserve territorial integrity and political independence. In judging political necessities in protecting its national interest, a state naturally tends to overcompensate in efforts to insure the national security. Because the national interests of different states are not always complementary, there is a conflict among the various nation-states as they pursue their primary interests. In fact, it is inevitable that such conflict should occur, if the goal of each nation is the maximization of its own chances of self-preservation. National interest is not only the starting point of foreign policy, it is the end result.

National interest is defined in terms of power. In pursuit of its national interest, a nation-state uses all available elements of power—military, diplomatic, economic, ideological, traditional, moral, technical, and geographical—to achieve its goals. The challenge of the international system is the management of power. Regardless of the ultimate aim of a foreign policy—be it freedom, security, or prosperity—the immediate aim is power. The fact that such goals are often defined in religious, philosophic, economic, or social terms does not alter their ultimate end—power. In evaluating any political alternative, the question of how it will affect the power of the nation must be asked. Legalistic and moralistic arguments are necessarily subordinated to political, that is, power considerations.

[4] The domination of this approach in American foreign policy is highlighted in Ronald J. Stupak, *The Shaping of Foreign Policy: The Role of Secretary of State as Seen by Dean Acheson* (New York: Odyssey, 1969), pp. 21–64.

It is power which separates the political from the nonpolitical. It has been said that a politician denying the importance of power is like a scientist ignoring gravity. It must be conceded that power is relative to time, to the problem toward which it is directed, and to the country applying it. There is no permanency to any power advantage. It is a common error to attribute too much weight to any one factor of power. Power must be accepted as the key element of politics; and the competition for, the allocation of, and the exercise of power is politics.

Taking into account the continued division of the world into nation-states, the primacy of national interest as the foremost determinant of national foreign policy, and the necessity of the recognition of the concept of power, the balance of power arrangement is essential in a system structured in accordance with principles of realism. It has been characterized as a system inimical to tyranny yet providing safeguards for the freedom of individual states. Changes in the system only supplement, they do not supplant, the existence of a balanced system. If there is a change in the relative balance, the system shifts to regain the balance. A nation's ability to shift is determined by national interest and a capability in defending that interest. Herein rests the key to success in the system: the ability to protect or advance one's national interest through adjustments in the balance of power. In the traditional sense, a balance of power system has a flexible element which acts as a balancer. The line between a balance of power and a favorable distribution of power is a fine one; most nations, especially superpowers, strive for the latter. Therefore, the system is in perpetual motion as each superpower looks for favorable readjustments. While it may appear that a universal bond exists among all members, such as a desire for peace, this appearance in its barest sense, is simply coincidence that each nation sees at that particular time that peace (i.e., often the status quo) will serve its own national interest. The ideal balance of power system builds on the mutual dependence among nations while at the same time overcoming strongly diverse forces and preserving, as much as possible, room for development and difference among societies and cultures.

The goal of a realistic foreign policy is to achieve the most favorable distribution of power in accordance with one's own national interest with "a minimum of foreign interference and minimal inconvenience or provocation to the interests of other nations,"[5] only in-

[5] Grayson L. Kirk, "In Search of the National Interest," *World Politics* (October 1952), p. 110.

sofar as such inconvenience would not be detrimental to one's own national interest. The axiom is therefore "the lesser evil," the rational maximization of one's goals and minimizations of one's losses.

Approaching the making of foreign policy in a realistic framework is a prudent and pragmatic process. To eliminate one danger at the expense of gravely enhancing another is not a solution. Principles cannot be applied in abstract formulations but must be filtered through the concrete circumstances of time and place. The facts of the situation—both the intentions and the capabilities of the parties involved—are examined; policy alternatives are outlined and evaluated in terms of both the facts of the problem and the national interests of all parties concerned—with primary concern for one's own national interests.

Realism is not the use of any means to justify ends, even noble ones. Yet, at the same time, a realist is aware that noble ends are always realized with imperfect means and methods. Often less than perfect means are used to achieve as well as justify ends. Realism must be interjected at every juncture of the policymaking cycle—in defining the problem, in relating it to the national interest, in evaluating alternative courses, in assessing the appropriateness of available means, in considering the power quotient, and in implementing and justifying the policy.

Realism in assessing intentions is a critical factor insofar as intentions dictate policy choices. Who seeks what, why, when, and how are vital questions about one's own course of action as well as that of one's allies and, of course, the opposition. How the opposition will interpret one's own moves is also a critical consideration. No foreign policy operates in a vacuum. The influences of internal political struggles and pressures are often key factors in international policy decisions.

In making such assessments, in order to insure against mere guesswork, intelligence becomes a key element in a realistic foreign policy process. As Roger Hilsman observed, intelligence is the manipulative instrument of foreign policy which is action conscious and policy oriented as it recasts the facts in terms of policy action.[6] While the Central Intelligence Agency may seem to be "dirty business," few actively engaged in the policymaking process will doubt the need for an intelligence gathering arm of government, if a realistic policy is to be followed. The accuracy and current nature of the data are

[6] Roger Hilsman, Jr., "Intelligence and Policy-making in Foreign Affairs," *World Politics* (October 1953), p. 1.

critical factors, but the key is interpretation of this data in policymaking terms. It is the responsibility of the decision makers to see that facts are not distorted or used selectively to support predicted outcomes.

The relationship between realism and diplomacy is *paper thin.* Diplomacy must never be played out in the trappings of a crusade. To load diplomatic activity with supercharged emotionalism is to cut down its effectiveness. The key to fruitful diplomatic endeavor is the ability to take the point of view of the host nation in terms of its own national interests. Taking the role of the host nation in policy debates, a diplomat can then anticipate reactions to foreign policy maneuvers and predict foreign policy offenses. The diplomat— with ceremonial, political, economic, and military resources in his repertoire—is the eyes, ears, mouth, and fingertips of foreign policy. The home office is the foreign policy brain center where data from the diplomats in the field and from their intelligence counterparts is gathered, evaluated, and fed into the policymaking process.

Within the realistic framework, alliances are entered into only when they are vehicles for expediting the national interest of a particular nation-state. Alliances are not joined as matters of principle or of good will. When a nation considers participation in an alliance with other nations it invariably seeks answers to some or to all of the following questions.[7] Is there a common threat to the primary national interest of each and every partner? Will this coincidence of primary interest overshadow conflicts of secondary national interests? Are there arrangements for sharing the responsibility for unpopular decisions so that no one party can be blamed? Are there built-in safeguards to insure that the organization remains a manageable size, keeping in mind that the larger the number of members, the more complex the consultation structure? Are there sufficient provisions to enforce sanctions against "independent" members?

The same realistic considerations apply to membership in international organizations. It is unrealistic to build such structures on the concept of a search for the perfect world order or a harbinger of peace, as if it were probable, or even possible, that conflict could be eliminated. The struggle for power is universal in time and space and the portrayal of unattainable goals contribute to cynicism about the possibilities of any international cooperation. No international organization is infallible. Instead it is simply a prudent choice for

[7] Louis J. Halle, *Civilization and Foreign Policy: An Inquiry for Americans* (New York: Harper & Row, 1952), p. 7.

a particular group of nation-states to join and observe its rules. In any case, sanctions or policy advances which jeopardize individual national interests, or compromise national sovereignty as in the case of collective security, are unworkable.

Realism in foreign policy also requires a recognition that international morality is nonexistent and that there is no concrete adherence to what is known as international law. Similarly, that body of thought referred to as international public opinion is a fiction of wishful thinking.

Assuming that the nation-state and its peculiar national interests prevail, the only limitation on policy actions is political expediency. It is conceded that the bulk of routine international contact takes place within the framework of international law, the codified reflection of custom, and according to its rules; it is not so much because of a respect for such law but as a result of policy cast out of habit in the interest of bureaucratic efficiency. Yet the greatest defect of international law continues to be the absence of effective and automatic sanctions. The procedural aspects of international law are much more highly developed than the more substantive facets. International codes are often effective justifications or excuses for a nation's policy actions, but are repeatedly ineffective against a renegade member of the community.

International law surrounds sovereignty with legal safeguards. It works only where complementary interests are identified and where the distribution of power is conducive to such adjustments. In any case, only those consenting to an agreement are bound, even morally, by it. Furthermore, codification of international law is ambiguous; no clear jurisdiction is outlined, and there is no hierarchy of decisions.

Only when national interests are complementary or when national ethical standards coincide does even a semblance of international moralism materialize. Even these occasional manifestations of what may appear to be international public opinion are most often temporary and subject to individual interpretation. And even if there is, to some small degree, a force called international public opinion, there is no empirical evidence of its restraining influence on national policies. If it does not affect the balance or distribution of power, it is not a major factor in determining realistic foreign policy.

While what appears to be a consensus is often the result of technical or philosophical unity, world public opinion is impossible given the lack of shared experiences of universal moral convictions and of common political aspirations among the peoples of the world. However, often peculiar national ethics claim to be aspirations of universal recognition. While public opinion rests upon such varied notions as "my country right or wrong," "self-preservation is the first rule of nations," upon ideas derived from Christian ethics, or upon United Nations humanitarian standards adjudged to operate in the consciences of individual men, it is assumed as the precondition for effective action in a system of international ethics that government is always by clearly identifiable persons who can be held personally accountable for their actions.

What sometimes passes for world public opinion is often nothing less than the universalization of certain aspects of nationalism—the elevation to the widest possible degree of the intellectual and moral conceptions which issue from diverse cultures. A tendency to draw universal implication from purely national experience is not an American monopoly. Each nation sees the whole of human aspiration through its own rose-tinted or devil-defining spectacles. Every nation sees the progress or the fate of mankind as parallel to its own and many times defines friends and enemies within this perverted, moralistic framework.

No description of an operational system of international ethics is adequate unless it makes sharp distinctions between ends and means. Although it has often been argued that some ends justify any means, there arises the suspicion that reasonable restraints establish the limits within which means are to be selected, however noble the ends. This is to suggest that in the analysis of the activities of nations vis-à-vis one another, realistic consideration must be given to the means as well as to the ends. Professor David Spitz, while I was a graduate student at The Ohio State University, once held forth on this theme. He made an analysis of the USSR, Germany, and Italy in terms of ends and means, and it came out something like this: The Soviet Union usually chooses noble ends (end of class conflict, class harmony, economic justice, etc.), but often seeks to realize them with horrible means (purges, liquidation of classes, harsh penal institutions designed to reconstruct citizens). Under Hitler, Germany chose ignoble ends (a society based on race) and chose to achieve such ends by the most ignoble means—the concentration camps, liquidation of Jews, Poles, etc. Italy, on the other hand, chose ignoble ends, but inefficient means to achieve them. Indeed, the criticism which seems most damaging against the Johnson administration with reference to American involvement in Southeast Asia comes from an analysis in terms of ends and means. However admirable was the notion that South Vietnam should have the right to determine its own political future, the means selected to achieve the end left too much to be desired on the part of those who did not understand the primary national objective. And to carry the point even further, it can be said that the Johnson administration began to invent ends in order to make them compatible with military, security means which had become, almost, ends in themselves.

With regard to realism and foreign aid decisions, national interest is once again the key factor. Aid is based not on generosity, but on national interest. All aid carries with it an aura of intervention no matter how veiled. Since the interests of donor nations and recipient nations are mutually served and reenforced, the introduction of claims of charity or generosity on the part of donor nations is a clear invitation to resentment on the part of recipients. It violates the receiver's self-esteem. Moreover, if the proclaimed basis for aid is charity or generosity, such help is generally unstable, for it could be withdrawn at the whim of the donor. On the other hand, when aid is based primarily upon mutual national interests, such aid is dependable and certain inasmuch as a nation's primary interest is less susceptible to change, being relatively inflexible.

Realism in foreign policy also involves a role for propaganda. The government of any nation-state must remain the leader of its public opinion, not its slave. Foreign policy is determined not by the masses, but by an elite group.[8] Domestic public opinion certainly does not make foreign policy, yet it is legitimate to question the extent to which policymakers, in their efforts to defend the national interest, express policies in moral and legalistic terms for maximum public support. At the same time, other policy scientists recognize the political wisdom of such a strategy, but question whether contemporary policymakers are clever enough to pull it off. On the other hand, excessive reliance in propaganda on moralism and legalism hampers diplomatic flexibility.

The effect on foreign policy in terms of realism of public opinion in the short run is not known. Realism of a foreign policy has no direct relationship to the number of people favoring it. Likewise there is no exact correlation between the truth of political philosophy and

[8] Public opinion analysts—from V. O. Key, Jr., onward—have wrestled with the matter of the informed citizenry, placing the number at no more than 15 percent of the population. Should the policymaker not show an extreme regard for understanding among this group—whatever he might feel toward the generally uninformed masses?

its effectiveness as political propaganda. Such propaganda must be relevant to the life experiences of the common man in the target state and play to popular aspirations.

THE TRUMAN DOCTRINE AND CONTAINMENT

A distinguished American writer, Norman Corwin, famous for his scripts in the Golden Age of Radio, once said that everything America learned during World War II was learned "trip hammer hard—between the blood transfusions and last rites." The movement away from moralistic considerations in international relations toward realism was step by step, painful, and slow. There was no sudden conversion experience, no light out of the blue, but a process lived through, a kind of slow dawning, a piecemeal gathering of evidence that the world did not correspond to American notions, and would not be responsive to them. Realism was the philosophical product of cumulative experience. Some things had to be endured, lived through, wrestled with, before the new policy stance was firm.

Both the United States and the Soviet Union were inexperienced in international diplomatic maneuvering. Each had had little contact with the other. Opposing ideologies with incompatible concepts of human behavior and the role of the state were further complicated by contrasting historical and cultural heritages. Finally, each had developed a favorite perception of and about the other's intentions, thus policy actions were based on erroneous assessments and tended to produce the predicted reaction as a self-fulfilling prophecy.

Our initial assessments of postwar Soviet intentions and capabilities were ambiguous and hotly debated. Nevertheless, once these intentions were reassessed and evaluated as a serious threat within the realism biases of the Trumans, the Achesons, and the Kennans, our reaction became both realistic and ingenious. This is not to say, however, that what was realistic with regard to the Soviet threat of 1945 or 1950 remains "realistic" in terms of the 1970s or, unfortunately, even the 1960s. Judgment as to the realism of continued containment policies will be offered at an appropriate spot in the narration. The concern here is with the realism of foreign policy decisions with regard to the Soviet Union in the years immediately following the war. This analysis is the key to the test of realism for the Truman administration since it was upon the policy of containment that all the other major foreign policy decisions were based. The question of the Soviet Union was always accorded the highest priority, and the question then, as now, would not go away. Wherever the policy-makers turned, somehow they felt they had to confront a new variant of Soviet power.[9]

It is almost incomprehensible that American leaders should have been so naive of Soviet interest in Europe after World War II. It is no less comforting that certain expert voices in our government were shouting warnings about the changing nature of America's role in international relations and being ignored as the government fumbled and hesitated in the immediate postwar period. The Henry A. Wallaces of the nation, obsessed with recollections of effective and close Soviet-American cooperation during the war, and fearful lest the disruption of such cooperation would hasten the coming of World War III, tended to initially prevail—a clear-cut example of the influence of a leadership elite out of all proportion to its numbers. At times it seemed as though the United States was once again revert-ing to its moralistic and legalistic assumptions that successful collabo-ration depended simply on the cordiality with which America entered new relationships. To intend the good was judged the guarantee of producing the good. Thus, the nation took a calculated risk on the good intentions of the Soviet Union—and lost much of its initial bar-gaining power. The situation was complicated by our compounding the risk by concurrent demobilization, thus inviting the USSR to flirt with its historical and cultural expansionism desires.

Before 1947, the United States policy was one of idealistic princi-ple overruling realism.[10] If it were expected that the Soviets would continue as loyal allies, then in order to maintain their confidence and consent, it would seem entirely proper to have restrained Western forces from the conquest of Berlin, Prague, and Vienna and to with-draw unconditionally from zones previously conceded to Soviet forces. If, however, it were indicated that the Soviets would revert to past rivalry, it would have been a mistake to hold forces back or to retreat until assurance of Soviet consent to its part of the bargain was demon-strated. Instead, the United States chose to follow-up at Potsdam with a hesitancy that left it at a disadvantage in relation to the Soviets.

[9] The author is not necessarily accepting the realism framework or the Truman policies flowing from it as good or bad, rather it is the author's contention that realism dominated the thinking and the policy patterns of the Truman years. Therefore, the description and analysis of the "creation years" is cast in this frame-work because of its relevance to what the Truman policymakers wanted to do and to what they thought they were doing.

[10] Halle, op. cit., p. 106.

When the German defeat seemed assured, the United States tried unsuccessfully to prevent the expansion of Russian power into Eastern and Central Europe. Language in the Yalta communique such as "freely elected, democratic regimes in Eastern Europe . . . in concert with the other Allied powers" ignored the factual distribution of power, the ambiguity of language which was bound to foment misunderstanding and ill will in later interpretations. Again at Potsdam, the word "democratic" flitted about indiscriminately in a formula which guaranteed that "interim governmental authority would broadly represent democratic elements in the population" and pledged "the earliest possible establishment through free elections of governments responsive to the will of the people."[11]

The Soviet Union appeared to want to consolidate its power as rapidly as possible in order to protect its homeland and to extend its political influence in Europe. There was no balance of power, in fact in Western Europe there was no power at all, since rapid United States demobilization had weakened America's position on the continent. The United States continued to act on the premise that the Soviet Union's objective was to reestablish national control and internal reconstruction with no major external advances.

Great Britain, supporting its claim with historical and practical arguments about Soviet national interest and international communism, continually warned the United States that the Soviet Union could not be expected to continue in practice the wartime alliance. The United States chose to believe that a desire for peace outweighed any individual national desires at that time. Furthermore, the American military, which after the war had disproportionate weight in the foreign policy process, let its pro-Soviet prejudice and its inherent distrust and smoldering jealousy of Great Britain's forces color its reactions to British pleas.[12]

It is curiously difficult to find documentation of official French assessments of Soviet postwar intentions and capabilities, or whether, indeed, the French were consulted at all on this question. However, it appears that the United States alone was responsible for wanting to "deal the Soviets in."

In April 1945, as FDR's death came suddenly, and the war in Europe was in its last month, Truman (an unknown quantity) took

[11] Cecil V. Crabb, Jr., *American Foreign Policy in the Nuclear Age* (New York: Harper & Row, 1972), p. 180.

[12] George F. Kennan, *Memoirs, 1925–1950* (Boston, Mass.: Little, Brown, 1967), p. 270.

over. The Truman administration protested the Soviet failure to live up to agreements on Poland, but did not back up its rhetoric with action. And the question remains whether the United States could have dared to do so with the still unfinished business pending in the Far East. At about this time, Ambassador Averill Harriman from his post in Moscow cabled recommendations for taking a hard line against the Soviets whom he judged to be acting completely from their own self-interest to the end of establishing total control over Eastern Europe.[13] Before Congress, Secretary of Defense James Forrestal was arguing that the Soviets in his view were following their own expansionary policies to the detriment of allied postwar strategy. Such statements were labeled alarmist and later their advocates, Harriman-Forrestal-Acheson, suffered personal retribution for their premature admonitions.

In May 1945, in an interpretative report from the United States Embassy in Moscow just a week before VE Day, diplomat George F. Kennan made the following observations about the "Soviet mood" at that time in a special telegram to the State Department in Washington: "They attach even greater importance to decisions of possible future peace conferences. For these later discussions, in the Soviet view, will be largely the product of the actual blows that will have been struck while the iron was hot."[14] In this same telegram, Kennan recommended prompt and clear reorganization of divided Europe into spheres of influence, since he was even then convinced that we were deceiving ourselves if we continued to hope for anything less than Communist dominance in those areas already under Soviet hegemony. We were wasting both money and time if we did otherwise, since such policies would be both undignified and misleading.

Up to this time, the debate over Soviet interventions had been largely private, carried on secretly by higher echelons of official United States and Great Britain representatives. In June 1947, with the publication of Kennan's "Mr. X" article in *Foreign Affairs*,[15] the American public and intellectual circles around the world entered the debate. As Kennan explains in his memoirs, the article's publication was intentional, but the disclosure of the identity of the author was accidental.[16]

---

[13] Arnold A. Rogow, *James Forrestal: A Study of Personality, Politics, and Policy* (New York: Macmillan, 1963), pp. 197–199.

[14] Kennan, op. cit., p. 265.

[15] See Appendix C for the full text of the important "Mr. X" article, "The Sources of Soviet Conduct."

[16] Kennan, op. cit., pp. 371–375.

The "Mr. X" article was originally a paper on Soviet intentions written for the personal enlightenment of Defense Secretary Forrestal. Kennan admits now that it was a careless and indiscriminately drafted piece insofar as his choice of words was concerned, since he most definitely was referring to political containment of a political threat, not military containment of a military threat. At the same time, the concept in Kennan's mind was limited geographically to Europe. His objective in writing the article was to highlight the danger of U.S. concessions to the Soviet Union and not to consolidate the status quo and the division of Europe. Misinterpretation of his article arose from the traditional failure of the American policymakers to understand the difference between political and military threats. In fact, it can be interpreted that the United States policymakers sealed the very division which their goal should have been to end.

In March 1946 in a speech in Fulton, Missouri, Winston Churchill made his reference to the "iron curtain" and called for joint action to oppose Soviet expansion. The U.S. government remained inert. Only after the Soviet pressures on Iran, the communization of Eastern Europe, and the tensions of Soviet obstructions in Germany did critical situations in Turkey and Greece spur the United States to action against Soviet expansionist tendencies. The result was a policy known as "containment" based fundamentally upon realism, and implemented initially by the Truman Doctrine. This explicit reorientation of American policy was based on the premise that the Soviets would mellow only after their expansionary designs had been frustrated for an extended period, thus forcing them to reevaluate their policies, adjust their capabilities, and modify their final objectives. A less dynamic, less hostile Soviet Union supposedly would have evolved. (Perhaps Kennan can argue that this is, in fact, what has happened in the 1970s.)

The Truman Doctrine was a strategic, not a moral instrument, despite military and State Department rhetoric to the contrary. In the Greek-Turkish case, action was taken by default to fill a vacuum of power left by Great Britain. What if Greece and Turkey had been left to their own devices? What would have been the impact on Europe of a communistic southeastern flank? Would Western Europe have been doomed to communism also? Was the United States whistling in the dark? The United States was realistic on these points, observing that aid to Turkey had to be militarily oriented while the Greeks were more in need of political and economic help. The policy per se is judged on balance to be realistic.

However, in announcing the policy as well as in "selling" it to a wary Congress, President Truman expanded its finite intentions, resulting in serious operational and rhetorical consequences for the entire future of American foreign policy: "It must be the policy of the United States to support free peoples who are resisting subjection by armed minorities or by outside pressures." In his *Memoirs* Truman recalled, "This was, I believe, the turning point in American foreign policy which now declared whenever aggression, direct or indirect, threatened the peace, the security of the United States [i.e., the national interest] was involved."[17]

The Truman Doctrine thus became a universalistic, open-ended policy for United States intervention, rather than a specific policy decision to aid Greece and Turkey with material and psychological support. One can well question the national interest of the United States in such interference. In addition, by defending the undemocratic regime of Greece, the United States was unable to make the democratic nature of the government in question a qualification for aid or intervention. The result was a careless blank check so that all a nation needed to do in order to get American aid was demonstrate the existence (or even sometimes, the illusion) of a Communist threat. In its negative sense, the Truman Doctrine became indiscriminately anti-Communist instead of prodemocratic. It fostered negative policies and a reaction-mentality by intervening in every threat, from aid to Greece and Turkey to military intervention in Korea and Vietnam, as it unrealistically treated communism as a monolithic, ideological structure.

It is also necessary to keep in mind that Soviet moves in the postwar years can be interpreted as simply defensive reactions to United States policy declarations and actions. According to Sokolovsky, the Soviets viewed the Truman Doctrine, the Marshall Plan, and NATO as instruments of American policy designed to enslave European countries, both economically and politically, after first transforming them into obedient tools in political-military blocs directed against socialist countries to the ultimate end of world domination.[18] It is therefore not so unreal to hypothesize that the Soviets practiced a Russian version of "containment" to keep the United States out of its legitimate spheres of influence.

[17] Harry S Truman, *Memoirs: Years of Trial and Hope,* vol. II (New York: Doubleday, 1956), p. 160.

[18] V. D. Sokolovsky, *Soviet Military Strategy* (Englewood Cliffs, N.J.: Prentice-Hall, 1963), p. 109.

The Berlin blockade could well have been a reaction to the announcement at the London Conference that the United States intended to set up a separate West Germany government. Similarly, the Soviet actions in the February 1948 Czechoslovakian coup were possibly a response to the Marshall Plan. As a last ditch Soviet attempt to consolidate all Europe under their hegemony, they played their final political cards by taking advantage of massive worker strikes in France and Italy. Even Korea might have been a reaction to the United States threat to sign a separate peace treaty with Japan, thus forcing the Soviets into a corner. We not only may have misread the Soviet intentions but we might have incorrectly assessed or failed to take into account genuine Soviet national interest interpretations of our policy moves.

The United States also failed in assessing Soviet military capabilities and intentions. Intelligence, the overlapping and loopholed responsibility of both the Department of Defense and the Department of State, was grossly inaccurate with regard to the level of Soviet atomic achievement. And American policymakers wrongly estimated the Soviet interpretation of and design for the United Nations, a miscalculation which is discussed later in this chapter.

A school of social scientists and contemporary historians who call themselves "revisionists" contend that Truman and his band of Cold Warriors led by Acheson precipitated the so-called Cold War by overestimating Soviet hostile intentions, thus forcing the Russians to respond with similar aggressiveness. Truman supposedly deliberately sabotaged Roosevelt's statesmanlike efforts (others would argue FDR was duped) at Yalta to establish a postwar *modus vivendi* with the Soviets and proceeded to preside over the creation of a vehemently anti-Communist United States, partly because of pressures from the military industrial interests, but also because of a national anticommunist neurosis.[19]

Certain revisionists charge Truman with "ignorance of Eastern Europe" and "a lack of sympathy for Soviet responsibilities for that

[19] These themes have gained numerous adherents. And the "respectability" of the revisionists has grown to such an extent that the *Foreign Service Journal* of May 1973 devotes its entire article section to revisionist critiques of post-World War II American foreign policy. However, it is the author's contention that realism dominated the perceptual lenses of the Truman policymakers, and that to operationally understand this period in historical context, realism must be used to describe and analyze post-World War II American foreign policy in order to understand its successes, failures, and excesses.

area."[20] However, most of them tend to underrate the Soviet role in helping to trigger the Cold War and the fact that the Truman administration, for the most part, ignored the Soviet sphere of influence in Eastern Europe except insofar as Soviet influence spilled over into Western Europe. In contrast to the Dulles rhetorical and ideological crusade of the 1950s to liberate the Soviet satellites, the Truman administration refused to take on this yoke—a realistic military and political choice.

Soviet intentions during the 1945–1947 period were understood by few inside or out of the Soviet Union. United States policy toward the Soviets after World War II initially seemed to represent a desire for agreement at almost any cost; any disagreements yielded United States concessions as it had bargained away real military capability advantages in exchange for imprecise Soviet promises of cooperation in the future. However, because of the delayed United States response, by 1947 the Soviets had made it clear that they were trying to establish a firm power position in Western Europe as well. The United States acted belatedly to stop them. The handling of the conflicts of interests with the Soviet Union as they were played out in Western Europe, in the Far East, and in Washington will be examined in the remaining sections of this chapter.

FROM ECONOMIC TO MILITARY STRATEGY: THE MARSHALL PLAN AND NATO

When it is clearly perceived that traditional idealistic and moralistic sentiments became an insufficient scaffold to support policymakers faced with the complexities, ambiguities, and duplicities of the early post-World War II years, one rightly searches for the specific policy decisions which rested upon a new philosophical base. Although there was an initial period of indecisiveness, a time of groping for friendly relations with the Soviet Union, especially so far as Western Europe was concerned, it finally became evident that on the most meager practical terms such collaboration appeared to the realists in the Truman administration to be impractical. Thereafter particular suggestions became the subjects of "in-house" debate, and subsequently—

[20] For example, see Athan G. Thoeharis, *The Yalta Myths* (Columbia, Mo.: University of Missouri Press, 1971); and Gar Alperovitz, *Atomic Diplomacy* (New York: Vintage, 1967).

after agonizing months—developed into clearly conceived policies which resulted in specific institutional formulation. The capstones of all such policies emanating from the Truman Doctrine were the Marshall Plan and the North Atlantic Treaty Organization (NATO).

The Marshall Plan was an outgrowth of United States national interest in restoring a favorable balance of power in Western Europe. It was conceived to thwart a shift in that balance toward the Soviet Union not unlike that which had already occurred in Eastern Europe. Immediately after the war, the Soviets had both quantitative and qualitative superiority in communications, transportation, and weaponry compared to the rest of Europe. The task was not to maintain or shore up, but to restore Western Europe to functional unity, economically and politically.

All so-called humanitarian interests of the United States were secondary. Anyone who might dispute this contention need only look at the time that elapsed between the defeat of Germany and the United States offer to aid, first economically, then militarily, the nations of Western Europe. Or one can look at the eighteen months it took Congress to pass the original Marshall Plan legislation even after Truman's initial decision on this question. Granted, the "selling" of the plan to the American public stressed the humanitarian aspects of economic aid, but this was only part of a tactical maneuver to build support. When the public demanded more than a "good will" gesture to justify such a massive economic outlay, the sales pitch shifted to the need to help Europe fight communism. Unfortunately, it mushroomed into the misperception that the Marshall Plan was, in fact, aimed directly and only at *stopping* communism instead of making Western Europe less vulnerable to communism. The real objective was to restore Europe, as an equal partner in the world order by rebuilding European economies, by increasing the European market, by reconciling France and Germany, by restoring shaken faith in the nation-state and therefore restoring the political balancer role of Europe—and all of this was to be accomplished in order to insure American national security interests as they pertained to the needed balance of power on the European continent. The Marshall Plan of economic aid will be discussed before moving on to an analysis of its military parallel, NATO. The latter extended American objectives to include a basis for direct United States participation in the affairs of Europe, assurance of a European military assistance bloc, and complete integration of a rebuilt Germany into the rest of Europe.

It was punctilious exactitude in Washington for the letter of the Lend-Lease arrangement which stopped the vital flow of American goods when they were needed most by Europe and the Soviet Union. At a time when it was appallingly clear that such support was critical, the United States withdrew its aid in favor of multilateral aid programs through the United Nations. The United Nations Rehabilitation and Relief Agency, in which we had publicly put our faith, also failed to do an adequate job in spurring economic recovery. It was clear that unless massive aid was offered immediately, the military and political threats would multiply uncontrollably. The only beneficiary of the continued stand-off was seen to be the Soviet Union.

Not until Marshall's visit to Moscow for the Foreign Ministers' Conference in April 1947 did the United States realize the gravity of the plight of Western Europe. The conference failed miserably and the United States along with its allies had to admit that collaboration with the Soviet Union was for the period under discussion a pipe-dream. France and Italy were threatened internally by Communist parties, and Germany was sliding toward economic bankruptcy. It had finally become clear that the Soviets were obviously banking on the United States inability and unwillingness to bail out Europe. Eventually it seemed as if Western Europe would turn to communism as Eastern Europe had done, leaving the Soviet Union to name its political price. The Marshall Plan broke through the aura of pro-Soviet thinking left among some American political decision makers and military leaders. At the same time, it shook loose the self-righteous punitivism of occupation policies in Germany—the leftovers from the anti-German mentality that was evident in the FDR administration.

The immediate problem was coal and industrial fuel. The long-range problems were the economic, political, and social structure of Europe. The enemy was the economic maladjustment which was making Western Europe vulnerable to communism, not communism itself.

The Marshall Plan idea was first aired as a trial balloon in Undersecretary of State Acheson's remarks in Cleveland, Mississippi, on May 8, 1947, in what Truman called "the prologue to the Marshall Plan," stressing that, after Moscow, General Marshall had concluded European recovery could not await "compromise through exhaustion" and must proceed without four-power agreement.[21] The "official" launching of the plan which had heretofore lain in the Clayton memoranda came on the occasion of Secretary Marshall's acceptance of an honorary degree from Harvard in June 1947. The speech, characterized as a

[21] Dean G. Acheson, *Present at the Creation* (New York: Norton, 1969), p. 228.

short, simple, and altogether brilliant statement of American resolve concentrated on the following points: The policy was directed not against any country or doctrine, but against hunger, poverty, desperation, and chaos; such assistance was not to be on a piecemeal basis but must be a cure rather than a mere palliative; the initiative would have to come from the Europeans themselves; and a central part of the plan would have to be the rehabilitation of Germany. It was understood that the Soviets were to be invited to participate so that if they refused the onus would be on their side for the responsibility of a divided Europe. Acheson has observed that "If General Marshall believed, which I am sure he did not, that the American people would be moved to so great an effort as he contemplated by as platonic a purpose as combating 'hunger, poverty, desperation, and chaos,' he was mistaken; but he was wholly right in stating this as the governmental purpose."[22]

While the government was preoccupied with restoring Western Europe's ability to thwart Communist designs, mention of a "united" Europe crept into its rhetoric. Such suggestions were simply not substantiated by events or policy decisions and later resulted in misunderstandings contributing to the cynicism surrounding the plan in general. It was taken for granted that the Soviets would refuse to participate in the European Recovery Program; therefore, it was unrealistic to portray the Marshall Plan as a vehicle for uniting Europe. While, with the aid of constant United States pressure for integration and unity in Western Europe, the Organization of European Economic Cooperation and the Schuman Plan were initiated in 1950, their accomplishments and aims were far short of European unity. In fact, it was dramatically clear that success of the plan would result in a permanently divided Europe. It was perhaps here that the Cold War really began as the Truman Doctrine caught fire in the Marshall Plan.

The plan sent $17 billion over a four year period, and by its end in 1951 production in each of the Western European states had reached or exceeded prewar levels, international trade was up 11 percent over the prewar period, and intra-European trade was on the upswing. The Marshall Plan had worked. It was perhaps the single greatest achievement of the Truman years, combining realistically assessed ends with available means with a view to serving the national interest by restoring the balance of power in Europe.

[22] Ibid., p. 233.

The successful operation of the Marshall Plan removed part of the threat which Soviet communism posed for Western Europe, for the reestablishment of the national economies closed out the possibility of Communist success stemming from economic chaos, hunger, unemployment and hopelessness. The plan, however, did not rule out the possibility of a Communist military takeover. It is now, therefore, necessary to recount the realistic effort to thwart perceived Soviet westward expansion. Thus, our attention is drawn to the creation of NATO, for by it an effective force came into being which forestalled further Soviet military aggression, or expansion by blackmail.

The United Kingdom took the lead in the move toward collective action which resulted in the Brussels Treaty—a fifty-year treaty of economic, social, and cultural collaboration and collective self-defense signed by the foreign ministers of Great Britain, France, and the Benelux countries in March 1948. Yet, despite the recognition of the common danger, there was unarguable recognition of the premise that Western Europe could not be defended, if attacked, without American participation in the defense effort. That the initiatives for such defense were European is readily understandable, for Western European countries had a close-up view of the Communist takeovers in Poland and Hungary in 1947. They witnessed the aftermath of Hungary's free election in which a conservative rural-agrarian party had won a clear majority, the tragic demise of Czechoslovakian democracy, and, of course, the Berlin blockade, which seemed to be a major catalyst that accelerated the resolve of both the Europeans and the Americans.

Great Britain's search for American assistance led to the consultations which in the course of time saw the start in Washington of negotiations on the drafting of the North Atlantic Treaty between the representatives of the Brussels treaty powers, Canada, and the United States. In the course of the negotiations it was deemed advisable to enlarge the membership of participating nations, and in March 1949 the negotiating powers invited Denmark, Iceland, Italy, Norway, and Portugal to adhere to the treaty. On April 4, 1949, the foreign ministers of all the above-named nations signed the treaty. It is interesting to recall even more emphatically that throughout the whole course of the negotiation, insistently footnoting its significance, the Soviet authorities applied the pressure of the Berlin blockade (June 24, 1948–May 9, 1949).

There were those, among them Ambassador George Kennan, who feared the establishment of NATO on the grounds of the military imbalance between the Soviet Union, which was not yet demobilized, and the United States, whose forces would obviously carry the bulk of the defense burden. They questioned whether the United States nuclear monopoly would continue. They felt that a written agreement tying the United States to the defense of Europe was unnecessary. After all, what had World War II been all about? Furthermore, when nations were struggling with economic recovery and political stability, rearmament seemed unnecessary, superfluous, and counter productive. Kennan would have preferred to keep the door open for an uncommitted and possibly demilitarized Germany and a united Europe with a view to reducing abnormal United States political and military responsibility around the world.[23]

The United States was well aware of the disproportionate burden of the NATO arrangement and was willing to assume the responsibilities. It also, by this time, had concluded that the time for reconciliation of East and West in Europe had passed leaving only two alternatives, a divided Europe or a united Europe under the Soviet Communist thumb. It is debatable whether the Trumanites grasped the permanency of the division NATO sealed.

With regard to the composition of NATO, one must look at the original membership. Although it was intended from the beginning that Germany should be a member, it was not until 1955 that the United States was able to obtain agreement to admit West Germany. The aborted European Defense Community was an effort to reconcile European misgivings about American insistence on German rearmament. It was admittedly realistic on the part of the United States to envision the leading role of Germany in Europe of the 1960s and 1970s. The Italians were included because their isolated position and complex domestic power struggle made them too vulnerable to go it alone. Likewise, it included Greece and Turkey, both of which are questionably European, and neither of which was "democratic" and/or "North Atlantic." Was this realism and national interest overruling pro- or antidemocratic feelings? Or was it a mockery of national interest?

Another open question was whether the Truman administration correctly estimated the British and French roles in the recovery of Europe. French plans were admittedly difficult to predict, but the United States failed to anticipate Charles de Gaulle's reemergence and the consequent revitalization of the nation-state philosophy. Such

[23] Kennan, op. cit., p. 231.

deep faith in the reality of the nation-state and an envisioned pyramid of power in Europe with France at the pinnacle with its force de frappe was a "wrench" in the United States design for postwar Europe. Many, including the Americans, failed to understand that the French nuclear force was a political, not a military, weapon aimed at making France and Europe a third force independent of the United States and the Soviet Union. It was timed to take advantage of the renewed self-confidence of European nations. To the French, it was the key to their independent status in the context of their national interests. It made American pressures for a supranational European alliance anathema. Nevertheless, during the immediate postwar years, internal French chaos frustrated attempts to restore French greatness. The continuation of the French democracy depended on outside assistance.

Great Britain, hailed after the war as an "equal partner in peace," was so regarded despite numerous warnings to the contrary, even in the serious intellectual British weeklies such as *New Statesman* and *The Nation*. Great Britain, as it recovered, had to adjust its perspective and objectives to the change in conditions as it emerged from the war more united as a nation, but declining steadily as a world power. As before the war, in the 1945–1957 period and after, Great Britain continued to be in an ambiguous position with regard to the rest of Europe. Traditionally, the British have avoided long-term foreign policy and eschewed continual commitments in an effort to retain their independent role as a balancer. The Commonwealth also presented a special problem for Great Britain's economic relationship with the rest of Europe. Its special ties to the United States unsettled the rest of the alliance, especially the French. Many of the British-American post-World War II agreements provoked political controversy and nurtured questions about United States' selective favoritism. Once again, the United States was caught in the role of closing the gap between European aspirations and credibility.

Problems in NATO multiplied. Success depended on perception of a common danger threatening the security and therefore the primary national interest of the member nations. Today, there is a question whether that common danger still exists or whether, more precisely, the European members believe it to be a primary threat to their national interest. In fact, there is even a segment of analysts who wonder if the threat ever existed at all. The thing that holds the alliance together is the continued conviction that the national interest of each party is most effectively served by working together through a cooperative framework of force. There is also the problem of the credibility of collective defense. Would the United States, then or now, have risked nuclear war over Europe? As soon as the Soviets developed "the bomb," in September 1949, wasn't the credibility of NATO fundamentally altered? Did we in 1949 believe our nuclear monopoly would continue indefinitely? There was then the question of the realism of the United States troop commitment in Europe. Did we anticipate a 20 year presence? Finally, did we take into account the internal politics of our allies? Were we able to share the responsibility for major decisions, especially the unpleasant ones?

NATO was a complete reversal of traditional American isolationism as the United States set out to organize defensively the rest of the world. NATO was the first in a complex set of regional alliances which ringed the globe, overextending American willingness and determination to defend all areas against Communist aggression and, at the same time, encouraging the Europeans to depend too confidently on United States commitments against possible Soviet aggression.

GERMANY: KEY TO POSTWAR EUROPE

The United States made its most costly errors in postwar foreign policy in its handling of the German question. Policy toward Germany immediately after the war showed a great lack of appreciation for the role of Germany in the balance of power in Europe. Due to our inability to perceive Soviet objectives, we were unable or unwilling to see the strategic, geographic, economic, and political importance of the German state in the power equation between East and West. We found it convenient to disregard the lessons of even recent history showing the natural force of the German nation in the political and economic profile of Europe. At the end of the war, no one took serious note of the advantages of preserving the German communications network linking all of modern Europe; instead, it, along with mountains of German research and intelligence data, was destroyed. Few saw the potential role of Germany as that buffer between East and West which at the same time could provide the most vivid example of face-to-face showcase demonstrations of democracy and communism. No one guessed that a politically and economically revitalized Germany would, within two decades, take the lead in economic, technical, and political cooperation within Western Europe and between Western Europe and the East. It is ironic that in its policy toward Germany, the West, particularly the United States, sealed the division of Germany, the division of Europe, and in part, the division of the world.

FDR's well-known aversion to discussing the politics of the postwar arrangements while the war continued, even though such considerations were uppermost in the Soviet planners minds, gave the Truman administration little to build on. The military took over and muddled through while a weak State Department shifted into gear in an attempt to regain control of what was now obviously, yet too belatedly appreciated—a political problem, not a military one.

The conduct of the American occupation, as well as that of the other allies, was almost disgraceful. Kennan's portrait of the military's dictation of the occupation presents it as being "directed by a characteristic love for pretentious generality, evangelical liberalism, self-righteous punitive enthusiasm, and pro-Soviet illusions."[24] The U.S. military in Germany operated almost as a sovereign power, often even expecting the government it represented to regard it as such. Too late the United States realized the enormity of the task it had undertaken and its inadequacy to fulfill it. The moralistic interpretation of "unconditional surrender," although perhaps justified psychologically, was totally unrealistic. Unconditional surrender was, in practice, an open invitation to a power vacuum in Central Europe. The terms of the Joint Chiefs of Staff Paper 1067 were administratively unworkable and politically and economically disastrous. Throughout this folly, the State Department did not do so much as to set up a separate German Desk in the Bureau of European Affairs. Instead the task of supervising our German operations was left to the Defense Divisions of Occupied Areas.

The policy was a negative one of complete disarmament, demilitarization, and dismemberment into its pre-Reich components. All our efforts as well as those of the other allies, were aimed at doing things to Germany, not for Germany. The Henry Morgenthau Plan to inflict pastoralization on the Germans by destroying the potential of the Ruhr and Saar forever was finally abandoned by Roosevelt, but only after heavy pressure from Harry Hopkins and the State Department.[25] JCS 1067, the "bible" of the United States occupation policies, was nevertheless heavily punitive, stating that "no action could be taken to support basic living standards in Germany higher than those existing in any one of the neighboring states." When the United States and Britain, eventually joined by France, decided to

---

[24] Ibid., p. 392.
[25] Cordell Hull, *Memoirs* (New York: Macmillan, 1948), p. 1610.

merge their zones economically, it was not surprising that sooner or later the Soviets would challenge our resolve. After the announcement of the allied intention to form a separate West German state which was followed by the Berlin currency reform which cut the ground from under the Russian-sponsored mark, the Soviets tried a squeeze play through the Berlin blockade to test allied patience and firmness. The airlift response was a realistic choice in that it accomplished the aim of continued viability of Berlin without risking a ground confrontation with the Soviet forces around Berlin. Germany was no longer an end in itself; it became the key to the Cold War, a symbol of the East-West confrontation and the frustrations of attempts at Four Power cooperation.

So far as Soviet intentions regarding Germany as a whole are concerned, the allies deceived themselves by trusting in Soviet cooperation and the myth of Four Power control. The Soviets had moved first among the four to "normalize" conditions in their zone. The Soviet walkout from the Berlin Kommandatura in July 1948, like the Soviet withdrawal from the Allied Control Commission in March, only formalized what had been an obvious fact for some time—that quadripartite cooperation was a myth. The Soviets appeared then, and continued to be, super-sensitive to events in Germany ever since the end of the war and have not always acted in their characteristic prudent manner in crisis cases.

By setting up a West German state in the London Protocol, the West ignored probable Soviet reactions. The result was the Berlin blockade. The West could have called a new Four Power Foreign Ministers Conference and abandoned the London program in exchange for retiring Soviet forces around Berlin, yet it was decided to stick by London and separate out the Berlin problem. Despite claims that a quadripartite compromise was considered, it is generally conceded that London was regarded a "fait accompli" in that General Lucius Clay, the American proconsul in Germany, regarded it as a last act of glory and never considered any alternatives despite the Soviet response. The result was the creation by the Soviets of a separate East German state.

In balance, America's German policies were only a partial success and, on balance, not totally realistic. The economic miracle was in large part due to American aid, but it was also the result of remarkable leadership and the characteristic energy of the German people. The success of the leadership projected the economic might of West Germany into the international political spotlight.

However, the question of Germany remains unsolved, even in the current period of detente. The United States has overextended its presence and power in West Germany, often overshadowing German decisionmakers in foreign policy matters. Finally, Germany, like Europe, remains divided. Yet it is not us, but the Germans, who are facilitating "normalization" of relations with the East, leaving us, along with the British and French, responsible for formally upholding the postwar Four Power agreements about Germany as a whole. Even today, despite German membership in the Common Market and NATO, Europeans, especially the French, are skeptical of German policies and demand a United States guarantee of security there. What had we gained?

KOREA: NEW WAR, OLD GENERAL, NO SOLUTION

Although the energies of the American president and his advisers in international affairs were focused upon Europe as they sought practical realistic responses to the ebb and flow of events, East Asia was not overlooked. The war had come to its dramatic ending with the flights of the Enola Gay and the Grand Artiste and their lethal cataclysmic atomic bombs for Hiroshima and Nagasaki, with the grand pageant of the final ceremonies bringing World War II to an end upon the broad deck of the U.S.S. *Missouri*. Much treasure and many a life had been lost since the fateful day at Pearl Harbor on December 7, 1941. Japan had been paid back double, and a proud military leader, General Douglas MacArthur, was in charge in the Dai-Ichi building facing the Imperial Palace in Tokyo. Surely, no more hostilities would erupt in East Asia.

Even as late as 1949, Americans saw little danger of new clashes in the Pacific, especially since the U.S. Air Force was established firmly on Okinawa, as well as in Japan itself. Most Americans rested assured that war in the Pacific was over. So far as public opinion was concerned, Korea was not vital to national interest, and there was little opposition to withdrawing our forces from that country.

The American public's lack of knowledge and understanding of the Asian problems and point of view often resulted in our failure to act, or in our taking the wrong course of action in Far East matters. In his "defense perimeter" speech, in which he drew the lines of the limits of vital U.S. defense areas, Secretary of State Acheson did not even mention Korea, seemingly a confirmation of American disinterest. Then suddenly in June 1950, we found ourselves at war.

Korea was not a crusade. American objectives were conservative—the status quo ante. Yet the war aroused public indignation about foreign policy, stimulated violent opposition in Congress, stained the political influence of the Joint Chiefs of Staff, and contributed to the ousting of the party in power in a national election.

While Korea was not specifically mentioned at Potsdam, it was clearly implied that Japan would not be allowed to resume administrative control of Korea, nor was it expected that the American or Soviet ground troops would occupy that area for any extended length of time. The 38th parallel was never a subject of interim discussion but merely a temporary solution to the void of control which the United States assumed would lead to joint supervision. In fact, the Soviets even refused a Japanese request to mediate the Pacific conflict. When the Soviets, in keeping with the pledge made at Yalta, entered the war two days after Hiroshima, they surprised the Japanese troops in Manchuria and the North Koreans, and even offered 20,000 Soviet troops to assist in the occupation of Japan. There was doubt and pessimism concerning their intentions, and the offer was refused.

According to Kennan, many United States officials viewed Korea as a first step in a Soviet grand design independent of any American policies to control the Far East.[26] Few were able to see it in a more realistic light as a defense of Soviet national interest in response to our announcement of a separate peace with Japan including agreement to retain U.S. military presence by forces and facilities in Japan and the Ryukyus. The unleashing of the war in Korea ended any possibility of Russian-American cooperation in neutralizing or demilitarizing Japan (an idea which in itself is open to serious question). In addition, throughout the Korean campaign, we appeared blind or insensitive to Soviet and Chinese interpretations of the tactics of General MacArthur as evidence of American policy objectives.

MacArthur viewed directives as statements upon which he could exert ingenuity like a scholar deciphering a palimpset which he could interpret according to his own established theories.[27] He had profound ignorance of the political ramifications as he decided to extend the war to China and even Russia by blockading Port Arthur, bombing railroads in Manchuria, and establishing himself as commander of

---

[26] Kennan, op. cit., p. 12.

[27] Robert Payne, *The Marshall Story* (Englewood Cliffs, N.J.: Prentice-Hall, 1951), p. 316.

the anticommunist forces in Asia. He was brave; he was dedicated; he was brilliant, but he was wrong. If one loses sight of political objectives, war becomes simply meaningless destruction. The personal frictions, the disagreements on strategy and foreign policy, the poor communications, the flouting of civilian control, the violations of the chain of command, and the independent offer to negotiate with the communists on the spot without orders or consultation were intolerable moves by MacArthur. Yet much of the public, as well as many congressmen, senators, and highly placed political leaders remained unconvinced that his independent actions threatened American national interests. But his removal was deemed imperative, and accordingly, President Truman relieved him of his command in April 1951.

The lessons of the Korean War were numerous, if not well learned. It was the first American experience with unconventional, undeclared, no-win war. The common soldier for the first time in the history of American military involvement regarded his duties with supreme indifference, devoid of any crusading spirit. His objective was rotation, and troop morale was bolstered only by the psychological comfort of knowing one would soon be returned home and replaced regardless of the course of the war.

Military leaders were frustrated by the "limited war" concept and resented civilian control. They lamented the futility of the stalemate and their "uneasiness because political considerations were overruling military factors."[28] The American public sided with the generals, a situation not unlike the responses of the garrison state of military domination so ominously predicted in the writings of Harold Lasswell. The dissidence of the military leaders became a focal point of public discontent; the result—the election of General Eisenhower who promised to "do something."

The omnipotence of our nuclear deterrent should have been shattered insofar, at least, as "ending" war was concerned. The American public was shocked into realizing the peace was not assured, and that security in the postwar era was a constant struggle. Our bungled military operation, in no small part the result of unrealistic premature demobilization, shook allied confidence in our conventional military superiority as well. Some people questioned the advisability of having dragged the question into the United Nations in view of the clear mandate for the United States in Korea as a result of occupation responsibility. The United Nations role was further abused when the

[28] Samuel P. Huntington, *The Soldier and the State* (New York: Random House, 1957), p. 390.

United States representative, in the midst of a heated debate, implied that MacArthur was on orders to proceed as far north as Vladivostok, triggering a vehement Soviet protest and further aggravating our position.[29]

At the same time, with the Korean conflict, we cracked the unity among non-Communist Asian nations by forcing them to declare themselves for or against United States-United Nations policy. By seeking an emotional, anti-Communist support bloc, the United States ignored the relevance of the Asian balance of power to United States national interest. Irrespective of the justifications in international law, American national interest, or the long-term interests of the Korean people, the immediate psychological effects of our intervention were unfavorable, especially in South Korea where the physical evidence of Soviet intervention was not perceptible. In addition, the decision by the United States to cross the 38th parallel to unify Korea became the subject of much domestic and international criticism. It is unfortunate that the United States was unable to anticipate these psychological countermeasures so that the Korean people would accept the anti-imperialist, democratic objectives of the United States. It was hoped that the lesson would not be lost in future non-Western encounters. Propaganda became an integral part of the intervention.

The most profound effect, as Acheson later observed, was that involvements like Korea "have a way of snowballing" beyond even our most pessimistic anticipations.[30] And, of course, in the 1970s we endure the uneasy truce accomplished in the tents of Panmunjon in 1953.

DEFENSE: FROM DEMOBILIZATION
TO A NUCLEAR ARMS RACE

In his *Memoirs*, Harry S Truman recalled that "one of the strongest convictions which I brought to the office of president was that the antiquated United States defense set-up had to be organized quickly as a step toward ensuring our future safety and preserving world peace."[31] The reforms in the defense establishment during the Truman years were concerned with both defense organization and military strategic planning.

The National Security Act of 1947 and its amendments in 1949

[29] Kennan, op. cit., p. 517.
[30] Acheson, op. cit., p. 649.
[31] Truman, op. cit., p. 46.

revolutionized the American military. The individual services were unified under a common, civilian Secretary of Defense. The individual services, organized in departments, likewise had civilian administrative leadership. An interdepartmental committee, the National Security Council (NSC), was established to achieve effective coordination of all policies relating to national defense, and the CIA was created to serve as a special information-gathering agency for the NSC. The Joint Chiefs of Staff were, by statute, given responsibility for the professional aspects of the military, the administrative-fiscal management of the military, and the political strategic function as well—a sweeping mandate. These innovations were designed to adjust the national security apparatus to fit the mold of the change in power realities in the international system.

In the selection of his secretaries of defense, more than anywhere else, Truman showed the boldness of his national security policies and politics. The burden of the defense realignment was borne primarily by his first Secretary of Defense, James A. Forrestal, who was driven to suicide as a defeated man. Forrestal was followed by his own arch-rival, super-Democrat Louis Johnson who was appointed to pay a political debt. He became a symbol of the popular cause of budget-cutting and was so despised by the military he commanded that the services issued an ultimatum for his resignation. The wisdom of this appointment was best illustrated by its brevity. Truman's final selection for the Defense post was former Secretary of State, General George C. Marshall, who might have epitomized the integration of State Department and Defense Department responsibilities for foreign policy planning. Marshall, however, leaned heavily toward the military perspective and military requirements as determined by the Joint Chiefs, often without sophisticated consideration for economic or political considerations.[32] It would be another decade, however, before civilian control of the military would be more clearly established.

One of Truman's personal crosses in the defense debate was the draft. In his *Memoirs*, he conjectured that he was "morally certain that if Congress had enacted the Universal Military Training Program (UMT) in 1945," when he first recommended it, "we would have had a pool of basically trained men which would have caused the Soviets to hesitate and perhaps not bring on a Berlin crisis or the Korean aggression." Such speculation is questionable, but no one could

---

[32] Huntington, op. cit., p. 442.

dispute the fact that the presence of a sizable standing force would have been to some extent a deterrent. Americans, up until Korea, had traditionally equated the draft with a national emergency, that is, war, and Congress was leery of risking its continuation. Such a decision was politically wise, but militarily questionable.

Defense planning under Truman was done on a time-projected basis. The initially secret National Security Policy Paper (NSC) 68 was a plan for extensive increases in armed strength during the late 1949 through mid-1950 period. Up until the outbreak of the Korean War the United States was following a dual-defense policy, one the clandestine NSC paper, the other, the small scale rearmament dictated by congressional and public demands for budget economies. A realistic approach to defense capabilities was overshadowed by political considerations. The price was paid in lack of trained, combat-ready troops at the beginning of the Korean conflict.

Another unique feature of the immediate post war years was the introduction of the "preventive attack" alternative. As the Trumanites took hold, the military balance was clearly in the United States' favor. Should the United States have taken advantage of the Soviet weakness? While such an alternative is morally repugnant, the deciding factor was the anticipated response. European confidence in the postwar years was in the American power to deter war, not in its capacity to win it. If we had won the conflict, what would the United States have done with a defeated Soviet Union? Occupation was already proving a monumental task. Wouldn't a scramble for the satellite countries have resulted? Would Europe be caught in the crossfire? The United States possessed the means, but projected no need to use them. The balance had shifted—capabilities outranged intentions.

This debate, however, was cut short by the Soviet success in its atomic adventures in the 1948–1949 time period that revolutionized American national security thinking. The result was a United States position marked by a foreboding rigidity of policy and a rapid accumulation of deadly munitions. The Soviet atomic bomb prompted the United States decision to go ahead with a hydrogen bomb in September 1949. Still, many assumed the American omnipotence was only "temporarily" challenged and rearmament became a distinct possibility and, later, a necessity. In fact, the arms race almost took on a life of its own.

Since it was impossible to calculate the defense needs in precise terms, the requirements were overestimated. Stockpiles were begun.

Research and development received new emphasis. Some scientists, represented by Robert Oppenheimer, refused to accept the burdens and frustrations of an indefinite nuclear arms race and demanded an end through negotiated disarmament. Plans for disarmament had crystalized earlier in the United Nations resolution known as the Baruch Plan, a pretentious and unrealistic guise for disarmament "our way." At the same time, it appeared to some that the advent of nuclear weapons had spelled the end of a need for conventional weapons. The Korean experience dispelled this misconception as well.

Finally, it was during the Truman years that the military-industrial alliance, inherent in wartime and dissolved in demobilization, was revitalized. The National Securities Industrial Association created by Forrestal was a first step. Project RAND created under contract by Douglas Aircraft in late 1945 was another. By 1948 it had set up an autonomous shop incorporated to further and promote science and education, for the welfare and security of the United States. The nuclear arms race of the 1950s and 1960s would bear the fruit, but the seeds were sown in the Truman years.

CHINA: EMERGENCE BY DEFAULT
OF THE "SLEEPING DRAGON"?

While American leadership was immersed in the day-by-day problems of occupation duties in Germany and the Asiatic offshore archipelagos, events of great moment were occurring on the Asiatic mainland. The withdrawal of Japanese forces from China uncluttered the battlefield for the showdown between Communist and Nationalist forces which ended in the flight of Chiang Kai-shek to Taiwan and the birth of the Chinese People's Republic in October 1949.

American official attitudes toward China dramatically revealed the inflexibility of American policies toward the Far East. The espousal of Chiang Kai-shek up until 1949 was a valid position as he was for the most part a real Asiatic power by comparison with others. But with his fall, the United States was unable to adapt, and clung with unprecedented tenacity to his cause, thereby losing in the process its ability to influence Asian politics. United States China policies were the most criticized segments of American foreign policy during the Truman adminstration. The bipartisan foreign policy stances evident up until late 1949 gave way to bloody partisan infighting with the advent of the Far East problems.

The contention of supporters of the Chiang regime was that if China fell to the Communists, there would be a sharp reversal of the cause of world peace and stability. The United States continued to be the major Western power in this area and was therefore primarily responsible for preventing any Communist success in the area. The British, French, and Dutch were preoccupied elsewhere in the Far East with colonial difficulties. China was "our baby." It was therefore assumed that when Nationalist China fell, it was because of something which had been wrong in our policies; the blame was placed squarely at the feet of the center of the American foreign policy process, the State Department.

This might have been a plausible explanation had China been some sort of United States province and if the State Department had been running it; or if it had been the State Department, and not the Chinese people themselves, who had decided that the Communist faction, superior in morale and discipline, was the stronger and therefore more capable of winning the civil war. The facts were quite the contrary. Earnest United States warnings to Chiang about political oppression, corruption, and misuse of aid were ignored. In his repeated visits to Chiang, Marshall noted that American advice was always politely listened to and not infrequently ignored when it seemed unpalatable.

The traditional American role vis-à-vis China was based on a strategy using economics to maintain political balance, spicing the efforts with an ideological-messianic flavor. The Potsdam Agreement had included a commitment to liberate China from Japan and to restore Manchuria to Chinese control. The Western interpretation of these statements was to equate "Chinese" with the Chiang regime. Support in the United States for the liberated and pro-American Nationalist government ran high and every time someone in Washington challenged our "all-out aid" to the Chiang regime, there was overwhelming opposition which gave the diehards in the China lobby new confidence and sabotaged American efforts to bring about peace in the Far East. The Wedemeyer Report, supposedly objective, included a warning to Chiang that "the fundamental and lasting solution to the China problem must come from the Chinese themselves," but remained silent on the failure of land reform and increasing Communist terrorism.[33] It concluded erroneously that American aid to the Nationalists should be of a military and economic nature on a larger

[33] Payne, op. cit., p. 302.

scale beginning in 1949. Saving face had become an American objective, albeit unrecognized, as we continued to be blind to the facts of the situation.

Finally, by June 1949, Marshall had admitted that China was no longer a fair risk, yet token aid would have to be continued. The United States had for long remained too timid to cut the aid sooner or to threaten abandonment unless Chiang agreed to follow American advice. Pressure politics again proved too difficult a step; political blackmail was still out of the question and unethical, even at the cost of losing face in the Far East. The United States should have forced the Nationalist hand in our own national interest. Our rhetoric became more vague as we continued to advocate "broadening the base of the Chinese government," skirting the issues of inadequate communications, falling industrial production, poor transportation facilities, uncontrollable inflation, an army spread too thin, and corruption and lack of self-discipline throughout.

Even after the fall of the Nationalist regime, American administrative leaders reasoned that China would never be a threat to world peace since it was not an industrial power, and was, in fact, not likely to become one under the new Communist regime. This attitude was a reversal, a face-saving device, a move away from the earlier "domino" contention. Japan continued to appear the sole military-industrial threat and potential power in the Far East. Moreover, it was assumed that Soviet designs upon the Far East were set within reasonable confines. Stalin had declared that the Chinese Communists were not truly Communists, and Madame Chiang Kai-shek had paid public tribute to the aid which the Soviet Union had rendered to the Nationalist cause. At the same time, Washington was primarily occupied with deterring the Soviet Union in Europe and chose to "let things ride" in the Far East.

Another complication in the China debate arose from the question of diplomatic recognition of the new regime, and the problem of the admission of China into the United Nations, with the attendant problem of the permanent seat on the Security Council. The president quickly dismissed the former, and cut off even the most tenuous ties with the mainland. Increased aid and attention was extended to the newly established Nationalist regime on Formosa. The strategy agreed upon was the isolation of the new Communist regime in Peking in order to force its hand—a policy which was regretted in little more than a year as the Chinese forces entered the conflict in Korea in November 1950 with almost disastrous results for the United States-

United Nations combined forces. Others recall that the American policy of nonrecognition took on a punitive character in retaliation for the treatment of former American consular and trade representatives, along with revulsion over the ideological nature of the new regime.

While the American president steadfastly refused to discuss any alteration of the situation which kept Nationalist China in possession of the seat on the Security Council on the grounds that the Communist Chinese neither held complete control of the mainland nor had the legal mandate of the people, the deeper reason for his adamant stand was a fear of adding another veto possibility to the already negative performance of the Soviet Union. Perhaps the sole favorable outcome of these questionable policies was the continuing friendship of Chiang—if that can truly be counted as a positive outcome.

Neither the Nationalist Chinese government nor its people were capable of using American aid effectively. The loss was squarely Chiang's responsibility. He was not overthrown, but ignored; he lost by default. The net effect was a decline in United States policies and influence in the Far East, and around the world. In an attempt to isolate the People's Republic of China, the Americans had given the Soviets and the Chinese another common cause, hatred for the United States—that common enemy element so essential to a successful alliance. The balance of power had not been restored in American favor and a net loss in the power quotient had evolved. As of late 1951, the American policy in the Far East was one of direct military support to Japan, Korea, and the Pacific Islands and indirect support to Formosa and French Indochina.

THE STATE DEPARTMENT: THE REVOLT
OF THE PRIMITIVES

The close of World War II marked the end of many traditional forms of international diplomacy. As the concept of national interest changed so did the role of the diplomat, whose primary function is to serve that national interest. Both the superpowers were new-comers in the play of polished diplomatic niceties. Both were now to tailor their efforts to their own needs in postwar competition—they alone wrote the rules. For 12 years, Franklin Roosevelt had almost singlehandedly made foreign policy. The Communists likewise had had little opportunity to practice diplomatic maneuvering. An official

Soviet philosophy which favors temporary expediency, and a government that punishes bitterly for failure, allows little flexibility for negotiators who simply respond to a chain of command.

Diplomacy had further been depreciated by the public image of "the honest man being sent abroad to lie for his country," and the feeling that secret diplomacy practiced by Hitler, Mussolini, Chamberlain, and Daladier at Munich in the autumn of 1938, and the Von Ribbentrop-Molotov exchanges of the summer of 1939, had precipitated World War II. Finally, diplomacy by partisan politics and parliamentary procedure brought with it a new philosophy of diplomats steered by peoples' elected delegates debating in open conference and resolving their negotiating limits by a vote. It became the nature of post-World War II world politics that persuasion was considered tantamount to trickery, that compromise was interpreted as treason, and any threat of the use of force was adjudged the equivalent of war. These transpositions of attitude overloaded an already complex international system. Observers failed to note the difference between the disclosure of the results of negotiations, and the disclosure of the course of diplomatic negotiations themselves. Traditional international bargaining usually began with statements of maximum demands by the bargainers, which were whittled down in the negotiating process until both sides sensed a mutual balancing of costs and benefits. Postwar negotiations now had as their audiences not only those directly concerned with the issues at stake but others, many of whom were not always capable of understanding what they saw and heard, or of absorbing what might be learned. Public crusaders, masquerading as diplomats, have more than once turned diplomatic intercourse into a propaganda match. The increasing complexity of the postwar years lifted the making of foreign policy from the realm of negotiations between ambassadors and foreign ministers to a level where tools of expertise from the political, economic, military, propaganda, cultural, and scientific arenas were needed.

Propaganda, sabotage, and infiltration replaced traditional diplomatic methods. The national interest was expanded to include influencing beliefs and attitudes abroad, and resisting similar attempts by the opposition. The Voice of America replaced the Office of War Information in 1948 and was more recently incorporated into the USIA, established in 1953. Such efforts, though meaningless in a policy vacuum, were found adept in preparing the way for substantive policies; for example, propaganda can assist with qualifying statements and insure comprehension, plus cushion the reception, or can serve to ameliorate the climate in which the policies are enunciated. Propaganda frequently descended to mere "name-calling" as it was used to "awaken the deluded masses to the evils of communist infiltration."[34] At home and abroad, it strengthened the unity of the United States for the cause of freedom, emphasized our determination to support other free nations in developing and maintaining psychological resistance to the Soviet Union. Propaganda was geared to increase a favorable balance of power by impressing our allies, by weakening any hostile coalition, and by winning the support of the uncommitted.

No nation in the world pays greater deference to public opinion than the United States. It seemed to bear out Morgenthau's contention that the need for popular emotional support for policies is a major factor in the foreign policies of democratic systems. While Walter Lippmann in *The Public Philosophy*, Gabriel Almond in his *The American People and Foreign Policy*, and James N. Rosenau in *Public Opinion and Foreign Policy* disagree on the amount of influence of public opinion, all agree that such opinion should not have a significant influence on foreign policy. The international relations of a democracy were no longer secret but subject to public scrutiny through mass communications. Vehement United States public debate arose over such Truman moves as the aborted appointment of an ambassador to the Vatican in November 1951, the Palestine question in 1947 and 1948, the China lobby, the political liability of Acheson in 1952, and the McCarthyism purge of the State Department.

At the same time that the State Department was crippled by the decline of traditional diplomacy, it was overshadowed by the rival Department of Defense which had gained the upper hand in postwar policymaking. State's role was minimal despite the fiction of joint military-political responsibility. Defense took the lead in occupation policy, in the formulation and operation of NATO, in the Korean development, in the adminstration of aid under the Marshall Plan, even as it had assumed the major policy responsibility for the allied response to the Berlin blockade. Such a course was particularly unrealistic, for it became evident that the military could not play the diplomatic role indefinitely—however qualified it might be to assume the role in the short run. At the same time it became increasingly clear that the lines between the political and military issues of foreign policy were becoming blurred in the matters of deterrence, collective

---

[34] William C. Johnstone, "Our Answer to the Big Lie," *Department of State Bulletin* (March 5, 1951), p. 373.

defense, crisis management, coercive diplomacy, limited warfare, foreign aid, and arms control.

Yet one must not labor under the misconception that much of the military's dominance was at State's request. Because the State Department was suffering from a lack of domestic constituency and was under increased partisan attack for being "soft on communism", its personnel were labeled incompetent and therefore unable to "sell" those policies they felt necessary to the national interest. Therefore, they called upon the military to explain and justify policies pleading for foreign aid, urging ratification of treaties, defending troop commitments, justifying MacArthur's dismissal, and defending the Korean War.•

Another shift in traditional United States diplomacy in an effort to meet more realistically the needs of the postwar era was the beginning of functional planning. The first priority was selection of a strategic framework of long-term objectives and priorities. The second function of such planning was the coordination of a program related to each specific country with which the United States engaged in formal diplomatic activities, identifying the major purposes and targets, and establishing priorities and guidelines for daily decisions. Country desks were set up, and country teams were formed, albeit belatedly for Germany. The third function of the new planning apparatus was to equip the State Department for the needs of the future through skills and instructions for conditions which could be foreseen.

The Policy Planning Staff (PPS), organized by George Marshall, was looking 10–20 years into the future while political leaders looked only at the immediate present. Its mission was to bring long-range implications to bear on current actions or problems. However, during the Truman years the PPS continued to have limited influences on day-to-day foreign policy. Likewise the National Security Council (NSC), organized to integrate foreign, economic, and military policies, was not a substitute for the continuous, able staff work done in the department. The trend toward policymaking by committee tended to turn substantive problems into administrative ones. It encouraged a thrust toward a standard of average performance, while at the same time encouraging the increase of bureaucratic politics.

President Truman, like FDR, remained the keystone of the arch of foreign policy decision making, but out of necessity he delegated most of the decisions and actions of foreign affairs, making the secretary of state the chief of staff of foreign affairs while the president set general guidelines and priorities. The secretary, as principal adviser to the president on foreign relations, must be privy to all the president's thoughts and must be allowed the last clear voice before action is taken. The secretary's staff, unlike the White House staff, it was discovered, could best provide the integration, constant supervision, and steady direction needed. The secretary had to be a man of great intellectual capacity, giving energetic leadership. His staff had to be imaginative, able, and expert, making other agencies respect the primacy of State, and State became increasingly able to exercise its role in the postwar period without restraint.

The foreign affairs personnel of the Truman adminstration can be divided into bankers and lawyers such as James Forrestal, Robert Lovett, Dean Acheson, and Averell Harriman, and soldiers and diplomats such as George Marshall, Omar Bradley, Dwight Eisenhower, David Bruce, and George F. Kennan. The foreign policy defense nucleus was composed of the president along with Forrestal, Marshall, Lovett, and Acheson. Of the secretaries of state, Acheson was certainly the most influential in a long-term policymaking sense. This lawyer's lawyer, versed in the military as well as the political elements of foreign policy, understood the intricacies of international finance, had an intimate knowledge of Congress and its foreign policy leaders, as well as enormous prestige among European diplomats. His predecessor, James S. Byrnes, was a former senator who had the advantage of experience in conferences abroad. His successor, George Marshall, viewed his position as that of chief of staff in a war fought without visible weapons. This combination of razor sharp minds known for their incisiveness, this innovative and experienced group contributed much to the adaptability of American foreign policy in the postwar years.

Most of the major foreign policy decisons of the Truman era were presidential, not congressional. Congress was faced with faits accomplis as its role became one of reviewing, not creating policy. Collaboration had occurred on Lend-Lease, the Marshall Plan, and NATO, but not even a pretense of consultation was made during the Berlin crisis or on the Korean War. The bitter duel between President Truman and Senator Taft persisted throughout Truman's presidency, and ended with the narrow defeat of an effort to amend the Constitution. For on the first day of the new Congress in 1953 Senator John Bricker of Ohio, with the support of 62 other senators, introduced the motion for an amendment which would have severely increased the power of Congress in the conduct of international diplomacy while reducing the powers of the president to enter into executive agreements. It would have prevented any treaty or other international agreement from having validity as internal law, except as supplmented by legislation, the constitutionality of which was supportable independently of the international commitment.[35]

Changes in the world order and the nature of diplomacy were also reflected in the type of staff the State Department needed and recruited. The traditional concept of the broad-based, intellectual, versatile Foreign Service Officer was slow to change, but the first ripples were seen during the Truman administration. The routine duties of answering cables, briefing congressional spokesmen, informing the press, answering press inquiries, liaison with Washington-based ambassadors from foreign nation states, and problems of administering the expanding bureaucracy both at home and abroad with authority and timeliness crystallized the need for a senior executive officer at the highest level. The creation of an under secretary for administration removed much of the departmental operation from the shoulders of the secretary, freeing time more appropriately devoted to policy formation. The Foreign Service Act of 1946 established the new structure of the foreign service, raised salaries, reduced the number of official categories, and set up the Foreign Service Institute, which in turn established a more professional atmosphere within the service on a broader base.

As the roles of the embassy officer and the desk officer changed, the making of foreign policy abroad was complicated by the proliferation of embassy-associated agencies. In addition to the Agency for International Development (AID), the United States Information Agency (USIA), the Military Assistance Advisory groups (MAAG), and assorted educational, cultural, agricultral, and scientific arms of the embassy—sixteen in all—the Central Intelligence Agency was undisputedly unique. Before the war, almost all overseas civilian personnel were State Department affiliates, the great majority of whom were in Europe. The shift, which today finds only $\frac{1}{5}$ of the overseas embassy personnel directly employed by the State Department, began during the Truman years. This organizational proliferation and growth brought conflicts of vested interests and bureaucratic competition, all of which slowed the policy process, stifled innovation, and hampered flexibility. It was here that Robert Lovett's "foul-up" factor was illustrated as everyone got the idea "that just because some decision may

[35] John P. Lovell, *Foreign Policy in Perspective* (New York: Holt, Rinehard & Winston, 1970), pp. 318–319.

affect you, you automatically have a right to take part in making it."

Before World War II, the United States had only a rudimentary foreign intelligence service. The Pearl Harbor debacle shockingly illustrated the importance of being able to organize techniques for evaluation and dissemination of available intelligence data. The creation of a formal, civilian agency responsible for coordinated intelligence gathering and interpretation was instituted under the Truman administration. The CIA was organized to increase the level of factual input into the foreign policy process. The military resented the cooptation of defense intelligence supremacy while the State Department found its intelligence arm inching toward an independent status tucked behind a security curtain. The objectives of the CIA were in part to seek out the secret intentions, plans, and capacities of other states, both allied and opposed, in order to take appropriate action, to use the opportunity for bargaining, or to counteract impending injury to our power position. The key was to make intelligence researchers policy-oriented.

The State Department needs most of all to remain free from an atmosphere of bullying, suspicion, intimidation, or officially prescribed values and attitudes in order to provide the criticism, innovation, and inspiration it is its nature to afford. Unfortunately, World War II and its aftermath brought into being conditions beyond the capability of American control (e.g., China), and some citizens—thoroughly frustrated—could only conceive of the nonresolution of certain problems as clear proof of treason and betrayal. In the shattered morale of the department under incessant fire from McCarthyism for being soft on communism, all kinds of charges and countercharges were hurled, and often accepted. Violations of confidences by individual officers were adjudged clear proof of departmental conspiracy. Personal indiscretions or behavioral deviance were seen as national scandal. It mattered little that charges were fabricated out of whole cloth. To make a charge was enough to cause some in government—and out—to believe it true. John Duncan Miller, writing in *The London Times,* characterized the unhappy period as "the revolt of the primitives against the intelligent."[36] It crippled the espirit de corps within the department and all but destroyed its credibility outside. The Foreign Service Officer in general became less critical in his reporting and more timid in his recommendations, while there was a ten-

---

[36] Elmer Davis, "The Crusade Against Acheson," *Harper's* (March 1951), pp. 23–29, quoting John Duncan Miller.

dency to spread responsibility as widely as possible for decisions on critical issues.[37]

As the Truman administration gained momentum, the State Department's responsibilities and influence had never been greater. By the end of this same administration, the department's image was at an all-time low, tarnished by the "fall of China," the "Korean fiasco," and the McCarthy allusions. The State Department had paved the way for the Republican Party's ride to victory on the Four Horsemen of Calumny—fear, ignorance, biogotry, and smear.[38]

UNITED NATIONS: SUPPLEMENTING BUT NOT SUPPLANTING THE BALANCE OF POWER

The United Nations was built on a Wilsonian fantasy of the banishment of war and the use of force bolstered by a continuation of the wartime alliance. It was to be a substitute for power politics, a harbinger of peace. Victory oriented, it was in practice government by the superpowers who would make the decisions in the Security Council which could then be presented as recommendations to the General Assembly for perfunctory approval. It was taken for granted that the great powers would act in unison to deal with any threat to peace. Their combined strength and wisdom were assumed sufficient to meet all threats to peace without recourse to war. A basic precondition which was also blithely accepted was that no such threats would emanate from one of the great powers themselves.

In an effort to avoid duplication of the League of Nations debacle, in the United States a veritable wave of educational propaganda was generated in behalf of American acceptance. The United Nations was to be "all things to all men" and the resolution to join it passed Congress with only two dissenting votes. The Truman administration had done a superb job in reading public opinion to mount support for this new "world government." The Soviet Union was also deluded. It had presupposed that the United Nations would in practice be merely an elaboration of the wartime coalition of the Big Three which would continue to make all major political and military decisions without consulting even their junior partners. The Soviets had also assumed that each of the Three Powers would control events in its own sphere of influence: the United States in the Western Hemi-

[37] Stupak, op. cit., p. 11.
[38] Acheson, op. cit., p. 364.

sphere, Great Britain in Western Europe and the Commonwealth, and the Soviet Union in Eastern Europe.

Both the United States and the Soviet Union quickly learned the limits of such an international organization. They were working within an undefined status quo, for, in the absence of a treaty settling the war, all remained provisional. Thus, even the peace they were attempting to keep was undefined and undelineated. From Dumbarton Oaks on, the issue of impingements on national sovereignty spelled difficult times to come. The constitutional scheme of the charter was defied by political reality as the General Assembly came into its own, declaring a majority vote could usurp the Security Council prerogatives and give the larger body increased jurisdiction as a result of the Uniting for Peace Amendment used on both the Korea and Palestine issues. The increasing number of member nations resulted in shifts making it increasingly difficult for either East or West to be assured of a two-thirds vote.

The United States dominance declined, Soviet influence increased. Diplomatic alliances in the United Nations were courted for a "vote" and not always based on moral judgments. Concessions were made to neutrals, not to one of the major declared powers. Regional groups took shape. An East-West deadlock resulted. The Secretary General in his attempts to settle disputes was restricted in his instruments of enforcement as his "punch" was limited to use of rational persuasion and the formalities of agreements for the most part already in force.

Collective security conformed to national interests. It was based on the assumption that virtually all nations would come to the defense of the status quo, herein forsaking national egotisms and national policies serving them. It is all too clear that individual national interests dictate the avoidance of any solution or conflict detrimental to one's cause and power position, thus paralyzing the collective security system. The United Nations had no permanent police force and no impact on arms limitation.

The United States was less unrealistic in its expectations concerning the United Nations during the late 1940s. With experience we diminished our grandiose dreams of a warless world and international cooperation, and began utilizing the United Nations forum in a more pragmatic manner in support of specific national interests. As the United Nations General Assembly debated the future of Palestine, the United States emerged as Israel's foremost advocate, using its influence to rally global support for the Israeli cause among uncommitted states.

As an ideological tool of American foreign policy, the United Nations became a means rather than an end in the policymaking process. It was a showcase for displaying our good intentions. Free world cooperation was pitted against Communist recalcitrance. The Soviet Union played its role to the hilt, and even walked out in protest, conveniently for the United States, before the Korean crisis in perfect tune with our national interest. Our success in using the United Nations to sanction our policies during the Truman years was as much a result of Soviet obtuseness as of our own adeptness.

The Truman years were ones of exploration and exploitation in the United Nations. By 1953, we had faced the fact that such an arrangement was practicable only if it supplemented, but did not supplant, the balance of power. Its nonpolitical specialized agencies such as the United Nations Educational Scientific and Cultural Organization were indeed effective. As Henry Cabot Lodge observed, "It is primitive. It is evolutionary. It has not brought nor will it bring the millennium. But it is useful; its cost is small; it is an intelligent first step. It and it alone stands between us and international anarchy."[39]

THIRD WORLD: NOT BLACK OR WHITE, BUT A MOSAIC OF GRAYS

It has been said that the United States' major strength against communism is the unity of the "free world." Yet, American foreign policy toward the less developed nations, from Truman's 1949 inaugural address through the innumerable foreign aid programs, was unrealistic in the economic, political, and social sense. As we attempted to buy votes for our side through foreign aid, we continued to disregard the realities of the national interests of third world countries by forcing them to look at the world in stark terms of black and white when it appeared to them to be a mosaic of grays. The arguments for our side were presented in terms of right or wrong, instead of the more convincing arguments of national security and viability. It was indeed a struggle for men's minds.

Furthermore, we unrealistically characterized such aid as charity instead of relating it to national interest as a weapon in the political armory of the donor nation. Foreign aid should be used with a coun-

[39] Much of the U.N. section is based on Lincoln P. Bloomfield, *The United Nations and U.S. Foreign Policy* (Boston, Mass.: Little, Brown, 1960).

try, not for it. Even the most benevolent aid has an aura of intervention. The United States failed to recognize publicly the façade of "humanitarian policies" of the Marshall Plan, the Point Four Program, the Berlin Airlift, and the Danube Flood Aid. One must distinguish between the motives of private industries, groups, or even individuals, and that of statesmen. One must first succeed in defining his own interests, if one expects to further them. To assume that the motive is anything but national interest only complicates relations with these allies. Calling a policy which promotes a mutual objective an act of charity unnecessarily emphasizes dependence and invites resentment. If it were mere generosity, it would be unwelcome since it could be withdrawn at a nation's whim. Aid based on appreciation of a common interest would be less susceptible to such whims. Charity, except in emergency, breeds despair and loss of self-esteem. Furthermore, it was eventually discovered that one need not be a docile ally to get aid. At the same time, aid must be based on the ability of the recipient to use it wisely in addition to the need factor. Short-term benefits must be balanced against long-range effects.

In the Truman administration, concern with third world countries, outside the Far East, focused on Latin America with additional support for newly independent entities such as India, Israel, and Egypt. In his inaugural address, President Truman overextended himself as his hyperbole outreached the provisions of the budget and the genuine concern of the American taxpayer. The Point Four Program was hailed as bold and novel. It captured the imagination of "world public opinion," but not of Congress or the American workers' pocketbook. In the fourth point of his address of January 20, 1949, Truman declared ". . . we must embark on a bold, new program for making our scientific advances and industrial progress available for improvement and growth of underdeveloped areas . . . the old imperalism . . . exploitation for foreign profit—has no place in our plans. What we envisage is a program of development based on the concept of democratic fair-dealing."[40] The program was to provide aid to 22 countries and place 2445 technicians in 35 countries, affecting everything from irrigation in Japan to industries in Egypt to malaria control in Peru. The trade policies had been liberalized in 1947 by American participation in the General Agreement on Trade and Tariffs—a far-reaching economic liberalization policy.

The administrative hang-ups and congressional infighting were complicated by anti-American demonstrations spelling doom for for-

[40] Truman, op. cit., p. 237.

eign aid in Latin America. For example, in Bogota, Columbia, during the Ninth International Conference of American States, the Communists staged a brief and bloody riot as a warning signal of the character of their presence on the American continent. Latin America remained low on the list of priorities and many concrete programs were terminated. There was an insufficient appreciation in the West of the deterioration in relations which would result from such a cutback and the concomitant reorientation of policies. When aid is cut out because of suspicion and pique, it is hardly conducive to the pragmatic, democratic objectives we espouse. Yet the West continued to be plagued by severe frictions and tensions, by diversity in outlook, by the complexities of modernization, and by the slowness of tangible results.

In addition to the foreign aid questions, there was the dilemma of how to court former allied colonies. There was also the role of third world countries and the United Nations. Finally, there was the revelation that Communist appeal was not only to those depressed in poverty, but that the middle class intelligentsia was now vulnerable. Economic aid was no longer enough. The concern was for the effect of these changes on the balance of power. Little action was taken in this regard during the Truman years when priorities were elsewhere: Europe was the "center," and the third world remained at the periphery.

CONCLUSION

The Truman revolution in American foreign policy and national security strategy should not be underrated. Looking back over the more than two decades since the end of World War II, one would have to concede that in view of the Trumanites' declared objectives and policy assumptions, the leadership of the Truman administration in foreign affairs was revolutionary, innovative, responsible, and realistic. The major stumbling blocks were the belated appreciation of Soviet intentions and interests, the inadvisability of rapid demobilization, and the need to rebuild a strong German state which precluded taking maximum advantage of the United States capabilities.

In November 1947, General George Marshall declared that the objective of the Truman policy was to restore the balance of power in both Europe and Asia, and that all actions would be viewed in the light of this objective. In an effort to preserve that which Americans most wished to keep—national security and freedom, that is the national interest—it was the opinion of the Truman administration that the only way to deal with the Soviet Union, which at that time was the only potential threat to American security, was to get tough by creating "situations of strength." Such bastions of anti-Communist power were built through armed alliances and by aiding vulnerable nations through economic means. The enemy, though, became systemically transformed from a rival nation-state, the Soviet Union, to a pervasive ideological adversary known only as "communism." With advances in military technology, the declared confrontation became a Cold War of deterrence and psychological warfare. Communication advances further aggravated the explosive international environment as rhetoric began to become more dominant than the operational policies themselves in defining the nature of international politics. Intermittent periods of calm and crisis in the superpower relationships ensued. Intelligence and propaganda became increasingly important while traditional diplomatic maneuvers had been rendered all but helpless.

During the Truman years for the most part the United States enjoyed unchallenged supremacy while undertaking a limited military and economic commitment to Europe and a hesitant extension of American power into Asia. In the 1970s the United States situation is all but reversed. American power and influence is declining. United States military and economic commitments have extended around the globe to a point where available power is outreached by the extent of these commitments. The problem today, as in 1945, is how to prudently balance objectives and capabilities. The first step is to define what we seek to accomplish and to set priorities within that list of objectives. In the 1970s, the United States must free itself from the burdens of obsolescent foreign policies and archaic, dangerous perceptions which were conceived in the late 1940s and which have become almost mechanistic routines. In so doing, American decision makers must then embark on a radical rethinking of the environment, of the issues, and of the policies adequate to deal with a transformed international system.

In the late 1940s and early 1950s, it was simpler to identify common interests among the Western powers in a bipolar world. The Soviet threat was defined as a clear-cut military-security threat. The lessons of the recent past were more relevant. The appropriate response was more obvious. The world leadership of the United States was taken for granted—internally and externally. Today, the problems are more subtle, more complex, and, maybe, even more dangerous.

VI

THE UNITED STATES AND ITS "WORLD POLICEMAN" PERIOD
Superactivism and the Use of American Combat Troops

With the revolution in American foreign policy since World War II and following the pattern set down in the Truman administration, the United States in the 1950s and 1960s began participating in the affairs of other nation-states in the international system at an ever-increasing rate at multidimensional levels and with a vast multitude of instrumentalities—all the way from foreign aid to direct military involvement. As one analyzes the thrust of U.S. combat troops into other nation-states, one beholds a microcosm against which the fundamental dislocations of American foreign policy (externally and internally) during the Cold War may be explained, and in the light of which one must judge the increasingly interventionist perceptions and activities which dominated American foreign policy until the enunciation of the Nixon Doctrine in 1969.

In retrospect, it appears that the Eisenhower, Kennedy, and Johnson administrations, though basically operating in the same parameters of the containment, Cold War framework of the Truman period, were guilty of bastardizing the fundamental restraint of realism that characterized the policies of the Truman-Marshall-Acheson entourage. This was done in ways that led rapidly to the bankruptcy of American foreign policy as the disillusionment of public opinion reached systematically dangerous dimensions toward the end of the 1960s. This tragic slide was culminated by the vulgarization of traditional American philosophical principles and the corresponding corruption of realism's axioms which was manifested in America's overcommitment to the

Vietnam conflict. In effect, the "world policeman" period of contemporary American foreign policy can be charted in a downward progression from Truman's containment to Dulles' rhetorical crusade, and Kennedy's activistic "machismo" to Johnson's paranoiac personalism.

Therefore, the most effective manner by which to highlight this progression of American foreign policy during the 1950s and 1960s is not to recount a superficial historical chronology of each presidential administration. It is to stress and explain the major declarative and operational themes of each administration which led to the superinterventionist mentality of American foreign policymakers during the 50s and 60s. This analysis of presidential administrations will then be extended into an investigation of the major factors which produced the ultimate interventions—the direct use of American combat troops. In this conceptual design a clearer understanding will be established as to: (1) why the initial successes and restraints of the "creation years" of the Truman administration became tainted; (2) why American international concerns led to a mentality of excessive interventionism and the massive power of the military in the American foreign policy process; and (3) why the Nixon-Kissinger foreign policy changes became necessary in the transformed international system of the 1970s.

THE EISENHOWER YEARS: OPERATIONAL REALISM OVERTAKEN BY THE VICTORY OF THE RHETORICAL CRUSADE

The Eisenhower years were operationally years of conserving the realism and power positions established during the Truman administration. Better than many of his contemporary critics in the 1950s, President Eisenhower understood the limits of presidential and national power, and he sought to conserve both.[1] In essence, the thrust of this section is that the operational realism of Eisenhower overwhelmed the rhetoric of Secretary of State John Foster Dulles whenever vital decisions had to be made; but, at the same time, the rhetoric of Dulles chipped away at the edges of operational restraint until finally the dam broke and the flood of moralistic slogans became accepted by audiences internally and externally as the essence of American foreign policy during the 1950s.

---

[1] *Foreign Service Journal* (May 1973), passim; but especially p. 30.

Nonetheless, the policies of the Truman administration remained the dominant thread of American foreign policy during most of the 1950s. The Republican administration of Dwight David Eisenhower cemented the restraint and institutional framework of the "creation years" to meet the perceived requirements of the postwar international environment. The 1950s marked an era of instability and insecurity in the bipolar world as each giant redefined world equilibrium. The growth in destructive power and technical rationality mushroomed the organizational bureaucracy begun under Truman, producing obdurate and functionally oriented policy. The realignment taking place in the international system solidified the interlocking of political, economic, military, and propaganda aspects of power and procedure. In reviewing these years it is crucial to understand the proper role of each of these components and where the locus of final control rested. The following analysis tries to place Eisenhower's foreign policy in perspective, hopefully correctly considering the role of self-interest, power, and morality, in order to cut through the rhetorical facade to reveal the realistic approach which at base continued to guide the nation.

Eisenhower as president was the control figure in American foreign policy from 1952 to 1961. Since the early beginnings of World War II the State Department had allowed its influence to degenerate, as it refused to challenge the alterations being demanded of diplomatic requirements. The department failed to seize control of the information processes and implementation avenues which were the key to policy power. The influence over foreign policy shifted increasingly to the Defense Department and to the White House with the NSC becoming the coordinating, governing body over U.S. foreign policy especially during the Eisenhower years. Thus, by 1952 the Department of State was being shattered by bureaucratic competition, White House centralization, and the batterings of McCarthyism. Therefore, the office of the president took it upon itself to regulate foreign policy according to the "rational" interdependent objectives of economics, security, and power. The State Department and its secretary were used to supply the rhetoric and propaganda necessary to gain political support at home and maintain national prestige abroad.

The president chose to create and institute policy according to the self-serving national interests of the United States. Very often programmatic policymaking was based on the ethos of modern organizational procedure and technological advancement. Unfortunately, the thrust of this bureaucratic culture was inconsistent with that of traditional American heritage and therefore the presidency and the national security advisers needed a figurehead to explain U.S policy in terms the public would support and understand. After his election the stalemate in Korea, the "loss of China," and the disillusionment of the American people (fanned by the "rightist" rhetoric of McCarthyism) with the "soft on communism" policies of the Truman administration set the stage for Eisenhower's presidency. A galvanizing of the American spirit seemed essential so that American foreign policy would have the internal support it needed in order to check Soviet power pressures around the world. Hence, the Eisenhower administration preached a strident ideological crusade, while at the same time operating in a fairly restrained, realistic, national self-interest manner on most basic issue areas. Eisenhower chose John Foster Dulles to be secretary of state. Dulles was the leading Republican spokesman on foreign policy and satisfied many domestic political prerequisits. The secretary was established as a proponent of internationalism, authoring two books both espousing the necessity of U.S. involvement in world affairs. Although his essays on the internatonal system appeared rather liberal, Dulles pleased the powerful right wing of Congress by filling his announcements with strident moralism and hardline conservative rhetoric.

John Foster Dulles had all the credentials needed to assuage the public's disillusionment. The son of a minister and a grandson of a statesman, Dulles had a long history of commitment to both diplomacy and national integrity. He was the perfect exegete to interpret the administration's policy for the public because of his lengthy career as an officer of the church coupled with his implacable trust in puritan morality. Dulles possessed the capability to preach a "special role" for the United States in bringing God's divine law to the world while justifying American foreign policy in virtuous oratory, thus concealing much of the commonplace national self-interest behind U.S. actions.

In an era of increasing organizational rationalism and bureaucratic control appointing an ideologue like John Foster Dulles perhaps appears inconsistent. But, as previously mentioned, Dulles fit the demands of the domestic political scene quite well. In addition, the president thought that Dulles could be controlled within the administration and specifically by his office. Under the Truman administration, Dulles was employed to work on the Japanese peace treaty. In the heat of negotiation Dulles seemed to become carried away with tactics, and thus served as an efficient instrumentality for pursuing national interests. Exploiting Dulles' talent and reputation with the public the Truman administration was able to insure the linkage of Japanese interests to ours when perceived security threats made it imperative, yet disguised these motives in cheers for human freedom and democracy in Asia. The incoming administration acknowledged Dulles's usefulness and, if controlled, felt he could become a valuable asset.

As secretary of state, Dulles was extremely conscious of public relations and popular support. He continually turned to the people in voicing policy decisions by flavoring his announcements with moral platitudes to guarantee a warm reception. In office the secretary held more press conferences than any of his colleagues and became the cardinal voice interpreting American foreign policy and action. To bring expertise in public relations to the department Dulles hired a newspaper man, Carl McCardle, to handle the press. Since his key function was to manipulate and draw support from the populace, Dulles chose to sacrifice some of the finest men in the department to protect his honorable and respected position in the eyes of the public and Congress. The secretary refused to protect the fate of his department employees from the highly explosive atmosphere of "McCarthyism" in order to avoid any rupture in public sentiment. The Republicans had been elected to purge the "Communists" from the Department, and with the assignment of Scott McLeod to clean out the "traitors," Dulles had to demand "positive loyalty" and publically immolate those who were tainted with the "soft on communism" charges to assure an untainted position within the domestic political arena.

Recent scholars of the Dulles era attack the secretary for yielding to McCarthy and sacrificing men such as Davies, Vincent, and Kennan. Reviewing the administration in a realist framework, however, illustrates that Dulles was only fulfilling what was thought to be a necessary role. Eisenhower needed Dulles to capture and control American support for the president's foreign policy. The secretary understood that the Department of State had lost its position of influence and therefore he did little to rejuvenate its policy planning organization and capabilities. He gave Bedell Smith the majority of the administrative responsibility and freed himself to act as the intellectual moralist Eisenhower had chosen to give the realist foreign policy of the United States a moralistic and universalistic façade.

The secretary of state also bestowed a sense of consistency and sagaciousness to foreign policy. In actuality the United States attempted to fashion its actions to the threats perceived in the changing power configuration of the international system. This precluded most long-range planning based on ideological objectives and fostered short-range crisis management. Since policy became a function of short-range situational choices in pursuit of realistic national interests, it was adjusted to power formations and security requirements. The American public, conventionally incurious about foreign affairs, needed to perceive a simplistic consonance in national action in order to offer its support to increased American involvement in world affairs. It would be too difficult if not impossible to explain the details of each separate international event to the public, so Eisenhower nominated Dulles to create a thread of coherence through foreign policy which the public could perceive and respond to with alacrity. Thus, John Foster Dulles built his interpretations on strident moralism and apocalyptic rhetoric, continually attacking communism as a monolithic and nefarious system endangering the world.

In reviewing the Eisenhower administration one must cut through the confusing morality of the decade and examine the actual policy produced. The president at all times was the final decider-in-chief of foreign policy as the State Department and legislative branch continued their slide away from policy creation. The nation's programs responded to national interests and short-term priorities, ignoring the intangibles of international law and universal codes. Power was the key element in international relations, and national security remained the chief objective of the Eisenhower administration. The use of ideology and morality was rhetorical as Dulles was used to promote internal support and unity. The 1950s witnessed the continuation of the realist framework forged in the Truman years. No matter what the declarative rhetoric demanded—rollback, liberation, massive retaliation—the operational policies of moderation, restraint, and containment continued. Eisenhower was sure that the United States had to contain the Soviet Union and, additionally, that it had to confront the belief system of communism in a changing world. But he understood the limitations of American resources and commitments and, as well, he warned against internal threats of presidential arrogance, institutional rigidities, and the military-industrial complex. He surely allowed Dulles too much forensic freedom, and he surely made some mistakes; but, overall he (personally) maintained a moderate, realistic stance toward the problems of the international system and the restraints on American resources.[2]

However, at the declarative, rhetorical level, the spokesman for the Eisenhower administration was Secretary of State John Foster Dulles. Dulles carried on an intense verbal confrontation with "international communism" at the level of a philosophical crusade. And, unfortunately, it was this either/or, good/evil framework which dominated the news media and the minds of the American public. In effect, the mind-set of a worldwide, universalistic confrontation between the "Communists and the free world" cultivated fertile ground upon which the Kennedy administration could' operationalize the rhetoric of the Dulles years by its strategy of flexible response.

THE KENNEDY YEARS

The Kennedy years began with the ringing pronouncements of the inaugural address[3] that the United States would go anywhere at any time to confront the Soviet program for world domination. Kennedy quickly followed this pledge with the interventionist-prone, flexible response strategy orchestrated under the direction of Secretary of Defense Robert McNamara. This strategy gave the United States the qualitative and quantitative military capabilities to go anywhere in the world to confront communism.

Wedded to this pledge and strategy were several other dimensions which accelerated America's dash into "globalism" under Kennedy. First, there was the interjection of the "Mr. Fix-it" strategic intellectuals with their overconfident academic game theories into the forefront of the policymaking process. Second, there was Kennedy's distrust of the "slow-moving" and self-interested bureaucracies (exacerbated, of course, by the Bay of Pigs disaster), coupled with his ex-

---

[2] This segment is basically my interpretation of the Eisenhower-Dulles framework. But also see Townsend Hoopes, *The Devil and John Foster Dulles* (Boston, Mass.: Little, Brown, 1973); Emmet John Hughes, *The Ordeal of Power: A Political Memoir of the Eisenhower Years* (New York: Atheneum, 1963); Dwight D. Eisenhower, *The White House Years: Waging Peace, 1956–61* (Garden City, N.Y.: Doubleday, 1962); Chalmers M. Roberts, "The Day We Didn't Go to War," *The Reporter* (September 14, 1954).

[3] See Appendix E for the full text of the speech.

cessive use of personal advisers—this policymaking pattern tended to accelerate into the dangerous treadmill of crisis diplomacy. Third, Kennedy believed that the third world was becoming the new battleground of the Cold War, forcing the United States to become involved in many areas of the world which both the Truman and Eisenhower administrations tended to ignore. Finally, when Kennedy's "macho" was bruised during his early meeting with Khrushchev in Vienna, a pattern was set in which Kennedy anxiously attempted to prove his masculine mettle by increasing the activism and initiatory policies of his administration[4]—a personal style that was to dominate his actions until the crucible of the Cuban missile crisis brought both him and Khrushchev to their senses. For with the Cuban missile crisis experience, there was a sign that Kennedy personally was moving toward policies of restraint and moderation—but then came the assassination.

THE JOHNSON ADMINISTRATION

The Johnson administration carried on many of the Kennedy policymaking traits, but under the influence of W. W. Rostow, Special Presidential Assistant for National Security Affairs, and Secretary of State Dean Rusk, the rhetoric of anticommunism and the fear of ideological wars of national liberation began to dominate the personalized policymaking framework of Lyndon Johnson. This led to the ultimate disaster in intervention—Vietnam. And in a way, Vietnam can be seen as the outcome of a simplistic liberal formula for foreign policymaking that no longer can or should guide America in the 1970s—an all-powerful central bureaucracy, an unhindered president, and military interventionism reached its peak in Vietnam—and it was found wanting.[5]

And yet, aside from administrative direction, it appears that the increased tempo of American intrusion into the affairs of other nations in the post-World War II period was inevitable for other reasons.

[4] On the Kennedy section, see Richard J. Walton, *Cold War and Counter-Revolution: The Foreign Policy of John F. Kennedy* (Baltimore, Md.: Penguin, 1972).

[5] On the bankruptcy of the liberal formula, see Ronald Steel, *Pax-Americana* (New York: Viking, 1967).

THE ENVIRONMENTAL IMPETUS
TO INTERVENTIONISM

First, the United States emerged from the war as the most powerful nation-state in world history. Britain and France came out bankrupt. Britain had lost its creditor nation status in India. Before the war Britain had great assets in Asia. After the war it had lost India, Burma, and Ceylon. Withdrawal from these areas was a "cutting of losses." For these reasons the United States took upon itself the responsibility to fill the power vacuums created in Europe, the Middle East, and Asia.

Second, the USSR emerged as a viable and ever-growing political, economic, and military power-center with its own intentions and desires for assuming a role in international relations that could increase its prestige and to make the conquered nations make good the physical damage inflicted on it during the war. This appetite for growth on the part of the Soviet Union was, however, rationalized in an ideological doctrine which rested upon a conflict-oriented base—it assumed conflict to be a normal condition of the twentieth century and to be ideologically aimed at a free enterprise system that had been practiced by Western capitalist nations from their inception. The United States was now the leader of these capitalist nations.

Third, the surge of revolution in the less developed regions within the international system manifested itself in an intense sense of national independence and/or formation, and in an intense desire for economic independence which Adlai Stevenson called "the revolution of rising expectations." The nature of this politicoeconomic struggle for growth in the Middle East, Southeast Asia, Africa, and Latin America generated politicoeconomic power vacuums of their own. These became areas of concern in a power struggle for the domination or the "filling" of such vacuums.

Due to the simultaneous existence of two superpowers, separated from each other by decades of cultural and ideological differences, and the existence of weaknesses in the developing areas, a growing conflict situation progressively resulted.

A fourth reason for such participation by the United States was a result of the magnitude of the other three. So vast and intricate were the problems, so complex and susceptible to multiple agency action, that the lines between domestic and international affairs became blurred, and then erased—in the United States, in the Soviet Union, and surely in the "mini-states" of the third world.

How were the United States and the Soviet Union to cope with this situation unique in the history of mankind? As Andrew Scott points out:

> Traditional statecraft was at a loss to deal with a situation that was neither war nor peace, and for a short period of time, American policy-making was at an impasse. A new set of policies, programs, techniques, and instruments had to be developed if the challenge was to be met.[6]

The use of such techniques and instruments and their resulting policies and programs have been examined by Scott and labelled as the process of informal penetration.

Although these covert activities do constitute an important dimension of relations between nation-states in the Cold War, when would this process of informal penetration be abandoned to the overt acts that have traditionally played the major role in international relations? One is forced to seek an explanation as to why the most overt of acts—direct combat troop intervention—has taken place unilaterally by the U.S. on three separate occasions. The landings made by combat troops in Lebanon, the Dominican Republic, and in South Vietnam cannot, however, be examined in isolation from the Korean decision. Nor can these three decisions be completely separated from the process of informal penetration that set the stage for their occurrence. A brief examination of the Korean decision in its inception and in its results will be combined with a description of the informal process perceived by the author as having the dominating influence in setting the stage for overt operations.

Since its earliest period of nationhood, the United States has had great anxiety and apprehension over the occurrence of violence and foreign intervention within the Western Hemisphere. It feared that the disturbing revolutionary upheavals in other parts of the hemisphere would invite European intervention into, and thereby control over, the power vacuums created by such instability. American decision makers in this period formulated the Monroe Doctrine as a definitive statement of American interests in containing intervention from abroad, and by doing so, restated their own policy of nonintervention in European affairs. Even though such a policy was made credible by the strength of the British Navy, the attitude accompanying this

---

[6] Andrew M. Scott, *The Revolution in Statecraft: Informal Penetration* (New York: Random House, 1965), p. 72.

policy had influence in the formation of the American outlook concerning international relations. It must be kept in mind that the nonintervention doctrine was postulated when it was in the American interest not to intervene. The United States could have lost much more than it could have gained by using intervention at that point. However, the nonintervention rhetoric was kept throughout the nineteenth century because "restraint in intervention was a hallowed concept, encrusted with moral and legal values; it was more politic to reinterpret it than to deny its validity entirely."[7]

The post-World War II environment forced the United States and the Soviet Union to enter new relationships within the international system if their growth as nation-states was to continue—indeed, if it was only to be maintained. This bipolar situation was, however, interpreted in much the same antiviolence, antiintervention perceptual framework that has generally guided United States policy, despite the unique nature of social, economic, and political upheavals and revolutionary movements that also came with the end of World War II. This interpretation took on a new, more sophisticated structure because of the reasons mentioned above and also because of the constantly rising communication-technological innovations that created new concepts of weaponry as well as the means of operationalizing the informal penetration process discussed earlier.

THE LATENCY OF ALLIANCE POTENTIAL CONCEPT

A concept from the physical sciences, that of "latent heat," might be of some value in describing this sophisticated version of our antiviolence policy. Latent heat is that heat which, even though present and increasing during the transformation process in the physical state of a material, is not manifested in an *overt* temperature change until the *material is on the verge of changing its state.*

The process of informal penetration has given a new, hidden dimension to international relations as practiced by both the Soviet Union and the United States. This method of operation within the international system has made the two superpowers acutely aware

[7] Doris A. Graber, "The Truman and Eisenhower Doctrines," *Political Science Quarterly* (September 1958), p. 327.

of how control over, and alliance with, other nation-states within the international system is to be accomplished. Much of it must begin on a concealed, hidden, or latent basis.

It is not difficult to demonstrate that American policymakers developed a foreign policy based on the assumption that control of a nation-state begun by a process of informal penetration initiated within another nation-state can and, if unchecked, will, lead to dominant control of the first nation-state by the second. This assumption can be called the "latency of alliance potential" concept. Assuming the validity of the assumption, it follows that major concerns about alliance formation with a major power must be resolved by policymakers as they fear lest latent heat (penetration and control) will change the very nature of the lesser state. Indeed, a small nation can undertake an alliance relationship with the United States and, as a consequence of American penetration and control, can be changed so dramatically by the relationship that the end result is the search for alignment with the USSR or the People's Republic of China. Note that this process of change is difficult to detect due to its concealed nature—the temperature change does not occur until a change of state is almost ready to occur. Violent action, revolution, and upheaval—*instability*—seem to be the thermometers by which American policymakers judge this point of change. In crisis situations this critical temperature point is perceived by American policymakers as almost being reached and the only recourse left to them is to recreate a temporary stability through a series of ad hoc reactions (not initiations), and one of these is the use of combat troops.

This latency of alliance potential seems to manifest itself through violent struggles within the target nation-state. This violence is perceived as leaving the nation-state susceptible to added penetration from an outside source and, along with this, control. The magnitude of the potential for alliance within the target nation-state, however, seems to depend on several key factors:

1. The degree of control presently held by a major power within the target nation-state itself. This need not be at a high point when combat troop intervention takes place, but its potential must be seen as so. However, if the control and penetration are currently at a very high point, the situation is perceived as having reached a lower point on the crisis scale and perhaps will be perceived as incapable of remedy without paying too exacting a price (e.g., the Hungarian, Polish, and Czech uprisings).

2. The degree of unified nationalism present in the state. When instability and division occur in a nation-state to a high degree, the United States will be more inclined to intervene more actively.

3. The degree of communism perceived as present in the ideology of one sect or another in the nationalist movement. When this is perceived as high, the United States is more apt to intervene, not because the United States is anti-Communist, per se, but because the degree of informal penetration of a powerful nation increases when activities work from a strong ideological base. As Scott states:

> The development of sharp ideological cleavages also helps explain the growth of informal access. Not all techniques of informal penetration rely on ideological appeal, but, when ideological cleavages do exist, a much broader range of possibilities is opened up. It is safe to say that the large-scale practice of informal attack requires an ideological base that can be exploited.[8]

4. The economic potential and the strategic position of the nation-state as perceived by both the United States and other powerful nations. When either one or both of these factors is perceived as high in value, intervention will be more likely to occur in a crisis situation (a situation in which these values would be lost to the penetrating nation and would be perceived as gained by another).

5. The degree of informal penetration already obtained by the United States in the target nation-state. When this is high, the United States will be more likely to intervene. If the degree of penetration has reached a point where a pro-American government is in power, instability in that nation-state will be looked upon as a crisis situation when the incumbent regime's existence is threatened. The incumbent regime is the key element in maintaining and increasing the United States capability for informal access on all levels—political, military, cultural, and economic.

Another aspect of the present degree of access held by the United States lies in its credibility as a nation-state. Once it decides upon a supportive role of a regime, it has declared an intention of will, the loss of which would indicate its incapability to gain further access or control for maintaining its national interest. In the words of Thomas

[8] Scott, op. cit., pp. 11–12.

Schelling, "We [are] not merely communicating an intention or obligation we already had but actually enhancing the obligation in the process."[9] Wishing to deter the Soviet Union and China from further attempts at informal access, the United States must indicate a willingness to risk an acceptable loss.

In summary, the strategy the United States uses to preserve its power, and its ability to increase power, lies in its capability to reduce the possibility of the latency of alliance potential as perceived by the United States between weaker nations and the Soviet Union by denying informal penetration to the Soviet Union (or China for that matter) on all possible levels. This will be attempted by a coordinated and combined effort of political, military, and economic policies that, along with deterring informal penetration to the Soviet Union, will simultaneously increase American informal penetration within the target nation-state.

The use of overt acts of intervention must be understood in the context of the above framework. An overt act such as the use of combat troops will only occur, however, when the earlier attempts of informal penetration have failed to preserve the objectives of United States policy. When the five factors listed above simultaneously present themselves in a combination conducive to intervention, a crisis situation will develop that makes a high degree of risk acceptable to the United States.

Another major element that must be considered when attempting to determine a crisis situation is the time factor itself, defined as the rate at which the above factors are perceived by the decision makers as approaching a critical point that threatens the national interests of the United States.

Historically the United States has used three major policy concepts to achieve the national interest. Because of space limitations only oblique reference can be made to the specific historic contexts within which such concepts found expression. Special recognition is acknowledged of the difficulty in determining at what specific point each factor reached the crisis situation, for such determination—on the theoretical level—changed with each policymaking group and depended upon unique personal inputs. However, certain conceptions of our policies remain rather rigid, even though each is managed in its own particular fashion by each policymaking group.

---

[9] Thomas C. Schelling, *Arms and Influence* (New Haven, Conn.: Yale University Press, 1966), p. 60.

POST-WORLD WAR II CATALYSTS
TO INTERVENTIONISM

The inception of American post-World War II foreign policy can be used as an indicator of what problems American policymakers perceived as having the greatest effect on the future of the United States in the international system. The first major statements of American concern over the process of informal access used by the Soviet Union came in the Truman Doctrine and the Point Four Program.

American aid to Greece and Turkey came as a result of certain assumptions held by President Truman and secretaries Marshall and Acheson These assumptions were first stated by Truman in his inaugural address of 1948:

> Communism maintains that social wrongs can be corrected *only by violence*. Democracy has proved that social justice can be achieved through peaceful change. . . .
>
> I state these differences, *not to draw issues of belief as such*, but because the actions resulting from the communist philosophy are a threat to the efforts of free nations to bring about *world recovery and lasting peace*.
>
> Since the end of hostilities the United States has invested its substance and energy in a great constructive effort *to restore peace, stability and freedom to the world*.[10] [Italics added.]

This was the beginning of an attitude that feared violent upheavals in any part of the world, especially in an area where a power vacuum existed and could possibly lead to an open opportunity for Soviet exploitation. Because of the lack of an ideological base from which to influence other nations, the United States was concerned over the distinct possibility of widening Soviet influence with its attendant potentiality for control over less developed nations via economic assistance and ideological penetration. Once this control was achieved, the possibility of future alliances between the Soviets and their newly won nation-states for further control within other regions was seen as having too great a potential. This was to be partially met by both the Truman Doctrine and the Point Four Program.

The Truman Doctrine stands as unique in United States foreign policy for three major reason:

First, the United States accepted the obligation to assume the

---

[10] Louis W. Koenig, *The Truman Administration* (New York: New York University Press, 1956), p. 275, quoting Harry Truman.

responsibility for containing unilaterally, if necessary, the perceived Stalinist drive for control over the eastern Mediterranean as Britain and France proved incapable of maintaining the balance of power in that area. That the United States might be left to cope unilaterally with such a situation was known to Truman since 1946.[11]

Second, Truman felt the countries of the eastern Mediterranean area, especially Greece, Turkey, and Iran, were resisting attempted subjugation by armed minorities (Communist parties) and by outside pressure (the Soviet Union). Truman was concerned that the violation of the Yalta agreements should extend no farther than Poland, Rumania, and Bulgaria. In essence, to Truman *Communist expansion was seen in simultaneity with Soviet quests for control.*

Third, the United States accepted use of economic aid as a method of counteracting Soviet influence. As the Marshall Plan would strengthen Europe, the Point Four Program would aim at reducing the potential conflict in the less developed nations while attempting to counteract any Communist-Soviet influence in these nations.

> This Point Four Program was on the President's mind from the time the Marshall Plan was first conceived. He realized that unless aid was extended, the poverty and despair existing in the world would provide a fertile field for communist infiltration. He realized that handsome slogans would do little good and that what was needed was food, clothing and shelter . . . by the end of 1951 Point Four was working in 35 different countries.[12]

Thus, precedents were set. These post-World War II policy guidelines were followed up to and into the Korean War. The Korean War itself was perceived by the Truman administration as proof of Soviet influence and its capability to instigate indirect aggression. The Korean War, however, added the military element as a method of counteracting indirect Soviet expansion to our policy program on a permanent basis. Military action now became an integral part of the containment policy. The Korean War was the first example of a military, economic, and political policy-fusion process which was to serve as another major precedent in American relations, and for this reason a brief examination of this decision is appropriate here.

---

[11] Herbert Druks, *Truman and the Russians* (New York: Speller, 1966), p. 132.
[12] Ibid., p. 162.

THE KOREAN DECISION

The most striking aspect of the Korean decision by the Truman administration was that the question of *whether* to repel the North Korean invasion was not really discussed—the attitude of the Truman Doctrine toward containing communism was accepted as a valid statement concerning Soviet Communist expansion in the Far East. "The only questions to be decided were the means, the timing, the various practical consequences of action."[13] Perhaps this was a justified assumption by Truman, as the Korean situation at the end of World War II left Soviet and American troops ominously facing each other as early as September 8, 1945. The strategic position of Korea also played some part in deciding its value to both the United States and the Soviet Union. Any Soviet attempts at aggression from this point into Japan or Indochina would have been against the interests of the United States, as perceived in this framework. However, the major concern of Truman at this time was the prospect of Korea serving as an example of a successful attempt of proxy aggression by the Soviet Union. Thus, South Korea "because symbolic of the West's struggle for freedom and the free world could not afford to capitulate to communist aggression."[14] For the possibility of a reduced latency of alliance potential for Korea with the Soviet Union, the *violence itself* would have to be contained. This brings on the interesting question of the means to this end.

"Not all conflicts are mortal challenges and not all should be made to appear so."[15] This attitude of Secretary of State Dean Acheson could well have represented the views of most of the decision makers in the Truman administration with the notable exception of John Foster Dulles. After some discussion with secretaries Pace and Acheson, Dulles was still confused by MacArthur's request for ground troops in an Asian war. It was hard for him to understand that a limited war

> does not seek unconditional surrender; it does not necessarily mean attaining all that we desire. The aim of limited war is to stop the infringement upon our interests. If, out of this, can come some gain to the opposing state as well, all the better.[16]

[13] Eleanor L. Dulles, *American Foreign Policy Making* (New York: Harper & Row, 1968), p. 219.
[14] Druks, op. cit., p. 228.
[15] Dean G. Acheson, *Power and Diplomacy* (New York: Atheneum, 1963), p. 55.
[16] Ibid., p. 56.

This new concept of limited war was, however, symptomatic of American concern with violent upheavals as being contrary to the national interest. It should be noted that when troop withdrawal from Korea occurred in 1949, President Rhee of South Korea was refused any military aid in *offensive* weapons as it was feared that he would invade the north. Our dealings with Chiang Kai-shek also indicated this same attitude. Once mainland China was accepted as "lost," Chiang was immediately *isolated* from further hostile actions on Formosa so that he could not move against mainland China. Even when the Korean invasion from the north began in June 1950, Chiang's offer of combat troops was not accepted by Acheson, as he feared further hostilities with Communist China and/or the Soviet Union. It was felt the latency for a Korean alliance with the Soviet Union and a direct confrontation with the Soviet Union could be reduced by limiting hostilities.

The Eisenhower administration tackled the Korean conflict with some of the same basic attitudes as the Truman administration even though campaign promises stressed an ending of hostilities so "the boys could come home." This is certainly born out by the adoption of the Eisenhower Doctrine[17] to extend the basic concepts behind the Truman Doctrine to the Middle East.

BEYOND THE KOREAN SITUATION: THE EISENHOWER DOCTRINE

It can be shown that from this point up through and including the Dominican and Vietnamese crises of 1965, United States policymakers kept the basic premises begun with the Truman Doctrine and the Korean War. From the end of the Korean hostilities to the present, the major alterations in foreign policies have come in management. The basic assumptions of violent upheavals being a grounds for Communist exploitation, and thereby raising the potential for a latent Soviet alliance, have been developed on a much more sophisticated basis. The most sophisticated development of these assumptions came with the Kennedy administration in 1960. However, the assumptions remained basically unchanged and thereby crisis situations continued to be responded to in much the same fashion as was done in Korea.

[17] See Appendix D for the full text of the Eisenhower Doctrine.

The added scope of the Eisenhower Doctrine developed from one consideration—the attempt to broaden the base of reasons why the United States should intervene in affairs overseas. World peace could be endangered by "the threat of military action, use of economic pressure, internal subversion, and other means to attempt to bring under their [USSR] domination peoples now free and independent."[18]

The threat of a Communist-backed Arab movement was a major concern to the United States in Middle Eastern affairs. A violent upheaval in the Middle East was seen as threatening the existence of the pro-Western nations in that area (Lebanon, Jordan, and Israel) and for this reason the United States saw the need for a faster reaction to any crisis situation. Consequently,

> the United States had given notice to the world that it claimed the right to intervene wherever communism was on the march, and it would do so whenever and wherever it saw fit, through the U.N. if possible, outside the U.N.—but within the confines of its legal rules—if necessary.[19]

This was the essence of the Eisenhower Doctrine.

THE KENNEDY ADDITIONS

The Kennedy outlook formalized many aspects of our past policies that were not yet defined in operational terms. Kennedy believed that the basic threat to American national interest lay in our confronting the determined Soviet program for world domination. Kennedy fully recognized the Soviets' capability for informal access on all levels, and for this reason was concerned with any Soviet attempts to use military might, political subversion, economic penetration (Kennedy called it Soviet imperialism), and ideological conquest as methods of control. Kennedy was still concerned with the possibility of a latent alliance being formed between penetrated nations and the Soviet Union. He was also concerned with preventing violent upheaval in any part of the world as Communist exploitation of an unstable period in a nation-state's history could make the possibility of alliance more credible.

What made the Kennedy method unique, outside of this sophisti-

[18] Graber, op. cit., pp. 310–311.
[19] Ibid., p. 315.

cated interpretation of the Communists' protracted conflict aspect of foreign affairs, was Kennedy's concept of gaining the initiative that the United States never really had over the Soviet Union. Kennedy attributed this to America's past policies being reactive in nature and not initiatory:

> We have reacted ad hoc to a crisis here and a crisis there, year by year, region by region. When the Latin Americans throw rocks at the Vice President, there is finally talk of a Latin American loan fund. When a friendly monarch is threatened in the Middle East, money is dispersed helterskelter while there is brave but brief talk about an Arab development fund.[20]

Kennedy was more concerned with preventing the potential for alliance taking place by preventing the violent upheavals that are capable of exploitation. This was to be done with major emphasis on aid and other economic development policies.

A second unique method came with the formal reliance upon the flexible response strategy as a method of deterring military aggression whether of a direct or indirect nature. This will be discussed later.

A third aspect of Kennedy policy dealt with his caution in labeling movements in the third world, or any of their leaders, as Communist. However, once a major political movement was considered to be Communist dominated, Kennedy would pledge the support of the United States to the anti-Communist forces of that nation. President Kennedy's diplomatic exchanges with Diem, the leader of South Vietnam, and his military commitment in the form of more advisers and aircraft pilots in 1962 certainly set "some" precedent for the Johnson "let us continue" policy of 1963–1965.

THE JOHNSON ADMINISTRATION: THE LOSS OF NUANCE

Two influential decision makers who were carried over with considerable trust into the Johnson administration were Dean Rusk and Walt Rostow. These men are separated from Kennedy on two counts: (1) both were more inclined to view *any type* of upheaval as more dangerous to American national security than did Kennedy, and (2)

[20] Allan Nevins, ed., *The Strategy of Peace* (New York: Harper & Row, 1960), p. 75.

both viewed "national wars of liberation" as more capable of *immediate* Communist domination than did Kennedy. Both of these decision makers reflected these attitudes on numerous occasions to a president who did not have the command or knowledge of foreign policy that Kennedy did, and for this reason was less capable of understanding the nuances of the Kennedy multidimensional outlook.

U.S. MILITARY STRATEGY: CAPABILITIES TOWARD INTERVENTIONISM

United States military policy evolved from a "balanced forces" concept in the post World War II years, through a "massive retaliation" concept that was never used and proved unsound in the Indochina decision of the Eisenhower administration in 1954, to a multifacted version of the balanced forces concept which became formally accepted as the flexible response strategy. It is not the purpose of this analysis to compare or contrast the worth of these concepts in themselves, but to show that these policies have much in common with each other and that each concept reflected the political outlook of its time, with the acceptance of the civilian attitudes on communism, conflict, and containment.

An often misunderstood aspect of the Dulles-Twining concept of "massive retaliation" centered on the use of ground combat troops. The difference here lies in a willing and full commitment of "national prestige":

> Matching the enemy hazard for hazard requires the creation of a political and military situation that can automatically involve a *full commitment of national prestige* if the enemy attempts aggression—either overtly or by subversion.
>
> The number and type of troops would, of course, *vary* with the geography, nature, and capability of friendly troops on the spot, *and the enemy threat.*
>
> These forces would create a pause for political reappraisal, and would *allow time* for our own reinforcement and subsequent action in event the enemy decided to broaden or escalate the War. More important the automatic commitment of U.S. prestige would be a power factor in deterring enemy action before it started.[21] [Italics added.]

[21] Nathan F. Twining, *Neither Liberty nor Safety* (New York: Holt, Rinehart & Winston, 1966), p. 64.

However, it should be noted that American decision makers felt no fear of such direct Soviet confrontation in the crisis situations of 1954 to 1960.

The big difference between the flexible response attitude and massive retaliation lies in the announcement of intention. U.S. Air Force generals Twining and LeMay claimed that indicating before our involvement that we would pursue "limited war" would give the enemy "room to maneuver" and thereby diminish the credibility of our deterrence. President Kennedy and U.S. Army generals Taylor and Gavin claimed deterrence would be lost if the United States did not maintain the recommended use of conventional forces outlined by Twining and Dulles *in depth*, with the capability to contain the Communist wars of national liberation *quickly* and *decisively* but at specific levels.

Why such a strategic split occurred within the military is a topic worthy of much research and inquiry and will not be dealt with here. What is of great importance to this study is the fact that *both* the massive retaliatory thinkers and the flexible response school depend upon conventional combat troops to maintain stability in troubled areas and to *deter* the protracted conflict aspect of the Communist threat which *all* agree was the major challenge facing the security of the United States since World War II.

ECONOMIC INTERDEPENDENCE AND
STRATEGIC INTERVENTION

The post-World War II era found American decision makers realizing fully that American foreign and domestic economic policies would clearly be incapable of separate consideration if an economic depression and stagnation like that of the 1930s was to be avoided. The major problem of such a consideration, however, was that any policy attempt to resolve economic difficulties had to be capable of being defined in political terms due to the unique, competitive bipolar framework perceived by American policymakers.

The two basic political attitudes, the maintenance of worldwide stability combined with the latency of alliance fear, created policies that would insure climates of investment abroad that could yield high rates of return with comparatively little risk to American investors in their intitial capital outlays, or for their long-term capital and property holdings abroad. The Truman Doctrine and the Point Four Program were the initiating policies formed in this framework.

Foreign policy considerations no matter how sound the analysis of the international situation upon which they rest must interlock with domestic politicoeconomic policies, if they are to contribute to the maintenance of national interest or advance national goals. Accordingly, the aspirations of those charged with the management of American overseas risk capital, as well as with the management of established overseas commercial-industrial activities, strongly insisted that American governmental decision makers search out policies which would tend toward the stability of emerging nations.

Senator J. W. Fulbright, although skeptical of many policy decisions made by the United States, seemed to support the need for stability in the third world as essential to American economic policy:

> Domestic and foreign policy lines have been wholly erased. The strength of the American economy, for example, enters directly as a factor in our power to build a versatile military establishment, or to *export capital* in a way that will contribute to the *orderly growth* of newly independent nations. In a reverse view, if these nations and their resources along with those of our European allies should ever be drawn into the communist orbit, it is difficult to see how we could for long maintain our present economy or, indeed, anything resembling our present way of life.[22] [Italics added.]

Dean Acheson brought this concept a little closer to home in a discussion of our foreign policy, "It is extremely difficult for constructive effort to develop in Cuba. This is *not* because Fidel Castro is or is not a communist, but because one cannot move forward in of State Bulletin (December 29, 1958), p. 1059.
the midst of upheaval."[23]

Former Under Secretary of State for Economic Affairs Douglas Dillon put the need for maintaining governmental stability overseas and our ability for "sound" investment in graphic terms: "Does anyone think for a moment that our expanding foreign trade and investment will be unaffected if these areas of the world fail to accomplish their economic growth or freedom?"[24] Mr. Dillon went on to state that "anticipatory investments" in underdeveloped areas were, in themselves, not enough to insure success to ourselves as to the developing nation. He indicated a "U-shaped curve" might be used to explain

[22] J. W. Fulbright, "What Makes U.S. Foreign Policy?" *The Reporter* (May 14, 1959), p. 19.

[23] Dean G. Acheson, "The Premises of American Policy," *Orbis* (Fall 1959), p. 275.

[24] Douglas Dillon, "Protecting American Investments Abroad," *Department*

the necessity of "a rounded, valid, and vital mutual security program whose operations can and should serve to prepare and smooth the way for private investment both of indigenous and foreign capital." Such a U-shaped curve would indicate when American investments had the best chance of surviving and yielding their highest returns. These returns will be highest when stability is maintained in the developing nation-states so that the "exaggerated nationalism" will not create a climate unconducive to American private investment. It seems as though the only "freedom" Mr. Dillon sees as acceptable for these areas is freedom of enterprise, as he insists, "we can and must find new ways to promote private investment."

All three portions of our foreign policy, the political, the military, and the economic, can now be seen as *mutually reinforcing each other* in an attempt to preserve stability, reduce the possibility of Soviet control and alliance with other nation states, and maintain American markets and resource areas abroad. Such a coordinated policy not only made the three combat troop involvements analysed below possible, but *highly probable,* when the five conditions mentioned in the first portion of this study were perceived as reaching the crisis point. The three case studies that follow will now be analyzed within the framework of the five factors described previously: (1) the degree of control presently held by a major power (the USSR and/or China) in the target country; (2) the degree of unified nationalism present in the target nation; (3) the degree of communism perceived as present in the ideological outlook of the target nation; (4) the economic value and strategic position of the target nation; and (5) the degree of informal penetration already obtained by the United States in the target nation. As long as the United States continued to operate in the framework of a sustained crisis environment, the treadmill of overreaction and superactivism leading to military interventions held centerstage.

THE CASE STUDIES

The Lebanon Crisis—*July 15, 1958*

1. American decision makers saw the Soviet Union as attempting to gain control by proxy of the newly formed United Arab Republic. John Foster Dulles saw Western influence in the area at an all-time

low after the 1956 Suez War, along with increasing Soviet penetration in the Middle East via arms sales to Egypt and Syria.

It should be noted, however, that there was no indication of direct Soviet control in Lebanon, or, for that matter, in any portion of the Middle East at that time. Dulles' major concern was his fear that "Soviet imperialism would in a twinkling envelop the Middle East."[25]

Indeed, it was almost inconceivable to Dulles that the Arab countries could side with anyone else outside the United States or the Soviet Union. Secretary Dulles perceived the formation of the U.A.R. after the combined British-French-Israeli attack on Egypt as being directly linked with the Soviet Union and international communism. Dulles chose to fit this new situation into the administration's containment policy rather than to modify that policy in the light of developing regional Arab nationalism that was forced by the United States to turn to the Soviet Union for arms after having been refused by the United States during the outbreak of hostilities on the Gaza Strip.

2. In the curious constitutional situation in Lebanon the offices of president and prime minister were alternated between Christian and Moslem groups, and at that time, the degree of unity within Lebanon itself was at an all-time low. Christian and Moslem elements divided the country almost in half with the Moslem elements in full support of the growing Arab nationalism. The incumbent regime, that of President Camille Chamoun, was a Christian, pro-West regime that was soon to end its regular term of office. However, Chamoun was planning to change the constitution so he could have another term in office, thereby aggravating the internal conflict even further.

The internal conflict in Lebanon centered on two factors. The first was a fear of Israel striking again, with or without British and French aid. This added fears to Arab elements of Lebanese politics, which felt security arrangements had to be made to protect against Zionist expansion.

The second and major conflict dealt with the fact of Lebanon being the only Arab nation to accept the Eisenhower Doctrine, which was viewed as suppressive to Arab nationalism. The Muslims of Lebanon, particularly the Sunnis, made the mistake of supporting Nasser and of even showing him greater loyalty than they showed to their own national leaders. Chamoun was then supported by the

---

[25] Leila Meo, *Lebanon—Improbable Nation* (Bloomington, Ind.: Indiana University Press, 1965), p. 109.

Christian elements more in self-defense, as they feared Lebanese nationalism would be lost in the rising surge of Arab unity.

3. The degree of internal Lebanese communism was almost non-existent and was not perceived as a major threat to American decision makers. President Chamoun sometimes banned the Lebanese Communist party, but for the most part its operations went undisturbed and attracted little following.

The major concern about communism as such came from the Dulles guideline which postulated that both nationalism and neutralism were dangerously susceptible to Communist pressure and could easily be subverted by communism acting through Arab nationalism.

4. Both the economic potential and strategic value of Lebanon can be rated as very high. The United States feared Soviet control over the warm water ports in both the Mediterranean and in the Persian Gulf. The oil rights of this entire region were feared capable of Soviet control via the United Arab Republic and its political closeness with Moscow. The 27 United States oil concessions in the Middle East would probably be nationalized if such an event took place. It should also be noted that 64 percent of the world's oil came from the Middle East, and 90 percent of Europe's oil passed through pipelines to Lebanese ports, or through the Suez Canal, the loss of this would have weakened the economies of Europe and for this reason it would have deprived the "center of power" of much of the strength needed to maintain itself as a strong ally of the United States.

5. The degree of U.S. informal penetration in Lebanon was at an all-time high when the crisis occurred. Of all the Middle Eastern countries, Lebanon had the longest history of continuous friendly association with the United States. Much of this realtionship dated back to the nineteenth century. Since 1950 the friendship had become even closer as Lebanon became the regional center of American business.

While the economic penetration in Lebanon was at an all-time high, diplomatic relations were at the same level. It must be restressed that Lebanon was the only Arab state in the Mideast which fully, without reservation, accepted the Eisenhower Doctrine. This in fact set the mold of U.S. involvement to the point where once aid was requested, the United States had to respond in order to maintain its credibility elsewhere in the area.

This brought an interesting modification of the crisis as American-Egyptian relations began to improve in early 1958 and presented

Washington with a difficult choice. Should it pursue this new approach to Mideast policy or should it fulfill its obligation to support Lebanon against armed aggression when asked to do so?

Eleanor Dulles indicates that, in fact, Washington saw no choice in this matter. "Our judgment of the importance of the area, widely evident at the time of the Suez Crisis, had been made explicitly part of our policy in early 1957. The question to be faced was not whether to act but when and how."[26] This indicates that the rigidity of U.S. policy allowed no feedback into the decision-making process so that change or the recognition of new facts could influence the decision.

With most major factors indicating that intervention would be highly likely, all that was needed was a catalyst, a precipitator, to bring the factor of time to a critical level of importance. This catalytic agent was introduced to the volatile mixture on May 13 and 14 when Lebanese Foreign Minister, Charles Malik, informed the State Department that Chamoun and he believed Egypt and Syria were attempting to destroy Lebanon by both subversive actions (mainly the smuggling of arms and terrorists across Lebanese borders) and frontal assault. On May 17 and 18, 1958, the United States ordered its naval amphibious forces of the Sixth Fleet temporarily doubled and stated that police weapons and possibly U.S. tanks would be airlifted into Lebanon. The "frontal assault" Malik spoke of might have been a rebel government which was formed in South Lebanon after riots occurred in Beirut on May 9.

By June the United Nations had been called in to observe the conflict and to determine whether or not Chamoun's and the United States' claim of smuggling and subversive activities existed. The United Nations report was negative, despite the State Department's claim that the opposite was true. In the midst of the poised violence in Lebanon, the Iraqi government was overthrown by a joint assault of pro-Nasser and "nationalist" Communist groups (July 14, 1958). Nuri Es Said and King Faisal and many in their government and among their political supporters were bestially murdered and their bodies desecreted. General Abdel Karrim al-Kassim's followers, the victors, were so fanatical and violent that a war of all against all in the Middle East, Arabs vs. Arabs, and Arabs vs. Israel, was rightly feared. The American and British governments acted at once by joint arrangement in response to appeals for help by Beirut and Amman.

[26] Dulles, op. cit., p. 274.

The United States landed marines as soon as this was physically possible without asking the U.N. for permission first, dispatching them, indeed, long before it even notified the U.N.

The Dominican Republic Crisis—*April 29, 1965*

1. As in Lebanon, the United States decision makers saw the potential for Soviet, and even Chinese, penetration in the Dominican crisis as very high via a proxy force. That force was the Cuban Communist regime which was believed by the military, the CIA, and the State Department to be a training center for members of all three Dominican Communist parties.[27]

Although not specifically mentioned by any United States sources, one cannot imagine Dean Rusk and Walt Rostow completely forgetting the informal penetration of the Soviet Union that had occurred in Cuba in 1962 and which subsequently led to a direct confrontation between the United States and the Soviet Union over the offensive missile sites in Cuba. One would expect that even the possibility of any such reoccurrence would have been looked upon by American policymakers as unacceptable to the national interest.

Again as in Lebanon, reducing the potential, not actual, Soviet penetration in the target nation seemed to be the major political objective of American decision makers.

2. Also as in Lebanon, the unity of nationalist factions was at an all-time low. Since the military overthrow of Juan Bosch in September 1963, a three-man junta headed by ex-Foreign Minister Donald Reid Cabral was in control. From the beginning Reid was a hard-liner on both the Communists and the military organization as he removed some of each from positions of power.

The Cabral regime was failing and for this reason it was suspected that Cabral would not hold elections in September 1965 as he had promised. The Cabral regime further split its own support by closing military post exchanges and by shutting off the "military-dominated smuggling racket" that had been in force for years.

The most unified faction in the Dominican nation was the armed forces; and clearly they were beginning to split with some in favor of returning Juan Bosch and others in favor of a new military junta.

---

[27] Georgetown University, *Dominican Action—1965* (Washington, D.C.: The Center for Strategic Studies, 1966), app. I and II; also, see p. 18.

3. The degree of communism present in the Dominican situation continues to be a central question of controversy:

The official explanations given by policy makers centered on the "protection of American lives and property," until April 30 when President Johnson explained that there were signs of outside forces seeking control of the revolution that were Communist-dominated and linked to an "international conspiracy."[28] However, studies that favored U.S. intervention pointed out that as early as March 1965, pro-Communist forces were planning for some time to reinstate Bosch and that all they were waiting for was the proper moment.[29] The failure of this fact to be communicated rapidly enough to both the press and the public was considered the major public information failure of the Dominican policy decision.

The earliest messages from Ambassador Tapley Bennett, Charge d'Affairs Connett, and from Under Secretary Thomas Mann stated as early as April 25 that the local Communist forces were ready to join forces in an attempt to take over the revolt itself. Much later evidence seems to refute this, but the fact remains that American decision makers believed, and were willing to believe, that a Communist takeover was inevitable and imminent—at least in the absence of American direct action or intervention.

4. Economically the Dominican Republic certainly has much valuable farmlands when combined with a cheap labor force and a government that favored a free enterprise system, it is certainly no surprise that American corporations hold millions of dollars in property assets in this small nation.

5. The degree of informal penetration held by the United States at the time of the turmoil was very high. The American Sugar Company and the United Fruit Company owned vast holdings, with the American Sugar Company controlling several subsidiary interests such as railroads and refineries. The very fact that there were 3000 Americans at the embassy in Santo Domingo waiting to be evacuated is indicative of the level of penetration that the United States had maintained for decades in the Dominican Republic.

It is also interesting to note that after the overthrow of Juan Bosch in 1963, the United States gave the Dominican Republic $100 million in direct and guaranteed loans—the most ever given to the

---

[28] Theodore Draper, *The Dominican Revolt* (New York: Commentary Press, 1968), pp. 21–24.

[29] Georgetown University, op. cit., passim.

Dominican Republic. Could it be that the Reid Cabral and military regimes of 1963 and 1964, having a strong free enterprise bias and a simultaneous anti-Communist stand, had influenced the decision for making the loan? More direct proof is needed, but this is one factor that must not be ignored.

The catalyst that precipitated the actual troop landings was the complete failure of any military faction to maintain law and order by April 26. The Boschist movement had completely collapsed and the projunta forces were fighting each other outside Santo Domingo, thus causing Bennett to fear that the expected, the anticipated Communist takeover would occur very soon. The temporary Molina Urena government collapsed about 5 P.M., after which Bennett was sure of Communist infiltration of the P.R.D. party which once was considered pro-Bosch but anti-Communist by Bennett. A complete fragmentation of military forces occurred as Colonel Benoit simply announced the rule of his four-man junta and began contacts with Bennett who called for troops "to restore public order in this country" at 2:36 P.M. on April 29. The Marines landed at 4:44 P.M.

The similarities with the Lebanon crisis are: (1) a predetermined assumption that Communist exploitation would follow violent upheaval, (2) the landing of combat troops to support a free enterprise oriented government, (3) a mixture of the above five factors triggered the use of troops to maintain stability as soon as a crisis situation was perceived to have developed, and (4) in quickly—out quickly.

The Vietnam Crisis—*Early Spring, 1965*

The very magnitude of the Vietnamese problem has been studied by many scholars and journalists and a review of the history of our involvement need not be given here. This analysis will simply point out a few of the major considerations that led to a favorable climate for large-scale intervention when a crisis situation of instability presented itself to the key decision makers of the Johnson administration in early 1965.

1. It is essential to realize that our Vietnam commitment came during a time when Soviet communism was seen as expanding through a method of "international conspiracy" that recognized no neutrals. The John Foster Dulles who saw a potential for Soviet alliance in Lebanon is the same Dulles who supported our initial commitments to South Vietnam in 1954. Furthermore, in 1965 this potential for a latent

alliance with the Soviet Union and/or China was perceived by Dean Rusk in more legalistic and power-oriented terms as "containing aggression" and as preventing the "dominoes from falling".

> If we were to abandon that idea, then the great powers would what?— Enter a race among themselves to gobble up those portions that are within their reach until they came into massive conflict with each other? That's the sure road to disaster.[30]

2. It is well known that South Vietnam has never been internally stable. The past 20 years have seen many regimes come and go with even the Diem regime falling to a coup. In essence, the stability factor was extremely low.

3. The brand of communism seen as existent in South Vietnam was a more sophisticated method of achieving its goals—the use of guerrilla warfare as exemplified in the strategic writings of Mao Tse-Tung, Ho Chi Minh, and General Vo Nguyen Giap. This point is essential in the type of war that the United States fought in terms of strategy and time in Vietnam.

For example, a key adviser to the Johnson administration on Vietnam policy who must not be overlooked is Walt Rostow. His perception of communism as "a disease to the transition of modernization" aided in formulating policy for the stable, long-range growth of the less developed nations based upon a basically free enterprise approach.

4. The strategic position of South Vietnam was seen as vitally important in containing Communist aggression to American decision makers. To them this corner of Asia was: (1) seen as geographically cutting across the East/West trade routes; (2) considered to be the rice bowl of Asia; (3) thought to be a dangerous base for further aggression, if held "in the wrong hands"; and (4) seen as economically potent in terms of raw materials necessary for supporting industrial growth.

5. U.S. informal penetration of South Vietnam begun in 1954

---

[30] In order to better understand the Vietnam situation in the early Johnson administration, for Rusk, see Ronald J. Stupak, "Dean Rusk on International Relations: An Analysis of his Philosophical Perceptions," *Australian Outlook* (April 1971), pp. 13–28; for W. W. Rostow, see W. W. Rostow, *The Stages of Economic Growth* (London: Cambridge University Press, 1960); and for guerrilla war, see Ronald J. Stupak and Donald Booher, "Guerrilla Warfare: A Strategic Analysis in the Superpower Context," *Studies on the Soviet Union* (Winter 1969), pp. 1–11.

is far too vast for us to go into in this analysis. U.S. military adviser programs under MAAG, our increased trade relations, our implicit commitment through the SEATO pact clearly set a precedent for our involvement at an extremely high level.

As in the Lebanese and Dominican crises, all that was needed was a rapidly developing crisis that would precipitate a large-scale involvement of American troops. This came when a "white paper" was released in February 1965 entitled "Aggression from the North: The Record of North Vietnam's Campaign to Conquer South Vietnam." The white paper became the turning point in the Vietnamese struggle according to Secretary of State Rusk. He and other key Johnson administration decision makers became convinced that if American troops were not greatly expanded at that time there would have been every prospect of a defeat of the South Vietnamese forces."[31] This was the catalyst, the reason, that led to a series of little yet emergency decisions which then led to a tremendously increased American troop strength in South Vietnam.

The accusations aimed at North Vietnam in the white paper gave the United States many specific reasons for entering the war on a larger scale: (1) the hardcore of Communists fighting in the South were trained in North Vietnam; (2) key leadership of the Viet Cong officer and enlisted personnel operated under Hanoi's direction; (3) Hanoi was a collecting point for Communist-made weapons from North Vietnam, China, and other Communist countries that were infiltrated into South Vietnam to support the Viet Cong; (4) the N.L.F. of South Vietnam was directed by Ho Chi Minh in the north; (5) in 1964, an estimated 7400 North Vietnamese regular combat troops infiltrated South Vietnam. At the paper's release an estimated 35,000 NVN regulars were in South Vietnam.

One can see that the United States policymakers feared that this guerrilla war was entering the second phase of guerrilla-warfare strategy—that of combined terrorist assaults with sporadic regular troop engagements on selected occasions.

This was also proof of outside interference on a grand scale. With the stated need of a ten-to-one ratio of counterinsurgent forces to insurgents needed to halt such actions, U.S. troop strength increased rapidly from 40,000 troops as of May 17 to 75,000 on June 16. Thus, the escalation of American combat troops exploded.

---

[31] Dean Rusk, "Our Purpose Is Peace," *Reader's Digest* (December 1967), p. 54.

Conclusions

Careful analysis of the major incursions of United States military forces into the affairs of other nations leads one to conclude that American foreign policy has remained basically unchanged since its significant modification in the years immediately following the close of World War II. The political, economic, and military means of achieving and sustaining such policy have become increasingly sophisticated, but the primary outlook has been constant: U.S. decision makers were looking for, or anticipating, a direct Communist involvement in the internal strife of less developed nations; and positive responses designed to forestall such involvement, or abate it, once started, were adjudged reasonable and acceptable risks in the American national interest.

Once this basic premise is recognized as operable within the foreign policymaking field, the action is all of a piece. The attempt to keep the "world safe from aggression," to keep the world "stable," is always done in an anti-Communist framework. And while policymakers did not fear a direct confrontation with the Soviet Union, they nonetheless perceived the Soviet Union as completely capable of aligning itself with any nation that had a potential for Communist exploitation.

American involvement in the affairs of other nations always followed a very logical, rationalistic, and manipulative framework which rested securely upon the premise of maintaining stability, on the one hand, and preventing the always possible alliance of the target nation with the Soviet Union, on the other. And this predilection on the part of the policymakers, in a sense, resulted in policies rigid to the point of ossification and in ignorance of the nuances of shifting power politics to the point of blindness.

Thus, we return to the original hypothesis of this chapter with renewed assurance of its fundamental descriptive accuracy. For the time period under consideration the major question was not so much whether the United States would become more involved in the affairs of the international system, but how the United States would act. The direct interventions in the affairs of Lebanon and the Dominican Republic were characterized by swiftness and relatively favorable outcomes. Success seemed to validate the underlying assumptions. Cost calculations were of secondary importance, for the trade-offs—stability for instability, brief military intervention for cessation of Communist aggression in two small countries—fell on the plus side of the ledger. Few there were to raise the question about the ability of the United States to afford the gross multiplication of the costs which would arise from a situation in which the assumptions underlying intervention would run aground on the hard rock of sustained military opposition to such intervention. Few there were, also, who foresaw that continued use of the assumptions would force the spread of the very alliance possibilities which the United States wished to prevent.

The continuing critical acceptance of the underlying assumptions for American intervention led to a total perversion of the most crucial problem faced by the United States since the end of World War II, as the nation maneuvered the Vietnamese situation within the framework of U.S.-USSR manipulations to insure their dominance in a growing bipolar international system. Within the larger dimensions of strategic-deterrence manipulations American involvement in Vietnam may yet be deemed successful, but in the more practical context of American politics, intervention and overcommitment created tremendous internal stresses and problems, and served to produce the agonizing domestic conflicts of the late 1960s, force the resignation of Lyndon Johnson,[32] and set the stage finally for the enunciation of the Nixon Doctrine in 1969—the announcement of planned American disengagement from its superactivist, interventionist role of the 1950s and 1960s.

VIETNAM: THE ARROGANCE OF
SUPERPOWER INTERVENTIONISM

To understand the significance of the transition toward deliberate disengagement, the whole Vietnamese episode must be viewed in the context of superpower arrogance in which it was played. The major problem which most Americans had with the Vietnam situation stemmed from the belief that the issue was joined between the United States and North Vietnam, or, more naively, that it was a problem between North Vietnam and South Vietnam.

The perceptual distortion of the situation gave most persons a false set of criteria by which to judge the conflict, and led correspondingly to recurring optimistic predictions concerning the probable outcome. On the other hand, no evaluation of the Vietnam puzzle is

[32] See Appendix F for an excerpt from the speech concerning Johnson's announcement not to run for the presidency in the 1968 election.

correct which omits an analysis in terms of the larger strategic framework of deterrence strategy, or which overlooks the insidious political manipulations of superpower diplomacy.

Vietnam was a problem, and only remained a problem of essential import in international politics as long as the United States and the Soviet Union believed that its resolution on North Vietnam's terms might redound to the credit of China's ideological and strategic position. To be sure, this formulation sets the outcome in most cynical, manipulative terms. Yet analysis tends to confirm this hypothesis.

The Soviet Union feared that a swift success for the North Vietnamese would present an ideological revolutionary threat to the USSR's doctrinal position of "peaceful coexistence." At the same time, the United States feared that a quick and cheap success of the strategic concept of guerrilla warfare within the context of the "wars of national liberation" idea would fuel a massive growth of revolutionary activity in areas such as Latin America, thus engendering a dangerously ripe escalatory environment of chaos and unpredictability.

In effect, both the USSR and the United States dreaded the Chinese revolutionary doctrine which each saw in a different way in the Vietnamese experience. Together they used Vietnam as a way of debunking the ideological pretensions of Maoism while, at the same time, exposing the power weakness which undergirded the intimidating Chinese rhetoric. Hence, the real tragedy of Vietnam is that both Vietnams were manipulated as pawns to assure the stability of the strategic balance by political leaders in Moscow and Washington.

To prostrate the Chinese in every way was the goal of both sides, and yet this was accomplished over the dead bodies of millions behind a veritable smoke-screen of candy-coated phrases such as self-determination, international justice, and socialistic brotherhood. Sadly, Vietnam was used and abused to serve the mutual self-interests of the Soviet Union and the United States.

When President Nixon went to the People's Republic of China, Vietnam was finished as an important American concern. And when the Soviet Union did nothing about American mining of Haiphong and other North Vietnamese ports, Vietnam was publicly dismissed as a Soviet concern. By its inaction, the Soviet Union permitted the North Vietnamese leaders to know that detente with the United States was now the official Soviet policy, and nothing was to be allowed to jeopardize the favorable outcomes to be derived from such a policy.

Both superpowers had achieved what they wanted. The United

States had persuaded the Chinese to abandon their dangerous rhetoric (at least, against the United States) and once China had consented to be admitted back into the rational, status quo dialogue of the deterrence framework, America knew that Vietnam was no longer necessary. Correspondingly, the Soviet Union had succeeded in replacing China as the "big brother" to North Vietnam. The guerrilla warfare idea had proven too costly and totally inadequate to the technological ante that the Americans had forced the North Vietnamese to pay.

In essence, the only problem left in the Vietnamese situation after the American-Chinese, American-Soviet agreements of 1972 was the manner of Soviet and American extrication from the morass. Of course, there was a parallel desire to accomplish the withdrawal with as little loss of image as possible.

Both the United States and the Soviet Union were willing to sell out their "allies" (at varying costs) now that China was no longer an ideological or strategic threat to the deterrence balance between them. At the same time, such a sell-out became even easier because China realized that it could no longer afford to use Vietnam as a demonstration showcase because China itself was economically weak, technologically outclassed, ideologically isolated, and strategically backward. Of course, the three major powers did not admit that they were anxious to dump the Vietnamese. They will not admit that they used and manipulated the Vietnamese for their own self-interests. They cover up this reality with rhetorical illusions.

Unfortunately, the real tragedy is that these three powerful states used the Vietnamese people as playthings. The cruel, rational, calculating strategic frameworks permitted the crisis managers, strategic intellectuals, and ideological programers in Moscow, Washington, and Peking to manipulate the Vietnamese people as calculatingly and as coldly as Bobby Fischer manipulates a pawn upon a chessboard. But Washington and Moscow are the superpower masters of the international political game, and they will bear the major brunt of historical condemnation. But even more revealing is the fact that neither of them could care less about what happens to Vietnam. With China back in the fold as a status quo actor in international policies, the United States and the USSR are not particularly concerned as to what happens in many of the third world nations after Vietnam—Ho is dead, Che is dead, the New Left is dead, and Mao is dying.

The rationality of strategic detente becomes easier and more confidently assured as the last revolutionary thrust capable of threatening the status quo rules of the deterrence game has been laid to rest with the death of the revolutionary dream of China—and to this very day, the Vietnamese themselves as well as most of the American public do not know how little freedom they had to influence anything in the 1960s murderous segment of the continuing rationalized nightmare called mutual deterrence played out in the Cold War context.

MOVING INTO THE 1970s

As active American troop involvement in Vietnam ended, a series of systemic transformations in the internal/national and external/international arenas began to emerge more clearly to American foreign policymakers in particular and to the American public in general. The bipolar, Cold War framework was shattered as both the United States and the Soviet Union realized they could not blatantly manipulate their allies or even depend upon them. In addition, the superpowers became increasingly apprehensive of the dangers, costs, frustrations, and risks associated with careless third world confrontations and spiraling nuclear weapons systems. The mutual interests of the superpowers began to compete with the a priori competitive interests associated with the Cold War mentality. Hence, both from within the corridors of official policymaking power and from without, demands were being made for new policies, different perspectives, and changing equilibriums in order to bring America into the realities of the multipolar nature of the contemporary international system.

Arms race complications, multinational arrangements, educational corporations, computer power, electronic battlefields, global village media, cultural inperialism, economic imbalances between the "haves" and the "have nots," ecological exploitations, and overpopulation required that America break out of its straitjacket of Cold War globalism.

A series of specific changes began to manifest themselves—and as they did, they began to suggest the need for new perceptual frameworks, restrained strategic doctrines, and the use of different instrumentalities for U.S. foreign policy and for international intercourse. Thus, as the United States moved into the 1970s, the following trends became accepted realities for both American policymakers and the general public.

First, the political and psychological intensity of the Cold War fell markedly since the early 1960s with a lessening of the fear that a setback anywhere might lead to disaster everywhere—witness the Nixon Doctrine.[33] While there were still ideological differences among the major powers, and the probability that they would continue, the nature of the confrontation was changing as were the means by which the differences were expressed in behavioral terms. The rhetoric of the ideologues was still close to pure conflict, but in practice, competitive coexistence better described the policies of the adversaries. There seemed to be a greater perception of interests that were shared by the major powers—the United States, the Soviet Union, and China—so that the nature of their confrontation was no longer seen as pure conflict or in zero-sum terms. There were some outcomes that were highly valued that could be achieved only through some form of negotiated cooperation. Foremost among these was the avoidance of nuclear war, but another that was becoming more important was the need to protect the status and perquisities of the rich and developed powerful countries against the encroachments of the developing nations. This was especially true in a world of finite resources. For some years we had been witnessing the development of a North-South confrontation to replace the East-West confrontation of the Cold War years. Increasingly, the lines were being drawn between the have-nations and the have-not-nations that were unwilling to supply the resources for the higher standards of living in the Northern Hemisphere. In essence, ideological confrontations were being replaced by negotiated national and global interests.

Second, technological developments confronted the advanced industrial countries of the Northern Hemisphere with a double problem: technology is an enormous consumer of talent and resources; it depends upon higher levels of stability, amalgamation, and cross-national integration than ever before. At the same time, by a curious logic, people are more mistrustful of technology and their mistrust extends to the nuclear strategists and technological militarists who orchestrated the questionable façade concerning the implicit rationality of nuclear deterrence and flexible response. At the same time that technological weapons systems were making negotiations more necessary, developments in the technology of communications were making them easier and more effective. This held true for communications in the diplomatic and intergovernmental realm, but also for communications on a people to people basis. The development of hot lines for communications between leaders of countries had shown some value as a means

---

[33] See Appendix G for the official introduction to the Nixon Doctrine.

of avoiding misunderstanding and misinformation. Technological developments facilitated contact between negotiators and the governments they represented. Instructions and offers could be transmitted more rapidly. Information was an important element in the diplomatic process. Improved communications instruments facilitated the dissemination of information on which to base negotiating positions. In addition, these facilities allowed negotiators to be kept apprised of situations as they changed.

Exchange of communications was having some impact on the publics of the negotiators. The utilization of television interviews by representatives of North Vietnam and the Vietcong during the Paris talks was a clear demonstration of the use of such communication techniques.

One of the major impediments to successful arms limitations agreements between the United States and the Soviet Union had always been the question of inspection and verification of compliance with the provisions of any treaty that could have been signed. This is a demonstration of the role of trust in the conclusion of any negotiated agreement. In an international system where there is not ultimate and effective executive and judicial power, the parties to a negotiation have always been dependent upon self-help in order to assure adherence to the provisions of an agreement. Consequently they went to great lengths to assure themselves of this capability. Disagreements over the mechanics of inspections and the inability to develop a sense of trust in the United States-USSR negotiations too often prevented their conclusion. The movement toward arms limitation in the beginning of the 1970s seemed at least in part to be the result of the fact that both parties felt that there were adequate assurances of compliance monitoring capabilities available to them, without the need to work out cooperative mechanisms. Given the advances in surveillance technology, the United States could monitor and detect any major quantitative deviations from possible agreements. The provisions that could be agreed to were those that could be monitored with the technology that was currently available. One of the reasons the Salt II sessions of the talks proved difficult to begin was the fear that it was much more difficult to detect from a satellite the number of warheads on a missile, while it was possible to detect the number of launch vehicles or silos or nuclear submarines that were constructed.

Third, the economic and strategic importance of much of the third world was fading as the mutual dependency of the developed societies—Communist and capitalist alike—became more manifest Hence, the value of engaging in every form of economic and military operation to win the third world to one's own side was diminishing. With China back in the fold as a status quo actor in international politics, the United States and USSR could care even less what happened to many of the third world nations after Vietnam—with the exception of those vital to their respective spheres of influence. The most they would do was cooperate to avoid being forced into confrontations by careless, irrational, less developed countries.

Fourth, in government, domestic problems began to take priority over foreign policy issues. After ten fat years the American military budget was finally being subjected to serious scrutiny and something resembling a ceiling was set upon spending for military manpower and hardware. Whether it would hold was another matter; but it was noteworthy that whereas spending for military and domestic programs was about equal in 1961, as the 1970s progressed the spending for domestic programs was rapidly increasing over military spending. This hinted that the restraint and "wait and seeism" of the diplomatic method might be more welcomed by a public that was less and less interested in military spending, "can do" interventionism, and defense alliance commitments.

The final change in the international system stemmed from the emergence of other actors in at least some major aspects of the international arena. With the increase in the number of relevant actors also came a broader range of conflict-cooperation mixes in the relationships among them. When the only two major actors were the United States and the Soviet Union, the relationship between them could be one of unmitigated hostility and mutual incompatibility. In such a situation military means were an important part of the relationship. With the emergence of Western Eruope and Japan as economic powers, and China as a potential economic and military power, other means had to come into play. Western Europe was no longer completely subservient to the wishes and instructions of the United States, but neither could it be considered a mortal enemy that had to be threatened with nuclear destruction to obtain its cooperation. Consequently, foreign policy instruments that could deal with situations of varying hostility appeared to be increasingly essential. Through negotiations and diplomatic means it seemed possible to deal with and secure the cooperation of special friends like Great Britain and West Germany, and to bring some pressure to bear on independent-minded France. An extension of this kind of instrumentality was seen in the development of increasing diplomatic contacts with the Soviet Union and China over a broad range of topics that ranged from military and security to economic, technological, and humanitarian.

What all of this seemed to augur was that the areas and activities which formerly provided the "military security operators" with their biggest justification no longer held the center of the stage—something had to be done to dovetail American foreign policy with the transformed environment. It was essential that America come home to deal with the domestic problems surfacing in this world's first post-modern society, while it also recast its philosophical guidelines and operational instrumentalities more carefully and systematically for dealing with the realities of the imploding international problems of the technetronic age. Surely, to move beyond the Cold War became a national necessity as the restive 1960s came to a close.

THE BANKRUPTCY
OF SUPERACTIVISM AND THE
RESURGENCE OF DIPLOMACY
AND THE DEPARTMENT OF STATE
An Interpretive Projection

As American leaders reflected upon the dire consequences of overseas military adventurism they came to sense the inconclusive, stopgap nature of the results. Puzzled by a failure to gain consistent widespread internal support for policies which seemed logically coherent to those who had devised them, and which seemed, also, in direct line of descent with policies which had met with at least majority approval, decision makers realized that the time for change had come. Moreover, in response to a chorus which grew ever louder, leaders sensed that more than specific policies had to give way. The established philosophy from which the policies had sprung needed overhauling as well. The Cold War framework no longer fitted the day of detente—the world was changing and a new set of policy lenses was needed to make sense of the changes. The key question thus came into focus: What could serve as a reasonable substitute for a militarily supported hard line? To that question we now turn.

The major thrust for an official change in the direction of American foreign policy is embedded in the Nixon Doctrine. It represents a reversal of the American formula of a do-it-ourselves world peace. From 1945 through the 1960s the United States perceived the world's problems and unilaterally established too many programs and expended too many resources to solve those problems. Thus, it is important to note that the Nixon Doctrine states emphatically that the Cold War is over and that the United States must enter into a period of partial disengagement in order to bring about a lower profile for

American foreign policy. No longer should or could the United States assume the role of world policeman. With our allies stronger, with parity at the nuclear level with the Soviet Union achieved, and with polycentrism in the Communist world a reality, it becomes essential for negotiation and bargaining (and their attendant instrumentalities) to replace coercion and the use of force to deal with the international problems of the 1970s. In effect, though ambiguity exists in the operational consistency and coherence of implementing the Nixon Doctrine, the overarching guidelines represent a rejection of the superactivism of post-World War II American foreign policy. A search for a new and viable balance of power compatible with the realities of the contemporary international system is the undergirding of the Nixon Doctrine. In essence, the "Kissinger-Nixon-Ford" approach is not revolutionary, but it *is* an attempt to structure a new balance of power beyond the outdated Cold War context. The Nixon vision is best explained in his own words of February 1972:

> There will always be conflict in the world, and turbulent change and international rivalries. But we can seek a new structure of global relationships in which all nations, friend and adversary, participate and have a stake. We can seek to build this into a world in which all nations, great and small, can live without fear that their security and survival are in danger, and without fear that every conflict contains for them the potential for Armageddon. In such a structure of peace, habits of moderation and compromise can be nurtured, and peoples and nations will find their fullest opportunities for social progress, justice, and freedom. This is what we mean by a generation of peace.[1]

The exit of American troops from Vietnam, the SALT I agreements, the Nixon trips to China and Russia, the ending of the draft and the cutbacks in military manpower are signs that major changes

[1] It is the author's opinion that no matter who would have been elected president in 1968, there would have been a major redirection toward restraint undertaken in American foreign policy—maybe more radical, maybe more conservative; but, in any case, Nixon became the president and he announced and orchestrated the directon and the pace of the change. Therefore, this analysis is not necessarily an endorsement of Nixon and the Nixon Doctrine; rather, it is considered to be an "accurate" historical, descriptive analysis of the current trend in American foreign policy. In addition, it is the author's further belief that as Ford follows Nixon to the presidency he will have to continue the low-profile, less activist foreign policy begun under Nixon's administration. Finally, the stupidity and dishonesty of Watergate may have an effect on policy specifics, but it will not bring about a change in the overall foreign policy guidelines of restraint and relaxation in the 1970s. Furthermore, President Ford has made it emphatically clear that he intends to continue the Nixon foreign policy trend in just about every respect.

occurred in American foreign policy under the Nixon administration—changes which the American attentive public and general public demanded and desired. Though arguments may ensue about the pace and the priorities of current American foreign policy, it is clear that the United States has turned its back on superactivism, universal interventionism, and Cold War globalism.

Henry T. Nash in his recent book, *American Foreign Policy: Response to a Sense of Threat,* extrapolates from the Nixon Doctrine a list of changes which he believes are essential for a new direction in American foreign policy: (1) a decreased dependence on the military for the implementation of foreign policy, (2) a more restricted role for intelligence collection and evaluation procedures, (3) an increased foreign policy participation by Congress, (4) the strengthening of the State Department, (5) a new approach to foreign aid, (6) an effort to raise the consciousness of the American electorate, and, finally, (7) assertive leadership by the president.[2]

The direction that American foreign policy must take is away from the perceptions, actions, and abuses of the excessive militarism and interventionism of the Cold War years. Policy must move toward a framework based on negotiations, bargaining, and coexistence. In essence, academics and policymakers alike are convinced of the general trends desired in American foreign policy, but the crux of the problem continues to arise on how to get there.

The answer lies in the traditions of diplomacy, the diplomatic method, and resurgence of the State Department. The end of American involvement in Vietnam signifies the transformation of power in the American foreign policy process out of the hands of the military-dominated institutions into the hands of those individuals and institutions proficient in and dedicated to the nonviolent perceptions and methods of defining and dealing with world problems.

Most contemporary academic and journalistic commentators have been proclaiming the death of the State Department as an essential and vital policymaking unit in the American foreign policy process. In fact, recent analyses make the point that the State Department has been eclipsed in the conduct of foreign policy by the emergence of rival theoretical frameworks and contending agencies which have

---

[2] Henry T. Nash, *American Foreign Policy: Response to a Sense of Threat* (Homewood, Ill.: Dorsey Press, 1973), pp. 199–212. In addition, see I. M. Destler, *Presidents, Bureaucrats, and Foreign Policy* (Princeton, N.J.: Princeton University Press, 1974), passim.

gutted the perceptual and operational power of the department and its personnel.

Traditionally foreign policy was thought to depend on negotiations that respected the sovereignty of separate nation-states. The principal means of exerting influence upon other states was from the outside through the intermediary of diplomacy backed by force. However, a new theoretical base for foreign policy emerged under the impact of the Cold War, in the wake of the revolution in weapons systems, and after the collapse of old European empires. This new approach was championed by ideologues, military managers, and programmatic operators of various sorts who felt that the United States had entered a new revolutionary age which rendered traditional diplomatic methods obsolete.

SUPERACTIVISM AND SECURITY MADNESS

This new theoretical base held that the revolutionary world situation could only be met by a massive mobilization of resources, weapons technology, and a vast array of manipulative techniques to win the battle for men's minds. In addition, this approach increasingly focused primarily on the emerging third world, which by the 1960s had surfaced as the essential ideological, strategic, and manipulative battleground. Furthermore, the new conceptual framework spawned a host of competing operational agencies—AID, the CIA, USIA, MAAGS, and the deterrent strategists—all of which consistently seemed to elevate the military and military-oriented instrumentalities to an unprecedented role in foreign policy deliberations. As a result of this operational acceptance of superactivism, the role and philosophy of diplomacy became subtly and not so subtly displaced in favor of "can do" military activists, crisis managers, and programmatic operators who acted as "Mr. Fix-its" with little or no profound understanding of, or commitment to, the tasks of diplomacy. The military ideological theorists, the clandestine superspies, and the dashing strategic intellectuals became Washington's main organizational planners for the 1960s and the early 1970s. In other words, the mood to move away from traditional procedures and channels and the traditions of isolationism to an overwhelming security-dominated almost imperialistic syndrome was a kind of governmental mood, widely supported, rarely opposed, and never effectively resisted.

As the Cold War deepened and the northern half of the global situation became increasingly stabilized, America's image of its role in the world became more and more oriented toward its acceptance of responsibility to help the struggling nations of the Southern Hemisphere. This, of course, was coupled with the growing perception of the Kennedy administration's "tough" crisis managers that the fate of the free world was at stake should the third world go Communist as the result of increasing Soviet-Chinese involvement in this area.

It was the essence of the Kennedy strategy to resist with vigor and passion every Soviet attempt to extend its influence into the third world. The revolutionary weapon of guerrilla warfare was to be struck down by "flexible response" and "counterinsurgency." This enterprise entailed unceasing attention to local upheavals which might allow the Russians to get a foot in the door. This need to solve the crises of the third world, lest catastrophe befall, spurred successive administrations into ceaseless and farflung activity and an ever deeper set of commitments and involvements in the third world.

Of course, this shift to a predominant third world emphasis was a progression that began with the worldwide economic and military assistance programs of the Truman administration. Thereafter it developed more with Dulles' pactomania and the Eisenhower Doctrine; then it was the Alliance for Progress to assist the Latin American nations, flexible response, and counterinsurgency civic action programs; and finally culminated in outright massive U.S. military intervention under Johnson. From desiring stability in new states in order to deny communism a chance to establish itself therein, it was an easy and deadly step to regard instability in itself as evidence of Communist activity. Under the impetus of this form of conceptualization, Washington expanded its multifarious operations in the third world with tools of ever greater manipulative sophistication. And yet, as strategy after strategy was tried they never seemed to achieve their purpose.

Instead of causing the policymakers to question their assumptions, each setback led to ever more grandiose conceptualizations, reaching their apotheosis in W. W. Rostow's logic that since third world countries would have to go through a stage in which "wars of liberation" were likely to sweep over a country's unsettled political and social structure, the United States had a responsibility to provide the indigenous governments with economic and political support at least, and with military intervention if deemed necessary by America. Such analyses spawned a heterogeneity of strategies and agencies, principally for dealing with the situation in the third world, which clearly displaced the emphasis from normal diplomatic dealings and international maneuvers to one upon economic and military aid programs, CIA-sponsored operations, counterinsurgency doctrines, and outright U.S. military intervention. These formal and informal penetration programs clearly took the play away from the normal agency of foreign policy—the State Department—at least in the conduct of U.S. policy vis-à-vis the third world or Southern Hemisphere states.

THE "CAN DO" MENTALITY

Here was an area with no experience in statehood, with weak and ineffective governments, of societies struggling to modernize and master their destiny but frequently racked by social and political convulsions, with political forces deemed dangerously susceptible to Communist blandishments whether of an economic, ideological, or military sort and therefore in which the normal rules of the diplomatic game were thought inapplicable. Here was an area in which only the most fundamental kinds of operations, including surgery, if necessary, would succeed if new nations were to survive and not succumb to communism.

The situation in many parts of the third world seemed to invite the newer mode of operations. Many third world states were woefully underdeveloped and in need of assistance; many had indigenous guerrilla movements that were eating at their vitals; many were ruled by leaderships whose values put them woefully out of touch with the needs of their people or with the currents of the time. These situations invited a policy of direct intervention.

Once it was decided that entirely new and more demonstrably effective techniques were needed if these areas were not to succumb to communism, the whole new set of bureaucratic agencies sprung massively into operation. Instead of the traditional "wait and see" philosophy of diplomacy, policymakers were relieved to hear the "can do" certainties of the CIA and of the military (attention is directed to the confident tone of many high-ranking military officers as they announced their promises and expectations regarding secret military operations in Laos and North Vietnam in the early 1960s). Given license to operate over this vast new terrain, the views of the newer agencies began first to compete with, and then clearly to, preempt the role of the State Department.

Instead of determining what was reasonably possible the new actors came to the scene with a "can do" operational philosophy. The goal of American economic and military assistance was to stabilize the particular societies undergoing modernization so as to prevent them from succumbing to civil war, revolution, or communism. That indigenous political and social factors might operate independently of and beyond the control of American assistance was not thoroughly understood. Or if it was understood, it was up to the CIA or the military to provide the means by which political change did not get out of hand. Under the guise of military assistance programs, MAAGs were expected to modernize and shape the national military establishments so as to insure that they would be able to cope with internal as well as external threats to the security of the country to which they were assigned. And if worse came to worse, the president could always call upon the Marines or units of the newly established Special Forces to help prevent coups or insurgencies which were beyond the power of the local forces to contain. Such was the scenario.

THE SUBORDINATION OF DIPLOMACY

Whether intended or not the philosophy behind these operations began to preempt the traditional role of diplomacy throughout much of the third world still open to American influence. Nor was the philosophy of such operations congenial to diplomacy. Even worse, diplomacy itself became bound up with or subordinated to the conduct of these operations:

> This proclivity for operating against all odds, leads to a milling about in the management of programs without advancing an inch toward goals. In 1967–1969, for example, the Department of State (and AID) were far more concerned with "staffing and running" CORDS (Civil Operations and Rural Development Support) than with analyzing what we were trying to do in Vietnam, and why. Programmatic approaches in foreign affairs are not only costly in economic terms and risky in political terms; they can also rapidly lose themselves in futility when the meaning of diplomacy becomes lost to the diplomats.[3]

Operations such as these and the philosophy behind them were in some profound sense the antithesis of diplomacy. Diplomacy deals with the external relations among states; it takes their competing

[3] Paul M. Kattenberg, "Vietnam and U.S. Diplomacy, 1940–1970," *Orbis* (Fall 1971), p. 838.

interests for granted and strives to find some basis for adjustment and accommodation. It assumes an element of uncertainty and contingency in every situation and does not believe that there can be any final and absolute answers. Diplomacy is rooted in the wisdom that states should not seek active intervention to shape the external and internal destiny of other states. Prudence warns that states involve themselves in other nations' internal affairs at their own risk. Beyond a certain point a state risks losing control of its own actions if it goes too far in the direction of intermixing itself in another state's internal development (see Chapter VI). Diplomacy like international law limits itself to manipulations of the international system via armaments, alliances, treaties, and even coercion; but it does not assume that international statecraft lends itself to direct intervention in and manipulation of the internal affairs of other states, at least not on a universal scale with the intent to manage the system via programs designated to mold and control the domestic affairs of other states.

Yet this is precisely what Amerian policymakers from Dulles and Kennedy forward have been striving to do. By insisting that the international system was unstable, bipolar, and so tightly coupled that Communist gains or instability of any magnitude anywhere would lead to disaster elsewhere, the United States put itself in the position of struggling to control change everywhere in a rigid zero-sum framework. Because in a world of a hundred developing nations there is no way of knowing which will benefit from development assistance, which will require military assistance or direct military intervention, the United States has been in the position of running around trying to put out fires everywhere. Instead of seeming active and in control, the United States often appeared insecure, reactionary, and on the defensive. In Cuba, in Indonesia, in Vietnam, and on the Indian subcontinent, the story has been the same.

THE QUICK-FIX SYNDROME OF CRISIS MANAGEMENT

The crisis managerial and programmatic operators' approach to international politics is the antithesis of diplomacy in yet another sense. Dean Acheson used to compare foreign relations to the art of the gardener. You work with nature over a long period of time before you can possibly get it to the point you want. You cannot force nature. The gardener variety of diplomatist knows that only rarely can you manage a crisis; the diplomatic art is to work with problems ahead of time so that they do not become crises. But the operator's philosophy does not allow for slow growth and accommodation to crisis. When failure overtakes his operations, as is far more likely to be the case when policy is based upon a recklessly assembled house of cards, the operator has no fallback position, no diplomatic arts to cushion his fall. Rather the situaton is such that the leadership becomes driven to a series of desperate expedients.

Slowly, but surely, the cautiousness and sobriety of the diplomatist's craft is eclipsed by the overwhelming confidence of the crisis manager. Each setback to the operator's assumptions in Vietnam was met by reliance upon a quick fix: first it was strategic hamlets; then it was the assassination of Diem; then it was escalation and the bombing of the north; then it was full-scale Americanization of the war; and finally, it was the mining of Haiphong and laying waste to North Vietnam in the holiday raids of 1972. This is not the only example. To quote again from Kattenberg:

> There is little in all this for which our military leadership can directly be blamed. Crisis swamped the reason and perception of top American civilian policy-makers in all key departments in 1964–1965. On the charitable side, one might adduce the physical and mental exhaustion that overtakes them in moments of "crisis management"—moments they abhor for their disorderliness (and tend to postpone as long as possible by deferring the necessary reviews and decisions that might avert them), yet embrace avidly because of their exhilaration when they inevitably occur.[4]

How insidious to know that our leaders, the "best and the brightest," when confronted by a shattering situation can take relief by the injection of another quick fix in the excitement of crisis situations.

Finally, the operators have been carried along by the primacy which the postwar American presidents have accorded to foreign policy and their commander in chief roles during the last two decades. Consequently, every conceivable weapon and every conceivable strategy has been amply financed by an unending stream of appropriations. Why bother to examine one's assumptions or the wisdom of one's course of action when one knows that if worst comes to worst new appropriations will be forthcoming with which to finance new programs and thereby redeem the shortcomings of the old?

[4] Ibid.

In dealing with the third world, there was never the determined or needed effort to define American objectives in terms relevant to international politics, apart from such concepts as dominoes, containment, and credibility. What relations might be had in traditional diplomatic terms of mutual interests, regional arrangements, international agreements, and international law were either only fleetingly cultivated (e.g., the Congo) or not considered at all. Even desired or acceptable outcomes tended to be bastardized in the meaningless rhetorical definitions of goals sometimes put forward for the benefit of domestic opinion, such as resistance to communism, self-determination for our allies, the capacity to develop a viable state, and the magic of counterinsurgency.

Perhaps it is harder for Americans than for most people to understand how they have been duped by their leaders' rhetoric—especially because of their relative neglect of foreign policy matters. They have been led away from the practical possibilities of the diplomatic situation by an endless stream of ideological and technological platitudes. Precisely because the stakes have not been as clear and unmistakable in our dealings with China and the third world as in our relations with the other nuclear superpower we have indulged ourselves with inflated fantasies of our good intentions towards the "peoples" of the third world and of our obligation to help out with their economic development, and at the same time save them from the virus of revolution and communism.

Because of the peculiarity of circumstances in the third world, for ten years the United States gave itself over to an orgy of operational strategies which were the very antithesis of the diplomatic method. The Department of State found itself harried and chivied in much of that part of the world by the "can do" antics of the CIA, AID, military advisory teams, and outright military intervention such as in Laos, Cambodia, Thailand, and South Vietnam.

The subtleties that differentiate one country or one situation from another are soon lost from sight when policy consists of applying the same program criteria across the board with little if any sensitivity. One regime was as good as another—an approach that had worked in one case could be applied just as easily somewhere else. In effect, the State Department personnel soon found themselves engaging in some of the same operational rat races as their competitors. In the scramble for influence and budget, State Department personnel often found themselves reluctantly engaging in the same arena.

THE STATE DEPARTMENT, THE DIPLOMATIC
METHOD, AND THE NORTHERN HEMISPHERE

Fortunately for the State Department the excesses of the operator's philosophy were mostly confined to the third world (Southern Hemisphere). In the Northern Hemisphere where relations essentially are between the more advanced industrial states no such faddish activism was as realistically possible. Relations were either between the two superpowers or between America and its allies—Canada, Japan, and Western Europe. In all these relations, the role of the State Department has remained the preeminent one. And it is in the context of the Northern Hemisphere bias of the Nixon Doctrine and the latest Soviet-American agreements that the embryo of the coming resurgence of the State Department as a coordinating institution of essential importance can be foreseen.

There diplomacy and the diplomatic method have remarried the dominant mode of conducting our foreign relations in these areas, but even here—perhaps especially here—the State Department has had to share its authority with the Treasury Department, the Pentagon, and not least the National Security Council. This was not true in the earlier postwar years. The "dollar shortage" was the dominant economic fact in the 1940s and 1950s, and economic policy was made to serve our diplomatic goals. Similarly NATO was created as an instrument of American foreign policy; later it became an end in itself with all the attendant strategic and institutional rigidities that were exemplified by the McNamara policy and by the ill-fated Multilateral Nuclear Force.

Naturally the role of the treasury and of the White House have been elevated as Europe and Japan have become America's economic competitors with the potential to upset our domestic economy. Because these matters have involved the political fortunes of successive administrations at the highest level, leadership has been taken away from the State Department and put in other hands. This has not guaranteed that it would produce any better trade and monetary policy.

William N. Turpin has made an interesting distinction in this regard between foreign policy and foreign relations:

> Just as no Chief of State can ignore the power position of his country in relation to others, so no American president can act in the foreign affairs field without reckoning the consequences to himself and to his party. For both these reasons while the President can, and indeed

must, leave "foreign relations" to be dealt with by the ordinary machinery of government, he cannot and the record shows, does not relegate foreign policy to the officials.[5]

The fact that such a distinction may exist or that other departments have shared and even dwarfed the role of the State Department does not mean that it works. Perhaps one reason why this distinction has become so pronounced is precisely because the State Department lost its foreign policy effectiveness under successive administrations and has not been able to get it back. It is a distinction between policymaking and diplomacy that certainly was not true under Acheson and only beginning to be true under Dulles. To be successfully executed the mass of international government activity cannot be separated from the "foreign policy" decisions of the president, nor can it be carried on successfully separated from the diplomacy and diplomatic methods of the Department of State. That successive presidents have been driven to the expedient of separating foreign policy and day-to-day foreign relations this way does not mean that it can be successfully employed indefinitely.

To be successful, policy in the trade and monetary realm must be negotiated with the interests of our allies and other states clearly in mind. And the same is true of a host of other issues which though technical by nature are eminently political (such as arms control, relations with the Common Market, the rule of the seabed, environment, oil prices, etc.). Unless the reporting, judgments, and negotiations that bear on these matters are diplomatic in character these policies can blow up in the president's face. Even if we concede that the distinction Turpin makes between foreign policy (the president's domain) and foreign relations (the professional diplomat's domain) may indeed exist, it is not one to be welcomed or treated as normal. It is not normal because it is an outgrowth of a period in our history when the shibboleths and routines of the Cold War stultified diplomacy in the traditional sense. The State Department cannot expect to be the only fountainhead of foreign policy, but for years it abdicated its vocation only to find its functions challenged by other departments and then taken over outright by the National Security staff. This is abnormal because there must be an organic connection between the advice the president is getting and the belief on the part of the people in the field that what they are doing makes

[5] William N. Turpin, "Foreign Relations, Yes; Foreign Policy, No," *Foreign Policy* (Fall 1972), pp. 50–61.

sense. It is time for the State Department to gain back for itself a coherent sense of what its vocation is: namely, to interpret to the president a useful sense of what is politically possible in the world beyond America's shores, and to do it in such a way as to take account of his needs. America is going to need more, not less, diplomatic skills in the coming years.[6]

SYSTEMIC TRANSFORMATIONS IN THE 1970s

In effect, the necessary and hoped for resurgence of the State Department is tied to a number of transitional changes occurring in the international system and at home. For the sake of clarity, let us repeat these changes and then explain how they affect the role of the State Department in its comeback as the principal architect in the future of American foreign policy. First, the political and psychological intensity of the Cold War has diminished. Secondly, technological society and its attendant systemic impacts have led people to mistrust technology and the nuclear strategists and technological militarists who have orchestrated it into a deterrence system of rationalistic violence. Thirdly, the economic and strategic importance of much of the third world is fading (though, surely, not all of it; i.e., the Middle East) as the dependency of the developed societies becomes more manifest. Finally, domestic problems such as inflation and Watergate have begun to take priority over foreign policy issues.

[6] This suggestion does not mean that all of a sudden the State Department is going to be preeminent in the foreign policy process. Rather it becomes an output demand on the American foreign policy process and on the State Department in light of the transformations and trends in the international and domestic environments outlined in the previous chapter and in the rest of this chapter. In other words, systemic demands will bring about institutional and instrumentality changes in the foreign policy process—and from all the signs analyzed above, the State Department and the diplomatic method should and must become the synthesizer of the multifarious faces of foreign policy in the 1970s.

There are those (though they too believe that different methods and instrumentalities are needed to take the lead in the foreign policy process of the 1970s) who think that the State Department is incapable of rising to the occasion demanded of it. See William I. Bacchus, "Diplomacy for the 70's: An Afterview and Appraisal," *American Political Science Review* (June 1974), pp. 736–748. But for a more quantitative analysis in support of the intermediate range, intuitive theses of this chapter, see David Harnham, "State Department Rigidity: Testing a Psychological Hypothesis," *International Studies Quarterly* (March 1974), pp. 31–39.

Quite apart from the fact that nation building in a counterinsurgency framework and protracted, semiconventional war on the Asian mainland have failed, it is simply no longer a relevant basis for American policy vis-à-vis the third world, and the sooner it comes to an end the better. Except for the Middle East (which is very much a leftover from the Cold War era) the political, ideological, and strategic significance of the third world is no longer as important as it was once thought to be. As the competitive incentive wanes the need for costly programatic operations will diminish in significance.

SITUATIONAL CIRCUMSTANCES REPLACING
IDEOLOGICAL UNIVERSALISMS

Increasingly the consequences of domestic upheaval and changes of regime in the third world can be left to diplomatic procedures to be worked out according to individual situational circumstances. This has always been true of America's relationship to a number of marxist-revolutionary and Moscow-leaning regimes in the third world (e.g., Algeria). When revolutionary change in the third world is simply no longer assumed to have major implications for American power and security, then the need for the "operators" will simply disappear. Their place will be taken increasingly by negotiators (not all of whose techniques are very nice—e.g., the U.S. threat to use its vote to cut off all loans by international lending agencies to Chile unless it agrees to just and speedy compensation for U.S. property nationalized by the Allende government), and the State Department will reassume its former role. Relations will be adjusted according to external criteria rather than by attempts to mold and shape the internal structures of third world countries. Henceforth, the U.S. commitment to third world countries will be shaped by the American economic and political stake in their respective development.

The real activity is increasingly likely to be centered, for the immediate future at least, in advancing the relations among the economic power centers of the Northern Hemisphere, the sphere where positive movement already exists. There the techniques of negotiation already have precedence over conflict and confrontation. Relations in the Northern Hemisphere are already preeminently diplomatic in character. They either involve the maintenance of security communities such as the North Atlantic Treaty Organization or the negotiation of understandings—about nuclear arms control, Berlin, and East-West relations—so as to avoid confrontation, escalation, and accidental war. The State Department has always retained its preeminent role in the conduct of U.S. foreign relations in the Northern Hemisphere (except when challenged from time to time by military opposition to arms control agreements). Now by fortunate happenstance, the Department of State is identified with the area in which positive movement and success have been achieved. Here State already has the inside track whereas it is less directly associated with the recent disaster areas of American foreign policy such as Cuba, Vietnam, Laos, and the Indian subcontinent. It is positively associated with whatever positive accomplishments have been realized in the Middle East and with West German's Ostpolitik.[7]

TECHNOLOGICAL AND ECONOMIC CONVERGENCE OF PROBLEM AND ISSUE AREAS IN INDUSTRIAL SOCIETIES

As technology imposes even greater restraints upon national foreign policies (not implying that the arms race is coming to an abrupt end, or that the dangers of nuclear war have been eliminated), there is bound to be a cumulative shift away from military rivalry and confrontation toward something approximating normal relations among the leading industrial states. The convergence that is taking place is not so much one of systems as of common arrangements, if Russia and America, Europe and Japan are to manage their affairs with a modicum of order and well-being. This is a situation ready-made for the exercise of diplomatic and negotiating skills rather than the arts and stratagems of war (cold or hot). The Pentagon is already lashing about with the implications of the summit agreements which confront it—witness the exhuming of the counterforce corpse by the Defense Department. A great deal depends, of course, upon the wisdom and restraint with which the Soviet leadership responds to the spirit of the arms agreements; but a great deal also depends upon

[7] Ostpolitik is the policy of the D.B.R. (West Germany) vis-à-vis the D.D.R. (East Germany). It recognizes that Germany, although one nation, is two nation-states; and that the eastern border of the Oder-Neisse rivers is fixed. This policy was established by a treaty signed in Bonn on November 8, 1972. The national debate on the issue demonstrated a national mood of detente, for the Social Democrats (SPD) gained a clear plurality in the Bundestag for the first time in its history in the election of November 19, 1972.

the efforts of Washington policymakers *not* to let the treaty limiting the number of strategic missiles encourage or legitimize a race to advance more and more deadly weapons outside the terms of the treaty.

Finally, the State Department is in a good position to regain the initiative in American foreign relations because, paradoxically, of the increasing inroads which domestic problems are making upon the resources and attention available for foreign policy programs. As both Russia and America confront the twin demands for more freedom and a better material environment, they are not going to have the time or resources to devote to the Cold War or the arms race (obviously a similar phenomenon is at work within China). Minority unrest and intellectual dissent are endemic within the Soviet Union. Moreover, the USSR is falling behind in the technological race with Europe, the United States, and Japan. Within the United States the political miscalculations in Vietnam, the consuming demands of Watergate, together with the failure of the government to deal (not to solve but simply to deal) effectively with the social and environmental problems have put the whole system into question. The magnitude of the backlash against the uncontrolled pace of technology is just beginning to be felt. We are living in the postindustrial society in which the major problem is not that of creating material well-being, but one of learning to live with the consequence of the scientific and technological revolution that is occurring. The traditional values are eroded, the center no longer holds, more and more people want the freedom and the means to live individualized lives, but the existing social and political system has not found a means of respecting those demands without losing all control.

The challenges of the domestic scene and the agonies of Watergate (and post-Watergate) are increasingly likely to draw resources and attention away from the international system, thereby returning diplomacy to the professionals. Nixon initially had to devote primary attention to foreign affairs because the delicate problem of retrenchment was one that required a great deal of effort and ballyhoo—and maybe even excessive summitry. But already a process of routinization and operationalization of many matters in the hands of the professional diplomats is under way. This does not mean to suggest that the volume of problems surging in upon Washington from the international arena will be lessened; in fact, it is likely to grow as the complexities of a technologically integrated Northern Hemisphere become more and more manifest. But these are the nonspectacular problems of trade, tariffs, international transport, standards, pollution, and air piracy, which civilized states will have in common, which manifestly can only be satisfactorily settled by common agreement, and which therefore will revert more and more to the skills of the professional diplomat and negotiator. In point of fact, foreign policy appears to be the driftwood in the current stream of domestic dominance in terms of political emphasis, technological-economic necessities, and governmental dislocations. Furthermore, the faith in technocrats to solve all our problems is diminishing as both the youth and the general public become outraged at many of the cultural ramifications of systems analysis, computer technology, domestic spying, and managerial conformity. Hence, the State Department, the least of the technetronic bureaucracies, should gain support for its more fundamental, qualitative approach to problems and issues in a world which is in danger of drifting toward a technological mono-culture.

A DIFFERENT APPROACH TO THE THIRD WORLD: "BENIGN NEGLECT" OR DIPLOMATIC MATURITY?

Clearly the crisis of the third world cannot be ignored. But henceforth the approach is much more likely to be one of how to minimize the damage and potential for disruption of the third world rather than how to win victories against the other side. If America's leaders have any wisdom at all, they will begin making serious efforts to channel the problems of the third world through the United Nations and other international agencies, such as the World Bank. Again this is not a terrain for the quick-fix operators in the Cold War sense, but rather for international lawyers, professional diplomats, and functional experts.

The Ford administration is presently constrained both by circumstances and public opinion from doing anything innovative about the third world. Most of its energies have had to go into the critical task of retrenchment (the Nixon Doctrine) and of reordering America's relations with Peking. But if and when this process is completed—and hopefully without irreparable damage to America's relations with Japan, Europe, and assorted other friends and allies—there are signs that the United States must take up the task of reestablishing its relations with the third world on a more stable, sane, and diplomatically productive basis. President Luis Echeverría Alvarez of Mexico recently made plain that neither his nor the other third world countries intend to be taken for granted.[8] Therefore, a new approach called a "Third World Averaging Strategy"[9] might be a way to recast U.S. policy toward the "new nations." It consists of:

1. A policy of abstaining from the internal politics of the underdeveloped countries in favor of dealing with each on the basis of tolerance and generous correctness.
2. An economic aid program in which a regular part of our national income would be committed through international agencies to genuine development.
3. An ability to resist overt military aggression by another superpower, but not to commit America to providing immediate assistance to nations undergoing revolution or who would use American participation as a weapon against internal opponents or against their neighbors. In essence, the United States would attempt to adjust its relations with all countries on the basis of diplomacy.

Here, too, such an approach would redound to the benefit of the Department of State. If adjustments in relations are limited to those that can be carried out by external means only, then this gives the play back to the diplomats rather than to the operators. We should see a diminution of foreign aid for Cold War purposes, or for purposes of maintaining bankrupt and repressive regimes in power; we will have an end to CIA-sponsored operations (internally and externally); we will have less need for manipulative informal penetration devices; we will have an end to American military advisers, American intervention, counterinsurgency, and even presidential arrogance in relation to congressional inquiries. Quite clearly the third world is going to settle for nothing less than a hands-off policy in their relations with the superpowers. Perhaps we will even see a return to respect by the superpowers for international norms in their dealings with the third world. There are indications that almost immediately upon taking office, Nixon recognized that military power could not be used in any and all circumstances without regard for the contextual situa-

[8] Echevarria's vitally important speech was made at a session of the OAS Permanent Council held in his honor June 16, 1972, during his state visit to Washington, D.C. The text is available in *Americas* (August 1972).

[9] Max Singer and Aaron Wildavsky, "A Third-World Averaging Strategy," in Robert W. Gregg and Charles W. Kegley, Jr., eds., *After Vietnam* (New York: Anchor Books, 1971), pp. 69–94.

tion. The limited war strategists assumed that force could be used in an instrumental fashion with little or no regard for the political and contextual situation. There was little if any understanding of the political might prudently and legitimately to be employed and for which it could not be legitimately and effectively employed. There is now a search about for such terms—witness the spate of America's appeals to the Soviet government for some kind of understanding about the limits to which the two superpowers will go in backing their respective allies and proteges. But this is not sufficient. The United States will have to take the lead, unilaterally if need be, in observing existing criteria governing the use of force in relations with states of the third world. George Modelski has suggested that: "The answer must be of course that (barring exceptional circumstances) force can safely be employed at the global level, if it is employed at all, for societal purposes alone . . . the threats to use such force, always dangerous, must be governed by purposes wider than national. This would mean that the means of coercion need to be tied to political structures of broader responsibility."[10] And this surely augurs a much enhanced role for traditional practices of statecraft and diplomacy in the third world.

CONCLUSIONS AND PROJECTIONS

The coming resurgence of the Department of State as the principal architect of American foreign policy and of diplomacy as the principal instrument of that policy is based upon all of the aforementioned trends. Surely, the overall retrenchment had to be made; now it will be essential to revitalize the Department of State as the coordinator of all the diplomatic and economic instrumentalities in order to give it the leadership role that is demanded of it in this transformation period "beyond the Cold War." Diplomacy and diplomatic methods will be the framework and the processes in working toward a multipolar structure of peace in the 1970s, especially as the role of the president shifts in emphasis from commander in chief to chief diplomat and domestic economic manager. And the conceptual insights of Henry Kissinger are essential in order to understand the

[10] George Modelski, "A Review of the Limits of Coercive Diplomacy . . .," *The American Political Science Review* (March 1972), p. 281.

vital need of diplomacy in the post-Vietnam international world and in the post-Watergate national search for domestic consensus:

> The logic of war is power, and power has no inherent limit. The logic of peace is proportion, and proportion implies limitation. The success of war is victory; the success of peace is stability. The conditions of victory are commitment, the condition of stability is self-restraint. The motivation of war is extrinsic: the fear of an enemy. The motivation of peace is intrinsic: the balance of forces and the acceptance of its legitimacy.[11]

The trend in American foreign policy has been from a pre-World War II isolationist position of total security to a Cold War interventionist search for national security and to the contemporary environment of ambiguity and hesitancy as we move into this transitional period in the 1970s when man must search for international security on this finite, increasingly interdependent "Spaceship Earth." Hopefully the extremes of isolationism and interventionism will form into a contemporary synthesis of mature diplomacy, cultural humility, governmental balance, instrumental restraint, and international sensitivity.

---

[11] Henry A. Kissinger, *A World Restored: Metternich, Castlereagh, and the Problems of Peace, 1812–1822* (London: Weidenfeld and Nicolson, 1957), p. 138.

APPENDIXES

APPENDIXES

APPENDIX A
The Truman Doctrine

Mr. President, Mr. Speaker, Members of Congress of the United States:

The gravity of the situation which confronts the world today necessitates my appearance before a joint session of the Congress.

The foreign policy and the national security of this country are involved.

One aspect of the present situation, which I wish to present to you at this time for your consideration and decision, concerns Greece and Turkey.

The United States has received from the Greek Government an urgent appeal for financial and economic assistance. Preliminary reports from the American Economic Mission now in Greece and reports from the American Ambassador in Greece corroborate the statement of the Greek Government that assistance is imperative if Greece is to survive as a free nation.

I do not believe that the American people and the Congress wish to turn a deaf ear to the appeal of the Greek Government.

Greece is not a rich country. Lack of sufficient natural resources has always forced the Greek people to work hard to make both ends meet. Since 1940 this industrious and peace-loving country has suffered invasion, four years of cruel enemy occupation, and bitter internal strife.

When forces of liberation entered Greece they found that the retreating Germans had destroyed virtually all the railways, roads, port facilities, communications, and merchant marine. More than a

Delivered by President Harry S Truman before a joint session of Congress on March 12, 1947. Printed as Department of State Publication 2785.

thousand villages had been burned. Eighty-five percent of the children were tubercular. Livestock, poultry, and draft animals had almost disappeared. Inflation had wiped out practically all savings.

As a result of these tragic conditions, a militant minority, exploiting human want and misery, was able to create political chaos which, until now, has made economic recovery impossible.

Greece is today without funds to finance the importation of those goods which are essential to bare subsistence. Under these circumstances the people of Greece cannot make progress in solving their problems of reconstruction. Greece is in desperate need of financial and economic assistance to enable it to resume purchases of food, clothing, fuel, and seeds. These are indispensable for the subsistence of its people and are obtainable only from abroad. Greece must have help to import the goods necessary to restore internal order and security so essential for economic and political recovery.

The Greek Government has also asked for the assistance of experienced American administrators, economists, and technicians to insure that the financial and other aid given to Greece shall be used effectively in creating a stable and self-sustaining economy and in improving its public administration.

The very existence of the Greek state is today threatened by the terrorist activities of several thousand armed men, led by Communists, who defy the Government's authority at a number of points, particularly along the northern boundaries. A commission appointed by the United Nations Security Council is at present investigating disturbed conditions in northern Greece and alleged border violations along the frontier between Greece on the one hand and Albania, Bulgaria, and Yugoslavia on the other.

Meanwhile, the Greek Government is unable to cope with the situation. The Greek Army is small and poorly equipped. It needs supplies and equipment if it is to restore authority to the Government throughout Greek territory.

Greece must have assistance if it is to become a self-supporting and self-respecting democracy.

The United States must supply that assistance. We have already extended to Greece certain types of relief and economic aid, but these are inadequate.

There is no other country to which democratic Greece can turn.

No other nation is willing and able to provide the necessary support for a democratic Greek Government.

The British Government, which has been helping Greece, can give no further financial or economic aid after March 31. Great Britain finds itself under the necessity of reducing or liquidating its commitments in several parts of the world, including Greece.

We have considered how the United Nations might assist in this crisis. But the situation is an urgent one requiring immediate action, and the United Nations and its related organizations are not in a position to extend help of the kind that is required.

It is important to note that the Greek Government has asked for our aid in utilizing effectively the financial and other assistance we may give to Greece, and in improving its public administration. It is of the utmost importance that we supervise the use of any funds made available to Greece, in such a manner that each dollar spent will count toward making Greece self-supporting, and will help to build an economy in which a healthy democracy can flourish.

No government is perfect. One of the chief virtues of a democracy, however, is that its defects are always visible and under democratic processes can be pointed out and corrected. The Government of Greece is not perfect. Nevertheless it represents 85 percent of the members of the Greek Parliament who were chosen in an election last year. Foreign observers, including 692 Americans, considered this election to be a fair expression of the views of the Greek people.

The Greek Government has been operating in an atmosphere of chaos and extremism. It has made mistakes. The extension of aid by this country does not mean that the United States condones everything that the Greek Government has done or will do. We have condemned in the past, and we condemn now, extremist measures of the right or the left. We have in the past advised tolerance, and we advise tolerance now.

Greece's neighbor also deserves our attention.

The future of Turkey as an independent and economically sound state is clearly no less important to the freedom-loving peoples of the world than the future of Greece. The circumstances in which Turkey finds itself today are considerably different from those of Greece. Turkey has been spared the disasters that have beset Greece. And during the war the United States and Great Britain furnished Turkey with material aid.

Nevertheless, Turkey now needs our support.

Since the war Turkey has sought additional financial assistance from Great Britain and the United States for the purpose of effecting that modernization necessary for the maintenance of its national integrity.

That integrity is essential to the preservation of order in the Middle East.

The British Government has informed us that, owing to its own difficulties, it can no longer extend financial or economic aid to Turkey.

As in the case of Greece, if Turkey is to have the assistance it needs, the United States must supply it. We are the only country able to provide that help.

I am fully aware of the broad implications involved if the United States extends assistance to Greece and Turkey, and I shall discuss these implications with you at this time.

One of the primary objectives of the foreign policy of the United States is the creation of conditions in which we and other nations will be able to work out a way of life free from coercion. This was a fundamental issue in the war with Germany and Japan. Our victory was won over countries which sought to impose their will, and their way of life, upon other nations.

To insure the peaceful development of nations, free from coercion, the United States has taken a leading part in establishing the United Nations. The United Nations is designed to make possible lasting freedom and independence for all its members. We shall not realize our objectives, however, unless we are willing to help free peoples to maintain their free institutions and their national integrity against aggressive movements that seek to impose upon them totalitarian regimes. This is no more than a frank recognition that totalitarian regimes imposed upon free peoples, by direct or indirect aggression, undermine the foundations of international peace and hence the security of the United States.

The peoples of a number of countries of the world have recently had totalitarian regimes forced upon them against their will. The Government of the United States has made frequent protests against coercion and intimidation, in violation of the Yalta agreement, in Poland, Rumania, and Bulgaria. I must also state that in a number of other countries there have been similar developments.

At the present moment in world history nearly every nation must choose between alternative ways of life. The choice is too often not a free one.

One way of life is based upon the will of the majority, and is distinguished by free institutions, representative government, free elections, guarantees of individual liberty, freedom of speech and religion, and freedom from political oppression.

The second way of life is based upon the will of a minority forcibly imposed upon the majority. It relies upon terror and oppression, a controlled press and radio, fixed elections, and the suppression of personal freedoms.

I believe that it must be the policy of the United States to support free peoples who are resisting attempted subjugation by armed minorities or by outside pressures.

I believe that we must assist free peoples to work out their own destinies in their own way.

I believe that our help should be primarily through economic and financial aid which is essential to economic stability and orderly political processes.

The world is not static, and the *status quo* is not sacred. But we cannot allow changes in the *status quo* in violation of the Charter of the United Nations by such methods as coercion, or by such subterfuges as political infiltration. In helping free and independent nations to maintain their freedom, the United States will be giving effect to the principles of the Charter of the United Nations.

It is necessary only to glance at a map to realize that the survival and integrity of the Greek nation are of grave importance in a much wider situation. If Greece should fall under the control of an armed minority, the effect upon its neighbor, Turkey, would be immediate and serious. Confusion and disorder might well spread throughout the entire Middle East.

Moreover, the disappearance of Greece as an independent state would have a profound effect upon those countries in Europe whose peoples are struggling against great difficulties to maintain their freedoms and their independence while they repair the damages of war.

It would be an unspeakable tragedy if these countries, which have struggled so long against overwhelming odds, should lose that victory for which they sacrificed so much. Collapse of free institutions and loss of independence would be disastrous not only for them but for the world. Discouragement and possibly failure would quickly be the lot of neighboring peoples striving to maintain their freedom and independence.

Should we fail to aid Greece and Turkey in this fateful hour, the effect will be far-reaching to the West as well as to the East.

We must take immediate and resolute action.

I therefore ask the Congress to provide authority for assistance to Greece and Turkey in the amount of $400,000,000 for the period ending June 30, 1948. In requesting these funds, I have taken into consideration the maximum amount of relief assistance which would be furnished to Greece out of the $350,000,000 which I recently requested that the Congress authorize for the prevention of starvation and suffering in countries devastated by the war.

In addition to funds, I ask the Congress to authorize the detail of American civilian and military personnel to Greece and Turkey, at the request of those countries, to assist in the tasks of reconstruction, and for the purpose of supervising the use of such financial and material assistance as may be furnished. I recommend that authority also be provided for the instruction and training of selected Greek and Turkish personnel.

Finally, I ask that the Congress provide authority which will permit the speediest and most effective use, in terms of needed commodities, supplies, and equipment, of such funds as may be authorized.

If further funds, or further authority, should be needed for purposes indicated in this message, I shall not hesitate to bring the situation before the Congress. On this subject the Executive and Legislative branches of the Government must work together.

This is a serious course upon which we embark.

I would not recommend it except that the alternative is much more serious.

The United States contributed $341,000,000,000 toward winning World War II. This is an investment in world freedom and world peace.

The assistance that I am recommending for Greece and Turkey amounts to little more than one tenth of one percent of this investment. It is only common sense that we should safeguard this investment and make sure that it was not in vain.

The seeds of totalitarian regimes are nurtured by misery and want. They spread and grow in the evil of poverty and strife. They reach their full growth when the hope of a people for a better life has died.

We must keep that hope alive.

The free peoples of the world look to us for support in maintaining their freedoms.

If we falter in our leadership, we may endanger the peace of the world—and we shall surely endanger the welfare of our own Nation.

Great responsibilities have been placed upon us by the swift movement of events.

I am confident that the Congress will face these responsibilities squarely.

APPENDIX B
The Six Principles of Realism: a Condensation

Principle One. There are objective laws governing political behavior that stem from human nature. These laws are eternal and can be discovered by analysis. Realism

> believes that the world, imperfect as it is from the rational point of view, is the result of forces inherent in human nature. To improve the world, one must work with these forces, not against them. Thus, being inherently a world of opposing interests, and of conflict among many of them, moral principles can never be fully realized, but must at best be approximated through the ever temporary balancing of interests and the ever precarious settlement of conflicts. This school, then, sees in a system of checks and balances a universal principle for all pluralist societies. It appeals to the historic precedent rather than to abstract principles, and aims at the realization of the lesser evil rather than of the absolute good.

Principle Two. Realism finds its main guide in the concept of interest defined in terms of power. Power unlocks the objective laws. Concern with interest and power leads realism to eschew the preoccupation with both the motives and ideological preferences of political actors.

Realism assumes "that statesmen think and act in terms of interest defined as power, and the evidence of history bears that assumption out." The purpose of realist theory

> is to present not an indiscriminate description of political reality, but a rational theory of international politics. Far from being invalidated

All quoted material in this section is from Hans J. Morgenthau, *Politics Among Nations*, 4th ed. (New York: Knopf, 1967), pp. 3–13.

by the fact that, for instance, a perfect balance of power policy will scarcely be found in reality, it assumes that reality, being deficient in this respect, must be understood and evaluated as an approximation to an ideal system of balance of power.

Principle Three. Realism does not claim an absolute and permanent meaning for its concept of power or interest. The objective laws are not fixed. The specific environment affects the shaping of interests and the emphasis upon power.

> Power may comprise anything that establishes the control of man over man. Thus power covers all social relationships which serve that end, from physical violence to the most subtle psychological ties by which one mind controls another.

Principle Four. Realism is not indifferent to morality. Universal moral principles cannot be realized, but, at best, approximated. There is ever-present tension between the requirements of successful political action.

> Realism maintains that universal moral principles cannot be applied to the actions of states in their abstract universal formulation, but that they must be filtered through the concrete circumstances of time and place . . . while the individual has the right to sacrifice himself in defense of a moral principle, the state has no right to let its moral disapprobation of the infringement of liberty get in the way of successful political action, itself inspired by the moral principle of national survival. Realism, then, considers prudence—the weighting of the consequences of alternative political actions—to be the supreme virtue in politics. Ethics in the abstract judges action by its conformity with the moral law; political ethics judges action by its political consequences.

Principle Five. States have no right to espouse their moral principles as moral laws that govern the universe. Realism conceives of all nations as political actors pursuing their interests defined in terms of power.

> It is exactly the concept of interest defined in terms of power that saves us from both . . . moral excess and . . . political folly. For if we look at all nations . . . as political entities pursuing their respective interests defined in terms of power . . . we are able to do justice to all of them in a dual sense: We are able to judge other nations as we judge our own and, having judged them in this fashion, we are then capable of pursuing policies that respect the interests of other nations, while protecting and promoting those of our own.

Principle Six. Realism is distinct from legalistic and moralistic approaches. "Political man" is a myth. In order to understand politics, it is necessary to free the study of politics from standards of thought appropriate to other spheres.

Political realism is based upon a pluralistic conception of human nature. Real man is a composite of "economic man," "political man," "moral man," "religious man," etc., . . . the human mind in its day to day operations cannot bear to look the truth of politics straight in the face. It must disguise, distort, belittle, and embellish the truth—the more so, the more the individual is actively involved in the processes of politics. . . . For only by deceiving himself about the nature of politics and the role he plays on the political scene is man able to live contentedly as a political animal with himself and his fellow men.

APPENDIX C
The Sources
of Soviet Conduct

The political personality of Soviet power as we know it today is the product of ideology and circumstances: ideology inherited by the present Soviet leaders from the movement in which they had their political origin, and circumstances of the power which they now have exercised for nearly three decades in Russia. There can be few tasks of psychological analysis more difficult than to try to trace the interaction of these two forces and the relative role of each in the determination of official Soviet conduct. Yet the attempt must be made if that conduct is to be understood and effectively countered.

It is difficult to summarize the set of ideological concepts with which the Soviet leaders came into power. Marxian ideology, in its Russian-Communist projection, has always been in process of subtle evolution. The materials on which it bases itself are extensive and complex. But the outstanding features of Communist thought as it existed in 1916 may perhaps be summarized as follows: (a) that the central factor in the life of man, the factor which determines the character of public life and the "physiognomy of society," is the system by which material goods are produced and exchanged; (b) that the capitalist system of production is a nefarious one which inevitably leads to the exploitation of the working class by the capital-owning class and is incapable of developing adequately the economic resources of society or of distributing fairly the material goods produced by human labor; (c) that capitalism contains the seeds of its own destruction and must, in view of the inability of the capital-owning class to adjust itself to economic change, result eventually

Article by "Mr. X." Reprinted by permission from *Foreign Affairs* (July 1947), pp. 566–582. Copyright 1947 by the Council on Foreign Relations, Inc., New York.

and inescapably in a revolutionary transfer of power to the working class; and (d) that imperialism, the final phase of capitalism, leads directly to war and revolution.

The rest may be outlined in Lenin's own words: "Unevenness of economic and political development is the inflexible law of capitalism. It follows from this that the victory of Socialism may come originally in a few capitalist countries or even in a single capitalist country. The victorious proletariat of that country, having expropriated the capitalists and having organized Socialist production at home, would rise against the remaining capitalist world, drawing to itself in the process the oppressed classes of other countries."[1] It must be noted that there was no assumption that capitalism would perish without proletarian revolution. A final push was needed from a revolutionary proletariat movement in order to tip over the tottering structure. But it was regarded as inevitable that sooner or later that push be given.

For 50 years prior to the outbreak of the Revolution, this pattern of thought had exercised great fascination for the members of the Russian revolutionary movement. Frustrated, discontented, hopeless of finding self-expression—or too impatient to seek it—in the confining limits of the Tsarist political system, yet lacking wide popular support for their choice of bloody revolution as a means of social betterment, these revolutionists found in Marxist theory a highly convenient rationalization for their own instinctive desires. It afforded pseudo-scientific justification for their impatience, for their categoric denial of all value in the Tsarist system, for their yearning for power and revenge and for their inclination to cut corners in the pursuit of it. It is therefore no wonder that they had come to believe implicitly in the truth and soundness of the Marxian-Leninist teachings, so congenial to their own impulses and emotions. Their sincerity need not be impugned. This is a phenomenon as old as human nature itself. It has never been more aptly described than by Edward Gibbon, who wrote in "The Decline and Fall of the Roman Empire": "From enthusiasm to imposture the step is perilous and slippery; the demon of Socrates affords a memorable instance how a wise man may deceive himself, how a good man may deceive others, how the conscience may slumber in a mixed and middle state between self-illusion and voluntary fraud." And it was with this set of conceptions that the members of the Bolshevik Party entered into power.

Now it must be noted that through all the years of preparation for revolution, the attention of these men, as indeed of Marx himself, had been centered less on the future form which Socialism[2] would take than on the necessary overthrow of rival power which, in their

---

[1] "Concerning the Slogans of the United States of Europe," August 1915, official Soviet edition of Lenin's works.

[2] Here and elsewhere in this paper "socialism" refers to Marxist or Leninist communism, not to liberal socialism of the Second International variety.

view, had to precede the introduction of Socialism. Their views, therefore, on the positive program to be put into effect, once power was
attained, were for the most part nebulous, visionary and impractical.
Beyond the nationalization of industry and the expropriation of large
private capital holdings there was no agreed program. The treatment
of the peasantry, which according to the Marxist formulation was
not of the proletariat, had always been a vague spot in the pattern
of Communist thought; and it remained an object of controversy and
vacillation for the first ten years of Communist power.

The circumstances of the immediate post-revolution period—the
existence in Russia of civil war and foreign intervention, together
with the obvious fact that the Communists represented only a tiny
minority of the Russian people—made the establishment of dictatorial
power a necessity. The experiment with "war Communism" and the
abrupt attempt to eliminate private production and trade had unfortunate economic consequences and caused further bitterness against
the new revolutionary regime. While the temporary relaxation of the
effort to communize Russia, represented by the New Economic Policy,
alleviated some of this economic distress and thereby served its purpose, it also made it evident that the "capitalistic sector of society"
was still prepared to profit at once from any relaxation of governmental pressure, and would, if permitted to continue to exist, always
constitute a powerful opposing element to the Soviet regime and
a serious rival for influence in the country. Somewhat the same situation prevailed with respect to the individual peasant who, in his own
small way, was also a private producer.

Lenin, had he lived, might have proved a great enough man
to reconcile these conflicting forces to the ultimate benefit of Russian
society, though this is questionable. But be that as it may, Stalin,
and those whom he led in the struggle for succession to Lenin's position of leadership, were not the men to tolerate rival political forces
in the sphere of power which they coveted. Their sense of insecurity
was too great. Their particular brand of fanaticism, unmodified by
any of the Anglo-Saxon traditions of compromise, was too fierce and
too jealous to envisage any permanent sharing of power. From the
Russian-Asiatic world out of which they had emerged they carried
with them a skepticism as to the possibilities of permanent and peaceful coexistence of rival forces. Easily persuaded of their own doctri-
naire "rightness," they insisted on the submission or destruction of
all competing power. Outside of the Communist Party, Russian society
was to have no rigidity. There were to be no forms of collective
human activity or association which would not be dominated by the
Party. No other force in Russian society was to be permitted to achieve
vitality or integrity. Only the Party was to have structure. All else
was to be an amorphous mass.

And within the Party the same principle was to apply. The mass
of Party members might go through the motions of election, delibera-
tion, decision and action; but in these motions they were to be ani-

mated not by their own individual wills but by the awesome breath of the Party leadership and the overbrooding presence of "the word."

Let it be stressed again that subjectively these men probably did not seek absolutism for its own sake. They doubtless believed— and found it easy to believe—that they alone knew what was good for society and that they would accomplish that good once their power was secure and unchallengeable. But in seeking that security of their own rule they were prepared to recognize no restrictions, either of God or man, on the character of their methods. And until such time as that security might be achieved, they placed far down on their scale of operational priorities the comforts and happiness of the peoples entrusted to their care.

Now the outstanding circumstance concerning the Soviet regime is that down to the present day this process of political consolidation has never been completed and the men in the Kremlin have continued to be predominantly absorbed with the struggle to secure and make absolute the power which they seized in November 1917. They have endeavored to secure it primarily against forces at home, within Soviet society itself. But they have also endeavored to secure it against the outside world. For ideology, as we have seen, taught them that the outside world was hostile and that it was their duty eventually to overthrow the political forces beyond their borders. The powerful hands of Russian history and tradition reached up to sustain them in this feeling. Finally, their own aggressive intransigence with respect to the outside world began to find its own reaction; and they were soon forced, to use another Gibbonesque phrase, "to chastise the contumacy" which they themselves had provoked. It is an undeniable privilege of every man to prove himself right in the thesis that the world is his enemy; for if he reiterates it frequently enough and makes it the background of his conduct he is bound eventually to be right.

Now it lies in the nature of the mental world of the Soviet leaders, as well as in the character of their ideology, that no opposition to them can be officially recognized as having any merit or justification whatsoever. Such opposition can flow, in theory, only from the hostile and incorrigible forces of dying capitalism. As long as remnants of capitalism were officially recognized as existing in Russia, it was possible to place on them, as an internal element, part of the blame for the maintenance of a dictatorial form of society. But as these remnants were liquidated, little by little, this justification fell away; and when it was indicated officially that they had been finally destroyed, it disappeared altogether. And this fact created one of the most basic of the compulsions which came to act upon the Soviet regime: since capitalism no longer existed in Russia and since it could not be admitted that there could be serious or widespread opposition to the Kremlin springing spontaneously from the liberated masses under its authority, it became necessary to justify the retention of the dictatorship by stressing the menace of capitalism abroad.

This began at an early date. In 1924 Stalin specifically defended the retention of the "organs of suppression," meaning, among others, the army and the secret police, on the ground that "as long as there is a capitalism encirclement there will be danger of intervention with all the consequences that flow from that danger." In accordance with that theory, and from that time on, all internal opposition forces in Russia have consistently been portrayed as the agents of foreign forces of reaction antagonistic to Soviet power.

By the same token, tremendous emphasis has been placed on the original Communist thesis of a basic antagonism between the capitalist and Socialist world. It is clear, from many indications, that this emphasis is not founded in reality. The real facts concerning it have been confused by the existence abroad of genuine resentment provoked by Soviet philosophy and tactics and occasionally by the existence of great centers of military power, notably the Nazi regime in Germany and the Japanese Government of the late 1930's, which did indeed have aggressive designs against the Soviet Union. But there is ample evidence that the stress laid in Moscow on the menace confronting Soviet society from the world outside its borders is founded not in the realities of foreign antagonism but in the necessity of explaining away the maintenance of dictatorial authority at home.

Now the maintenance of this pattern of Soviet power, namely, the pursuit of unlimited authority domestically, accompanied by the cultivation of the semi-myth of implacable foreign hostility, has gone far to shape the actual machinery of Soviet power as we know it today. Internal organs of administration which did not serve this purpose withered on the vine. Organs which did serve this purpose became vastly swollen. The security of Soviet power came to rest on the iron discipline of the Party, on the severity and ubiquity of the secret police, and on the uncompromising economic monopolism of the state. The "organs of suppression," in which the Soviet leaders had sought security from rival forces, became in large measure the masters of those whom they were designed to serve. Today the major part of the structure of Soviet power is committed to the perfection of the dictatorship and to the maintenance of the concept of Russia as in a state of siege, with the enemy lowering beyond the walls. And the millions of human beings who form that part of the structure of power must defend at all cost this concept of Russia's position, for without it they are themselves superfluous.

As things stand today, the rulers can no longer dream of parting with these organs of suppression. The quest for absolute power, pursued now for nearly three decades with a ruthlessness unparalleled (in scope at least) in modern times, has again produced internally, as it did externally, its own reaction. The excess of the police apparatus have fanned the potential opposition to the regime into something far greater and more dangerous than it could have been before those excesses began.

But least of all can the rulers dispense with the fiction by which the maintenance of dictatorial power has been defended. For this fiction has been canonized in Soviet philosophy by the excesses already committed in its name; and it is now anchored in the Soviet structure of thought by bonds far greater than those of mere ideology.

II

So much for the historical background. What does it spell in terms of the political personality of Soviet power as we know it today?

Of the original ideology, nothing has been officially junked. Belief is maintained in the basic badness of capitalism, in the inevitability of its destruction, in the obligation of the proletariat to assist in that destruction and to take power into its own hands. But stress has come to be laid primarily on those concepts which relate most specifically to the Soviet regime itself: to its position as the sole truly Socialist regime in a dark and misguided world, and to the relationships of power within it.

The first of these concepts is that of the innate antagonism between capitalism and Socialism. We have seen how deeply that concept has become imbedded in foundations of Soviet power. It has profound implications for Russia's conduct as a member of international society. It means that there can never be on Moscow's side any sincere assumption of a community of aims between the Soviet Union and powers which are regarded as capitalist. It must invariably be assumed in Moscow that the aims of the capitalist world are antagonistic to the Soviet regime, and therefore to the interests of the peoples it controls. If the Soviet Government occasionally sets its signature to documens which would indicate the contrary, this is to be regarded as a tactical manoeuvre permissible in dealing with the enemy (who is without honor) and should be taken in the spirit of *caveat emptor*. Basically, the antagonism remains. It is postulated. And from it flow many of the phenomena which we find disturbing in the Kremlin's conduct of foreign policy: the secretiveness, the lack of frankness, the duplicity, the wary suspiciousness, and the basic unfriendliness of purpose. These phenomena are there to stay, for the foreseeable future. There can be variations of degree and of emphasis. When there is something the Russians want from us, one or the other of these features of their policy may be thrust temporarily into the background; and when that happens there will always be Americans who will leap forward with gleeful announcements that "the Russians have changed," and some who will even try to take credit for having brought about such "changes." But we should not be misled by tactical manoeuvres. These characteristics of Soviet policy, like the postulate from which they flow, are basic to the internal nature of Soviet power, and will be with us, whether in the foreground or the background, until the internal nature of Soviet power is changed.

This means that we are going to continue for a long time to find the Russians difficult to deal with. It does not mean that they should be considered as embarked upon a do-or-die program to overthrow our society by a given date. The theory of the inevitability of the eventual fall of capitalism has the fortunate connotation that there is no hurry about it. The forces of progress can take their time in preparing the final *coup de grace*. Meanwhile, what is vital is that the "Socialist fatherland"—that oasis of power which has been already won for Socialism in the person of the Soviet Union—should be cherished and defended by all good Communists at home and abroad, its fortunes promoted, its enemies badgered and confounded. The promotion of premature, "adventuristic" revolutionary projects abroad which might embarrass Soviet power in any way would be an inexcusable, even a counter-revolutionary act. The cause of Socialism is the support and promotion of Soviet power, as defined in Moscow.

This brings us to the second of the concepts important to contemporary Soviet outlook. That is the infallibility of the Kremlin. The Soviet concept of power, which permits no focal points of organization outside the Party itself, requires that the Party leadership remain in theory the sole repository of truth. For if truth were to be found elsewhere, there would be justification for its expression in organized activity. But it is precisely that which the Kremlin cannot and will not permit.

The leadership of the Communist Party is therefore always right, and has been always right ever since in 1929 Stalin formalized his personal power by announcing that decisions of the Politburo were being taken unanimously.

On the principle of infallibility there rests the iron discipline of the Communist Party. In fact, the two concepts are mutually self-supporting. Perfect discipline requires recognition of infallibility. Infallibility requires the observance of discipline. And the two together go far to determine the behaviorism of the entire Soviet apparatus of power. But their effect cannot be understood unless a third factor be taken into account: namely, the fact that the leadership is at liberty to put forward for tactical purposes any particular thesis which it finds useful to the cause at any particular moment and to require the faithful and unquestioning acceptance of that thesis by the members of the movement as a whole. This means that truth is not a constant but is actually created, for all intents and purposes, by the Soviet leaders themselves. It may vary from week to week, from month to month. It is nothing absolute and immutable—nothing which flows from objective reality. It is only the most recent manifestation of the wisdom of those in whom the ultimate wisdom is supposed to reside, because they represent the logic of history. The accumulative effect of these factors is to give to the whole subordinate apparatus of Soviet power an unshakeable stubbornness and steadfastness in its orientation. This orientation can be changed at will by the Kremlin but by no other power. Once a given party line has been laid down on a given issue of current policy, the whole Soviet governmental machine, including the mechanism of diplomacy, moves inexorably along the prescribed path, like a persistent toy automobile wound up and headed in a given direction, stopping only when it meets with some unanswerable force. The individuals who are the components of this machine are unamenable to argument or reason which comes to them from outside sources. Their whole training has taught them to mistrust and discount the glib persuasiveness of the outside world. Like the white dog before the phonograph, they hear only the "master's voice." And if they are to be called off from the purposes last dictated to them, it is the master who must call them off. Thus the foreign representative cannot hope that his words will make any impression on them. The most that he can hope is that they will be transmitted to those at the top, who are capable of changing the party line. But even those are not likely to be swayed by any normal logic in the words of the bourgeois representative. Since there can be no appeal to common purposes, there can be no appeal to common mental approaches. For this reason, facts speak louder than words to the ears of the Kremlin; and words carry the greatest weight when they have the ring of reflecting, or being backed up by, facts of unchallengeable validity.

But we have seen that the Kremlin is under no ideological compulsion to accomplish its purposes in a hurry. Like the Church, it is dealing in ideological concepts which are of long-term validity, and it can afford to be patient. It has no right to risk the existing achievements of the revolution for the sake of vain baubles of the future. The very teachings of Lenin himself require great caution and flexibility in the pursuit of Communist purposes. Again, these precepts are fortified by the lessons of Russian history: of centuries of obscure battles between nomadic forces over the stretches of a vast unfortified plain. Here caution, circumspection, flexibility and deception are the valuable qualities; and their value finds natural appreciation in the Russian or the oriental mind. Thus the Kremlin has no compunction about retreating in the face of superior force. And being under the compulsion of no timetable, it does not get panicky under the necessity for such retreat. Its political action is a fluid stream which moves constantly, wherever it is permitted to move, toward a given goal. Its main concern is to make sure that it has filled every nook and cranny available to it in the basin of world power. But if it finds unassailable barriers in its path, it accepts these philosophically and accommodates itself to them. The main thing is that there should always be pressure, unceasing constant pressure, toward the desired goal. There is no trace of any feeling in Soviet psychology that that goal must be reached at any given time.

These considerations make Soviet diplomacy at once easier and more difficult to deal with than the diplomacy of individual aggressive leaders like Napoleon and Hitler. On the one hand it is more sensitive to contrary force, more ready to yield on individual sectors of the diplomatic front when that force is felt to be too strong, and thus more rational in the logic and rhetoric of power. On the other hand it cannot be easily defeated or discouraged by a single victory on the part of its opponents. And the patient persistence by which it is animated means that it can be effectively countered not by sporadic acts which represent the momentary whims of democratic opinion but only by intelligent long-range policies on the part of Russia's adversaries—policies no less steady in their purpose, and no less variegated and resourceful in their application, than those of the Soviet Union itself.

In these circumstances it is clear that the main element of any United States policy toward the Soviet Union must be that of a long-term, patient but firm and vigilant containment of Russian expansive tendencies. It is important to note, however, that such a policy has nothing to do with outward histrionics: with threats or blustering or superfluous gestures of outward "toughness." While the Kremlin is basically flexible in its reaction to political realities, it is by no means unamenable to considerations of prestige. Like almost any other government, it can be placed by tactless and threatening gestures in a position where it cannot afford to yield even though this might be dictated by its sense of realism. The Russian leaders are keen judges of human psychology, and as such they are highly conscious that loss of temper and of self-control is never a source of strength in political affairs. They are quick to exploit such evidences of weakness. For these reasons, it is a *sine qua non* of successful dealing with Russia that the foreign government in question would remain at all times cool and collected and that its demands on Russian policy should be put forward in such a manner as to leave the way open for a compliance not too detrimental to Russian prestige.

III

In the light of the above, it will be clearly seen that the Soviet pressure against the free institutions of the western world is something that can be contained by the adroit and vigilant application of counter-force at a series of constantly shifting geographical and political points, corresponding to the shifts and manoeuvres of Soviet policy, but which cannot be charmed or talked out of existence. The Russians look forward to a duel of infinite duration, and they see that there was a time when the Communist Party represented far more of a minority in the sphere of Russian national life than Soviet power today represents in the world community.

But if ideology convinces the rulers of Russia that truth is on their side and that they can therefore afford to wait, those of us on whom that ideology has no claim are free to examine objectively the validity of that premise. The Soviet thesis not only implies complete lack of control by the west over its own economic destiny, it likewise assumes Russian unity, discipline and patience over an infinite period. Let us bring this apocalyptic vision down to earth, and suppose that the western world finds the strength and resourcefulness to contain Soviet power over a period of ten to fifteen years. What does that spell for Russia itself?

The Soviet leaders, taking advantage of the contributions of modern technique to the arts of despotism, have solved the question of obedience within the confines of their power. Few challenge their authority and even those who do are unable to make that challenge valid as against the organs of suppression of the state.

The Kremlin has also proved able to accomplish its purpose of building up in Russia, regardless of the interests of the inhabitants, an industrial foundation of heavy metallurgy, which is, to be sure, not yet complete but which is nevertheless continuing to grow and is approaching those of the other major industrial countries. All of this, however, both the maintenance of internal political security and the building of heavy industry, has been carried out at a terrible cost in human life and in human hopes and energies. It has necessitated the use of forced labor on a scale unprecedented in modern times under conditions of peace. It has involved the neglect or abuse of other phases of Soviet economic life, particularly agriculture, consumers' goods production, housing and transportation.

To all that, the war has added its tremendous toll of destruction, death and human exhaustion. In consequence of this, we have in Russia today a population which is physically and spiritually tired. The mass of the people are disillusioned, skeptical and no longer as accessible as they once were to the magical attraction which Soviet power still radiates to its followers abroad. The avidity with which people seized upon the slight respite accorded to the Church for tactical reasons during the war was eloquent testimony to the fact that their capacity for faith and devotion found little expression in the purposes of the regime.

In these circumstances, there are limits to the physical and nervous strength of people themselves. These limits are absolute ones, and are binding even for the cruelest dictatorship, because beyond them people cannot be driven. The forced labor camps and the other agencies of constraint provide temporary means of compelling people to work longer hours than their own volition or mere economic pressure would dictate; but if people survive them at all they become old before their time and must be considered as human casualties to the demands of dictatorship. In either case their best powers are no longer available to society and can no longer be enlisted in the service of the state.

Here only the younger generation can help. The younger generation, despite all vicissitudes and sufferings, is numerous and vigorous; and the Russians are a talented people. But it still remains to be seen what will be the effects on mature performance of the abnormal emotional strains of childhood which Soviet dictatorship created and which were enormously increased by the war. Such things as normal security and placidity of home environment have practically ceased to exist in the Soviet Union outside of the most remote farms and villages. And observers are not yet sure whether that is not going to leave its mark on the overall capacity of the generation now coming into maturity.

In addition to this, we have the fact that Soviet economic development, while it can list certain formidable achievements, has been precariously spotty and uneven. Russian Communists who speak of the "uneven development of capitalism" should blush at the contemplation of their own national economy. Here certain branches of economic life, such as the metallurgical and machine industries, have been pushed out of all proportion to other sectors of the economy. Here is a nation striving to become in a short period one of the great industrial nations of the world while it still has no highway network worthy of the name and only a relatively primitive network of railways. Much has been done to increase efficiency of labor and to teach primitive peasants something about the operation of machines. But maintenance is still a crying deficiency of all Soviet economy. And in vast sectors of economic life it has not yet been possible to instill into labor anything like that general culture of production and technical self-respect which characterizes the skilled worker of the west.

It is difficult to see how these deficiencies can be corrected at an early date by a tired and dispirited population working largely under the shadow of fear and compulsion. And as long as they are not overcome, Russia will remain economically a vulnerable, and in a certain sense an impotent, nation, capable of exporting its enthusiasms and of radiating the strange charm of its primitive political vitality but unable to back up those articles of export by the real evidences of material power and prosperity.

Meanwhile, a great uncertainty hangs over the political life of the Soviet Union. That is the uncertainty involved in the transfer of power from one individual or group of individuals to others.

This is, of course, outstandingly the problem of the personal position of Stalin. We must remember that his succession to Lenin's pinnacle of preeminence in the Communist movement was the only such transfer of individual authority which the Soviet Union has experienced. That transfer took 12 years to consolidate. It cost the lives of millions of people and shook the state to its foundations. The attendant tremors were felt all through the international revolutionary movement, to the disadvantage of the Kremlin itself.

It is always possible that another transfer of preeminent power may take place quietly and inconspicuously, with no repercussions anywhere. But again, it is possible that the questions involved may unleash, to use some of Lenin's words, one of those "incredibly swift transitions" from "delicate deceit" to "wild violence" which characterize Russian history, and may shake Soviet power to its foundations.

But this is not only a question of Stalin himself. There has been, since 1938, a dangerous congealment of political life in the higher circles of Soviet power. The All-Union Congress of Soviets, in theory the supreme body of the Party, is supposed to meet not less often than once in three years. It will soon be eight full years since its last meeting. During this period membership in the Party has numerically doubled. Party mortality during the war was enormous; and today well over half of the Party members are persons who have entered since the last Party congress was held. Meanwhile, the same small group of men has carried on at the top through an amazing series of national vicissitudes. Surely there is some reason why the experiences of the war brought basic political changes to every one of the great governments of the west. Surely the causes of that phenomenon are basic enough to be present somewhere in the obscurity of Soviet political life, as well. And yet no recognition has been given to these causes in Russia.

It must be surmised from this that even within so highly disciplined an organization as the Communist Party there must be a growing divergence in age, outlook and interest between the great mass of Party members, only so recently recruited into the movement, and the little self-perpetuating clique of men at the top, whom most of these Party members have never met, with whom they have never conversed, and with whom they can have no political intimacy.

Who can say whether, in these circumstances, the eventual rejuvenation of the higher spheres of authority (which can only be a matter of time) can take place smoothly and peacefully, or whether rivals in the quest for higher power will not eventually reach down into these politically immature and inexperienced masses in order to find support for their respective claims? If this were ever to happen, strange consequences could flow for the Communist Party: for the membership at large has been exercised only in the practices of iron discipline and obedience and not in the arts of compromise and accommodation. And if disunity were ever to seize and paralyze the Party, the chaos and weakness of Russian society would be revealed in forms beyond description. For we have seen that Soviet power is only crust concealing an amorphous mass of human beings among whom no independent organizational structure is tolerated. In Russia there is not even such a thing as local government. The present generation of Russians have never known spontaneity of collective action. If, consequently, anything were ever to occur to disrupt the unity and efficacy of the Party as a political instrument, Soviet Russia might be changed overnight from one of the strongest to one of the weakest and most pitiable of national societies.

Thus the future of Soviet power may not be by any means as secure as Russian capacity for self-delusion would make it appear to the men in the Kremlin. That they can keep power themselves, they have demonstrated. That they can quietly and easily turn it over to others remains to be proved. Meanwhile, the hardships of their rule and the vicissitudes of international life have taken a heavy toll of the strength and hopes of the great people on whom their power rests. It is curious to note that the ideological power of Soviet authority is strongest today in areas beyond the frontiers of Russia, beyond the reach of its police power. This phenomenon brings to mind a comparison used by Thomas Mann in his great novel *Budden-brooks.* Observing that human institutions often show the greatest outward brilliance at a moment when inner decay is in reality farthest advanced, he compared the Buddenbrook family, in the days of its greatest glamour, to one of those stars whose light shines most brightly on this world when in reality it has long since ceased to exist. And who can say with assurance that the strong light still cast by the Kremlin on the dissatisfied peoples of the western world is not the powerful afterglow of a constellation which is in actuality on the wane? This cannot be proved. And it cannot be disproved. But the possibility remains (and in the opinion of this writer it is a strong one) that Soviet power, like the capitalist world of its conception, bears within it the seeds of its own decay, and that the sprouting of these seeds is well advanced.

IV

It is clear that the United States cannot expect in the foreseeable future to enjoy political intimacy with the Soviet regime. It must continue to regard the Soviet Union as a rival, not a partner, in the political arena. It must continue to expect that Soviet policies will reflect no abstract love of peace and stability, no real faith in the possibility of a permanent happy coexistence of the Socialist and capitalist worlds, but rather a cautious, persistent pressure toward the disruption and weaking of all rival influence and rival power.

Balanced against this are the facts that Russia, as opposed to the western world in general, is still by far the weaker party, that Soviet policy is highly flexible, and that Soviet society may well contain deficiencies which will eventually weaken its own total potential. This would of itself warrant the United States entering with reasonable confidence upon a policy of firm containment, designed to confront the Russians with unalterable counter-force at every point where they show signs of encroaching upon the interests of a peaceful and stable world.

But in actuality the possibilities for American policy are by no means limited to holding the line and hoping for the best. It is entirely possible for the United States to influence by its actions the internal developments, both within Russia and throughout the international Communist movement, by which Russian policy is largely determined. This is not only a question of the modest measure of informational activity which this government can conduct in the Soviet Union and elsewhere, although that, too, is important. It is rather a question of the degree to which the United States can create among the peoples of the world generally the impression of a country which knows what it wants, which is coping successfully with the problems of its internal life and with the responsibilities of a World Power, and which has a spiritual vitality capable of holding its own among the major ideological currents of the time. To the extent that such an impression can be created and maintained, the aims of Russian Communism must appear sterile and quixotic, the hopes and enthusiasm of Moscow's supporters must wane, and added strain must be imposed on the Kremlin's foreign policies. For the palsied decrepitude of the capitalist world is the keystone of Communist philosophy. Even the failure of the United States to experience the early economic depression which the ravens of the Red Square have been predicting with such complacent confidence since hostilities ceased would have deep and important repercussions throughout the Communist world.

By the same token, exhibitions of indecision, disunity and internal disintegration within this country have an exhilarating effect on the whole Communist movement. At each evidence of these tendencies, a thrill of hope and excitement goes through the Communist world; a new jauntiness can be noted in the Moscow tread; new groups of foreign supporters climb on to what they can only view as the band wagon of international politics; and Russian pressure increases all along the line in international affairs.

It would be an exaggeration to say that American behavior unassisted and alone could exercise a power of life and death over the Communist movement and bring about the early fall of Soviet power in Russia. But the United States has it in its power to increase enormously the strains under which Soviet policy must operate, to force upon the Kremlin a far greater degree of moderation and circumspection than it has had to observe in recent years, and in this way to promote tendencies which must eventually find their outlet in either the break-up or the gradual mellowing of Soviet power. For no mystical, Messianic movement—and particularly not that of the Kremlin— can face frustration indefinitely without eventually adjusting itself in one way or another to the logic of that state of affairs.

Thus the decision will really fall in large measure in this country itself. The issue of Soviet-American relations is in essence a test of the over-all worth of the United States as a nation among nations. To avoid destruction the United States need only measure up to its own best traditions and prove itself worthy of preservation as a great nation.

Surely, there was never a fairer test of national quality than this. In the light of these circumstances, the thoughtful observer of Russian-American relations will find no cause for complaint in the Kremlin's challenge to American society. He will rather experience a certain gratitude to a Providence which, by providing the American people with this implacable challenge, has made their entire security as a nation dependent on their pulling themselves together and accepting the responsibilities of moral and political leadership that history plainly intended them to bear.

APPENDIX D
The Eisenhower Doctrine

First may I express to you my deep appreciation of your courtesy in giving me, at some inconvenience to yourselves, this early opportunity of addressing you on a matter I deem to be of grave importance to our country.

In my forthcoming State of the Union Message, I shall review the international situation generally. There are worldwide hopes which we can reasonably entertain, and there are worldwide responsibilities which we must carry to make cerain that freedom—including our own—may be secure.

There is, however, a special situation in the Middle East which I feel I should, even now, lay before you.

Before doing so it is well to remind ourselves that our basic national objective in international affairs remains peace—a world peace based on justice. Such a peace must include all areas, all peoples of the world if it is to be enduring. There is no nation, great or small, with which we would refuse to negotiate, in mutual good faith, with patience and in the determination to secure a better understanding between us. Out of such understandings must, and eventually will, grow confidence and trust, indispensable ingredients to a program of peace and to plans for lifting from us all the burdens of expensive armaments. To promote these objectives our government works tirelessly, day by day, month by month, year by year. But until a degree of success crowns our efforts that will assure to all nations peaceful

Special Message by President Dwight David Eisenhower to the Congress, January 5, 1957; printed in *American Foreign Policy, Current Documents, 1957,* Department of State Publication 7101.

existence, we must, in the interests of peace itself, remain vigilant, alert and strong.

I

The Middle East has abruptly reached a new and critical stage in its long and important history. In past decades many of the countries in that area were not fully self-governing. Other nations exercised considerable authority in the area and the security of the region was largely built around their power. But since the First World War there has been a steady evolution toward self-government and independence. This development the United States has welcomed and has encouraged. Our country supports without reservation the full sovereignty and independence of each and every nation in the Middle East.

The evolution to independence has in the main been a peaceful process. But the area has been often troubled. Persistent cross-currents of distrust and fear with raids back and forth across national boundaries have brought about a high degree of instability in much of the Mid East. Just recently there have been hostilities involving Western European nations that once exercised much influence in the area. Also the relatively large attack by Israel in October has intensified the basic differences between that nation and its Arab neighbors. All this instability has been heightened and, at times, manipulated by International Communism.

II

Russia's rulers have long sought to dominate the Middle East. That was true of the Czars and it is true of the Bolsheviks. The reasons are not hard to find. They do not affect Russia's security for no one plans to use the Middle East as a base for aggression against Russia. Never for a moment has the United States entertained such a thought.

The Soviet Union has nothing whatsoever to fear from the United States in the Middle East, or anywhere else in the world, so long as its rulers do not themselves first resort to aggression.

That statement I make solemnly and emphatically.

Neither does Russia's desire to dominate the Middle East spring from its own economic interest in the area. Russia does not appreciably use or depend upon the Suez Canal. In 1955 Soviet traffic through the Canal represented only about there fourths of 1% of the total. The Soviets have no need for, and could provide no market for, the petroleum resources which constitute the principal natural wealth of the area. Indeed, the Soviet Union is a substantial exporter of petroleum products.

The reason for Russia's interest in the Middle East is solely that of power politics. Considering her announced purpose of communizing the world, it is easy to understand her hope of dominating the Middle East.

This region has always been the crossroads of the continents of the Eastern Hemisphere. The Suez Canal enables the nations of Asia and Europe to carry on the commerce that is essential if these countries are to maintain well-rounded and prosperous economies. The Middle East provides a gateway between Eurasia and Africa.

It contains about two thirds of the presently known oil deposits of the world and it normally supplies the petroleum needs of many nations of Europe, Asia and Africa. The nations of Europe are peculiarly dependent upon this supply, and this dependency relates to transportation as well as to production. This has been vividly demonstrated since the closing of the Suez Canal and some of the pipelines. Alternate ways of transportation and, indeed, alternate sources of power can, if necessary, be developed. But these cannot be considered as early prospects.

These things stress the immense importance of the Middle East. If the nations of that area should lose their independence, if they were dominated by alien forces hostile to freedom, that would be both a tragedy for the area and for many free nations whose economic life would be subject to near strangulation. Western Europe would be endangered just as though there had been no Marshall Plan, no North Atlantic Treaty Organization. The free nations of Asia and Africa, too, would be placed in serious jeopardy. And the countries of the Middle East would lose the markets upon which their economies depend. All this would have the most adverse, if not disastrous, effect upon our own nation's economic life and political prospects.

Then there are other factors, which transcend the material. The Middle East is the birthplace of three great religions—Moslem, Christian and Hebrew. Mecca and Jerusalem are more than places on the map. They symbolize religions which teach that the spirit has supremacy over matter and that the individual has a dignity and rights of which no despotic government can rightfully deprive him. It would be intolerable if the holy places of the Middle East should be subjected to a rule that glorifies atheistic materialism.

International Communism, of course, seeks to mask its purposes of domination by expressions of good will and by superficially attractive offers of political, economic and military aid. But any free nation, which is the subject of Soviet enticement, ought, in elementary wisdom, to look behind the mask.

Remember Estonia, Latvia and Lithuania. In 1939 the Soviet Union entered into mutual assistance pacts with these then independent countries;[1] and the Soviet Foreign Minister, addressing the Extra-ordinary Fifth Session of the Supreme Soviet in October 1939, sol-emnly and publicly declared that "we stand for the scrupulous and punctilious observance of the pacts on the basis of complete reciproc-ity, and we declare that all nonsensical talk about the Sovietiza-tion of the Baltic countries is only to the interest of our common enemies and of all anti-Soviet provocateurs."[2] Yet in 1940, Estonia, Latvia and Lithuania were forcibly incorporated into the Soviet Union.[3]

Soviet control of the satellite nations of Eastern Europe has been forcibly maintained in spite of solemn promises of a contrary intent, made during World War II.[4]

Stalin's death brought hope that this pattern would change. And we read the pledge of the Warsaw Treaty of 1955[5] that the Soviet Union would follow in satellite countries "the principles of mutual respect for their independence and sovereignty and non-interference in domestic affairs." But we have just seen the subjugation of Hungary by naked armed force. In the aftermath of this Hungarian tragedy, world respect for and belief in Soviet promises have sunk to a new low. International Communism needs and seeks a recognizable success.

Thus, we have these simple and indisputable facts:

1. The Middle East, which has always been coveted by Russia, would today be prized more than ever by International Communism.
2. The Soviet rulers continue to show that they do not scruple to use any means to gain their ends.
3. The free nations of the Mid East need, and for the most part want, added strength to assure their continued independence.

III

Our thoughts naturally turn to the United Nations as a protector of small nations. Its charter gives it primary responsibility for the

[1] Pact of Sept. 28, 1939, with Estonia (198 LNTS 223); pact of Oct. 5, 1939, with Latvia (ibid., 381); and pact of Oct. 10, 1939, with Lithuania (De-partment of State *Bulletin*, Dec. 16, 1939, pp. 705–707).

[2] *Soviet Peace Policy: Four Speeches by V. Molotov* (London, 1941), p. 36.

[3] Estonia was incorporated in the USSR by a decree of the Supreme Soviet of Aug. 6, 1940; Latvia, by a decree of Aug. 5, 1940; and Lithuania by a decree of Aug. 3, 1940.

[4] See the Declaration on Liberated Europe in the Protocol of Proceedings of the Crimea (Yalta) Conference; *A Decade of American Foreign Policy: Basic Documents, 1941–1949*, p. 29.

[5] Text in *American Foreign Policy, 1950–1955: Basic Documents*, pp. 1239–1242.

maintenance of international peace and security. Our country has given the United Nations its full support in relation to the hostilities in Hungary and in Egypt. The United Nations was able to bring about a cease-fire and withdrawal of hostile forces from Egypt because it was dealing with governments and peoples who had a decent respect for the opinions of mankind as reflected in the United Nations General Assembly. But in the case of Hungary, the situation was different. The Soviet Union vetoed action by the Security Council to require the withdrawal of Soviet armed forces from Hungary. And it has shown callous indifference to the recommendations, even the censure, of the General Assembly. The United Nations can always be helpful, but it cannot be a wholly dependable protector of freedom when the ambitions of the Soviet Union are involved.

IV

Under all the circumstances I have laid before you, a greater responsibility now devolves upon the United States. We have shown, so that none can doubt, our dedication to the principle that force shall not be used internationally for any aggressive purpose and that the integrity and independence of the nations of the Middle East should be inviolate. Seldom in history has a nation's dedication to principle been tested as severely as ours during recent weeks.

There is general recognition in the Middle East, as elsewhere, that the United States does not seek either political or economic domination over any other people. Our desire is a world environment of freedom, not servitude. On the other hand many, if not all, of the nations of the Middle East are aware of the danger that stems from International Communism and welcome closer cooperation with the United States to realize for themselves the United Nations goals of independence, economic well-being and spiritual growth.

If the Middle East is to continue its geographic role of uniting rather than separating East and West; if its vast economic resources are to serve the well-being of the peoples there, as well as that of others: and if its cultures and religions and their shrines are to be preserved for the uplifting of the spirits of the peoples, then the United States must make more evident its willingness to support the independence of the freedom-loving nations of the area.

V

Under these circumstances I deem it necessary to seek the cooperation of the Congress. Only with that cooperation can we give the reassurance needed to deter aggression, to give courage and confidence ·to those who are dedicated to freedom and thus prevent a chain of events which would gravely endanger all of the free world.

There have been several Executive declarations made by the United States in relation to the Middle East. There is the Tripartite Declaration of May 25, 1950,[6] followed by the Presidential assurance of October 31, 1950, to the King of Saudi Arabia.[7] There is the Presidential declaration of April 9, 1956, that the United States will within constitutional means oppose any aggression in the area.[8] There is our Declaration of November 29, 1956, that a threat to the territorial integrity or political independence of Iran, Iraq, Pakistan or Turkey would be viewed by the United States with the utmost gravity.[9]

Nevertheless, weaknesses in the present situation and the increased danger from International Communism, convince me that basic United States policy should now find expression in joint action by the Congress and the Executive. Furthermore, our joint resolve should be so couched as to make it apparent that if need be our words will be backed by action.

VI

It is nothing new for the President and the Congress to join to recognize that the national integrity of other free nations is directly related to our own security.

We have joined to create and support the security system of the United Nations. We have reinforced the collective security system of the United Nations by a series of collective defense arrangements. Today we have security treaties with 42 other nations[10] which recognize that their, and our, peace and security are intertwined. We have joined to take decisive action in relation to Greece and Turkey[11] and in relation to Taiwan.[12]

Thus, the United States through the joint action of the President and the Congress, or, in the case of treaties, the Senate, has manifested in many endangered areas its purpose to support free and independent governments—and peace—against external menace, notably the menace of International Communism. Thereby we have helped to maintain peace and security during a period of great danger. It is now essential that the United States should manifest through joint action

[6] Ibid., p. 2237.

[7] A letter expressing U.S. interest in the independence of Saudi Arabia, delivered by U.S. Ambassador Raymond A. Hare at the time he presented his credentials. [Footnote in source text.]

[8] *American Foreign Policy: Current Documents*, 1956, pp. 592–593.

[9] Ibid., p. 2237.

[10] For a list of these 42 countries, see the map facing p. 788, *American Foreign Policy, 1950–1955: Basic Documents*.

[11] See *A Decade of American Foreign Policy: Basic Documents, 1941–1949*, pp. 1253–1267.

[12] See *American Foreign Policy, 1950–1955: Basic Documents*, pp. 2483–2487.

of the President and the Congress our determination to assist those nations of the Mid East area which desire that assistance.

The action which I propose would have the following features.

It would, first of all, authorize the United States to cooperate with and assist any nation or group of nations in the general area of the Middle East in the development of economic strength dedicated to the maintenance of national independence.

It would, in the second place, authorize the Executive to undertake in the same region programs of military assistance and cooperation with any nation or group of nations which desire such aid.

It would, in the third place, authorize such assistance and cooperation to include the employment of the armed forces of the United States to secure and protect the territorial integrity and political independence of such nations, requesting such aid, against overt armed aggression from any nation controlled by International Communism.

These measures would have to be consonant with the treaty obligations of the United States, including the Charter of the United Nations and with any action or recommendations of the United Nations. They would also, if armed attack occurs, be subject to the overriding authority of the United Nations Security Council in accordance with the Charter.

The present proposal would, in the fourth place, authorize the President to employ, for economic and defensive military purposes, sums available under the Mutual Security Act of 1954, as amended,[13] without regard to existing limitations.

The legislation now requested should not include the authorization or appropriation of funds because I believe that, under the conditions I suggest, presently appropriated funds will be adequate for the balance of the present fiscal year ending June 30. I shall, however, seek in subsequent legislation the authorization of $200,000,000 to be available during each of the fiscal years 1958 and 1959 for discretionary use in the area,[14] in addition to the other mutual security programs for the area hereafter provided for by the Congress.

VII

This program will not solve all the problems of the Middle East. Neither does it represent the totality of our policies for the area. There are the problems of Palestine and relations between Israel and the Arab States, and the future of the Arab refugees. There

[13] See sec. 401 (a) of the Mutual Security Act of 1954, as amended through 1955 (*American Foreign Policy, 1950–1955: Basic Documents*, p. 3119); and sec. 8 (a) of the Mutual Security Act of 1956 (*American Foreign Policy: Current Documents, 1956*, p. 1269).

[14] See the president's message of May 21, 1957, to Congress requesting appropriations for the Mutual Security Program for FY 1958; *post*, doc. 487.

is the problem of the future status of the Suez Canal. These difficulties are aggravated by International Communism, but they would exist quite apart from that threat. It is not the purpose of the legislation I propose to deal directy with these problems. The United Nations has made clear, notably by Secretary Dulles' address of August 26, 1955,[15] that we are willing to do much to assist the United Nations in solving the basic problems of Palestine.

The proposed legislation is primarily designed to deal with the possibility of Communist aggression, direct and indirect. There is imperative need that any lack of power in the area should be made good, not by external or alien force, but by the increased vigor and security of the independent nations of the area.

Experience shows that indirect aggression rarely if ever succeeds where there is reasonable security against direct aggression; where the government possesses loyal security forces, and where economic conditions are such as not to make Communism seem an attractive alternative. The program I suggest deals with all three aspects of this matter and thus with the problem of indirect aggression.

It is my hope and belief that if our purpose be proclaimed, as proposed by the requested legislation, that very fact will serve to halt any contemplated aggression. We shall have heartened the patriots who are dedicated to the independence of their nations. They will not feel that they stand alone, under the menace of great power. And I should add that patriotism is, throughout this area, a powerful sentiment. It is true that fear sometimes perverts true patriotism into fanaticism and to the acceptance of dangerous enticements from without. But if that fear can be allayed, then the climate will be more favorable to the attainment of worthy national ambitions.

And as I have indicated, it will also be necessary for us to contribute economically to strengthen those countries, or groups of countries, which have governments manifestly dedicated to the preservation of independence and resistance to subversion. Such measures will provide the greatest insurance against Communist inroads. Words alone are not enough.

VIII

Let me refer again to the requested authority to employ the armed forces of the United States to assist to defend the territorial integrity and the political independence of any nation in the area against Communist armed aggression. Such authority would not be exercised except at the desire of the nation attacked. Beyond this it is my profound hope that this authority would never have to be exercised at all.

[15] Text in *American Foreign Policy, 1950–1955: Basic Documents*, pp. 2176–2180.

Nothing is more necessary to assure this than that our policy with respect to the defense of the area be promptly and clearly deter- mined and declared. Thus the United Nations and all friendly govern- ments, and indeed governments which are not friendly, will know where we stand.

If, contrary to my hope and expectation, a situation arose which called for the military application of the policy which I ask the Con- gress to join me in proclaiming, I would of course maintain hour-by- hour contact with the Congress if it were in session. And if the Con- gress were not in session, and if the situation had grave implications, I would, of course, at once call the Congress into special session.

In the situation now existing, the greatest risk, as is often the case, is that ambitious despots may miscalculate. If power-hungry Communists should either falsely or correctly estimate that the Middle East is inadequately defended, they might be tempted to use open measures of armed attack. If so, that would start a chain of circum- stances which would almost surely involve the United States in mili- tary action. I am convinced that the best insurance against this danger- ous contingency is to make clear now our readiness to cooperate fully and freely with our friends of the Middle East in ways consonant with the purposes and principles of the United Nations. I intend promptly to send a special mission to the Middle East to explain the cooperation we are prepared to give.[16]

IX

The policy which I outline involves certain burdens and indeed risks for the United States. Those who covet the area will not like what is proposed. Already, they are grossly distorting our purpose. However, before this Americans have seen our nation's vital interests and human freedom in jeopardy, and their fortitude and resolution have been equal to the crisis, regardless of hostile distortion of our words, motives and actions.

Indeed, the sacrifices of the American people in the cause of free- dom have, even since the close of World War II, been measured in many billions of dollars and in thousands of the precious lives of our youth. These sacrifices, by which great areas of the world have been preserved to freedom, must not be thrown away.

In those momentous periods of the past, the President and the Congress have united, without partisanship, to serve the vital interests of the United States and of the free world.

[16] See *post*, doc. 207.

APPENDIX E

Inaugural Address
of President John F. Kennedy

Mr. Chief Justice, President Eisenhower, Vice President Nixon, President Truman, reverend clergy, fellow citizens, we observe today not a victory of party, but a celebration of freedom—symbolizing an end as well as a beginning—signifying renewal, as well as change. For I have sworn before you and Almighty God the same solemn oath our forebears prescribed nearly a century and three quarters ago.

The world is very different now. For man holds in his mortal hands the power to abolish all forms of human poverty and all forms of human life. And yet the same revolutionary beliefs for which our forebears fought are still at issue around the globe—the belief that the rights of man come not from the generosity of the state, but from the hand of God.

We dare not forget today that we are the heirs of that first revolution. Let the word go forth from this time and place, to friend and foe alike, that the torch has been passed to a new generation of Americans—born in this century, tempered by war, disciplined by a hard and bitter peace, proud of our ancient heritage—and unwilling to witness or permit the slow undoing of those human rights to which this Nation has always been committed, and to which we are committed today at home and around the world.

Let every nation know, whether it wishes us well or ill, that we shall pay any price, bear any burden, meet any hardship, support

Delivered by President John F. Kennedy at the Capitol, Washington, D.C., on January 20, 1961; printed as Document No. 9, Senate, 87th Congress, 1st Session, 1961.

any friend, oppose any foe, in order to assure the survival and the success of liberty.

This we pledge—and more.

To those old allies whose cultural and spiritual origins we share, we pledge the loyalty of faithful friends. United, there is little we cannot do in a host of cooperative ventures. Divided, there is little we can do—for we dare not meet a powerful challenge at odds and split asunder.

To those new States whom we welcome to the ranks of the free, we pledge our words that one form of colonial control shall not have passed away merely to be replaced by a far greater iron tyranny. We shall not always expect to find them supporting our view. But we shall always hope to find them strongly supporting their own freedom—and to remember that, in the past, those who foolishly sought power by riding the back of the tiger ended up inside.

To those peoples in the huts and villages across the globe struggling to break the bonds of mass misery, we pledge our best efforts to help them help themselves, for whatever period is required—not because the Communists may be doing it, not because we seek their votes, but because it is right. If a free society cannot help the many who are poor, it cannot save the few who are rich.

To our sister republics south of our border, we offer a special pledge—to convert our good words into good deeds, in a new alliance for progress, to assist free men and free governments in casting off the chains of poverty. But this peaceful revolution of hope cannot become the prey of hostile powers. Let all our neighbors know that we shall join with them to oppose aggression or subversion anywhere in the Americas. And let every other power know that this hemisphere intends to remain the master of its own house.

To that world assembly of sovereign states, the United Nations, our last best hope in an age where the instruments of war have far outpaced the instruments of peace, we renew our pledge of support—to prevent it from becoming merely a forum for invective—to strengthen its shield of the new and the weak—and to enlarge the area in which its writ may run.

Finally, to those nations who would make themselves our adversary, we offer not a pledge but a request: that both sides begin anew the quest for peace, before the dark powers of destruction unleashed by science engulf all humanity in planned or accidental self-destruction.

We dare not tempt them with weakness. For only when our arms are sufficient beyond doubt can we be certain beyond doubt that they will never be employed.

But neither can two great and powerful groups of nations take comfort from our present course—both sides overburdened by the cost of modern weapons, both rightly alarmed by the steady spread of the deadly atom, yet both racing to alter that uncertain balance of terror that stays the hand of mankind's final war.

So let us begin anew—remembering on both sides that civility is not a sign of weakness, and sincerity is always subject to proof. Let us never negotiate out of fear. But let us never fear to negotiate.

Let both sides explore what problems unite us instead of laboring those problems which divide us.

Let both sides, for the first time, formulate serious and precise proposals for the inspection and control of arms—and bring the absolute power to destroy other nations under the absolute control of all nations.

Let both sides seek to invoke the wonders of science instead of its terrors. Together let us explore the stars, conquer the deserts, eradicate disease, tap the ocean depths, and encourage the arts and commerce.

Let both sides unite to heed in all corners of the earth the command of Isaiah—to "undo the heavy burdens and to let the oppressed go free."

And if a beachhead of cooperation may push back the jungle of suspicion, let both sides join in creating a new endeavor, not a new balance of power, but a new world of law, where the strong are just and the weak secure and the peace preserved.

All this will not be finished in the first 100 days. Nor will it be finished in the first 1,000 days, nor in the life of this administration, nor even perhaps in our lifetime on this planet. But let us begin.

In your hands, my fellow citizens, more than in mine, will rest the final success or failure of our course. Since this country was founded, each generation of Americans have been summoned to give testimony to its national loyalty. The graves of young Americans who answered the call to service are found around the globe.

Now the trumpet summons us again—not as a call to bear arms, though arms we need; not as a call to battle, though embattled we are; but a call to bear the burden of a long twilight struggle, year in, and year out, "rejoicing in hope, patient in tribulation"—a struggle against the common enemies of man: tyranny, poverty, disease, and war itself.

Can we forge against these enemies a grand and global alliance, North and South, East and West, that can assure a more fruitful life for all mankind? Will you join in that historic effort?

In the long history of the world, only a few generations have been granted the role of defending freedom in its hour of maximum danger. I do not shrink from this responsiblity—I welcome it. I do not believe that any of us would exchange places with any other people or any other generation. The energy, the faith, the devotion which we bring to this endeavor will light our country and all who serve it—and the glow from that fire can truly light the world.

And so, my fellow Americans, ask not what your country can do for you: Ask what you can do for your country.

My fellow citizens of the world: Ask not what America will do for you, but what together we can do for the freedom of man.

Finally, whether you are citizens of America or citizens of the world, ask of us the same high standards of strength and sacrifice which we ask of you. With a good conscience our only sure reward, with history the final judge of our deeds, let us go forth to lead the land we love, asking His blessing and His help, but knowing that here on earth God's work must truly be our own.

APPENDIX F

An Excerpt from President Lyndon B. Johnson's Broadcast to the Nation

THE HEART OF U.S. INVOLVEMENT

But let it never be forgotten: Peace will come also because America sent her sons to help secure it.

It has not been easy—far from it. During the past 4½ years, it has been my fate and my responsibility to be Commander in Chief. I have lived daily and nightly with the cost of this war. I know the pain that it has inflicted. I know perhaps better than anyone the misgivings that it has aroused.

Throughout this entire long period, I have been sustained by a single principle: that what we are doing now in Viet-Nam is vital to the security of every American.

Surely we have treaties which we must respect. Surely we have commitments that we are going to keep. Resolutions of the Congress testify to the need to resist aggression in the world and in Southeast Asia.

But the heart of our involvement in South Vietnam under three different Presidents, three separate administrations—has always been America's own security.

And the larger purpose of our involvement has always been to help the nations of South Asia become independent and stand alone, self-sustaining as members of a great world community—at peace with themselves and at peace with all others.

With such an Asia, our country—and the world—will be far more secure than it is tonight.

Delivered by President Lyndon B. Johnson on March 31, 1968; printed as Department of State Publication 8376.

I believe that a peaceful Asia is far nearer to reality because of what America has done in Viet-Nam. I believe that the men who endure the dangers of battle—fighting there for us tonight—are helping the entire world avoid far greater conflicts, far wider wars, far more destruction than this one.

The peace that will bring them home some day will come. Tonight I have offered the first in which I hope will be a series of mutual moves toward peace.

I pray that it will not be rejected by the leaders of North Viet-Nam. I pray that they will accept it as a means by which the sacrifices of their own people may be ended. And I ask your help and your support, my fellow citizens, for this effort to reach across the battlefield toward an early peace.

A CALL FOR NATIONAL UNITY

Finally, my fellow Americans, let me say this:

Of those to whom much is given, much is asked. I cannot say, and no man could say, that no more will be asked of us.

Yet, I believe that now, no less than when the decade began, this generation of Americans is willing to "pay any price, bear any burden, meet any hardship, support any friend, oppose any foe to assure the survival and the success of liberty." Since those words were spoken by John F. Kennedy, the people of America have kept that compact with mankind's noblest cause.

And we shall continue to keep it.

Yet I believe that we must always be mindful of this one thing, whatever the trials and the tests ahead: The ultimate strength of our country and our cause will lie not in powerful weapons or infinite resources or boundless wealth but will lie in the unity of our people.

This I believe very deeply.

Throughout my entire public career I have followed the personal philosophy that I am a free man, an American, a public servant, and a member of my party, in that order always and only.

For 37 years in the service of our nation, first as a Congressman, as a Senator, and as Vice President, and now as your President, I have put the unity of the people first. I have put it ahead of any divisive partisanship.

And in these times as in times before, it is true that a house divided against itself by the spirit of faction, of party, of region, of religion, of race, is a house that cannot stand.

There is division in the American house now. There is divisiveness among us all tonight. And holding the trust that is mine, as President of all the people, I cannot disregard the peril to the progress of the American people and the hope and the prospect of peace for all peoples.

So I would ask all Americans, whatever their personal interests or concern, to guard against divisiveness and all its ugly consequences.

Fifty-two months and 10 days ago, in a moment of tragedy and trauma, the duties of this office fell upon me. I asked then for your help and God's, that we might continue America on its course, binding up our wounds, healing our history, moving forward in new unity, to clear the American agenda and to keep the American commitment for all of our people.

United we have kept that commitment. United we have enlarged that commitment.

Through all time to come, I think America will be a stronger nation, a more just society, and a land of greater opportunity and fulfillment because of what we have all done together in these years of unparalleled achievement.

Our reward will come in the life of freedom, peace, and hope that our children will enjoy through ages ahead.

What we won when all of our people united just must not now be lost in suspicion, distrust, selfishness, and politics among any of our people.

Believing this as I do, I have concluded that I should not permit the Presidency to become involved in the partisan divisions that are developing in this political year.

With America's sons in the fields far away, with America's future under challenge right here at home, with our hopes and the world's hopes for peace in the balance every day, I do not believe that I should devote an hour or a day of my time to any personal partisan causes or to any duties other than the awesome duties of this Office—the Presidency of your country.

Accordingly, I shall not seek, and I will not accept, the nomination of my party for another term as your President.

But let men everywhere know, however, that a strong, a confident, and a vigilant America stands ready tonight to seek an honorable peace—and stands ready tonight to defend an honored cause—whatever the price, whatever the burden, whatever the sacrifices that duty may require.

Thank you for listening.

Good night and God bless all of you.

APPENDIX G
The Nixon Doctrine

INTRODUCTION

A nation needs many qualities, but it needs faith and confidence above all. Skeptics do not build societies; the idealists are the builders. Only societies that believe in themselves can rise to their challenges. Let us not, then, pose a false choice between meeting our responsibilities abroad and meeting the needs of our people at home. We shall meet both or we shall meet neither.

The President's Remarks at the Air Force Academy
Commencement, *June 4, 1969*

When I took office, the most immediate problem facing our nation was the war in Vietnam. No question has more occupied our thoughts and energies during this past year.

Yet the fundamental task confronting us was more profound. We could see that the whole pattern of international politics was changing. Our challenge was to understand that change, to define America's goals for the next period, and to set in motion policies to achieve them. For all Americans must understand that because of its strength, its history and its concern for human dignity, this nation occupies a special place in the world. Peace and progress are impossible without a major American role.

This first annual report on U.S. foreign policy is more than a record of one year. It is this Administration's statement of a new

A report to Congress by President Richard M. Nixon on February 18, 1970. Printed as *United States Foreign Policy for the 1970's.*

approach to foreign policy, to match a new era of international relations.

A NEW ERA

The postwar period in international relations has ended.

Then, we were the only great power whose society and economy had escaped World War II's massive destruction. Today, the ravages of that war have been overcome. Western Europe and Japan have recovered their economic strength, their political vitality, and their national self-confidence. Once the recipients of American aid, they have now begun to share their growing resources with the developing world. Once almost totally dependent on American military power, our European allies now play a greater role in our common policies, commensurate with their growing strength.

Then, new nations were being born, often in turmoil and uncertainty. Today, these nations have a new spirit and a growing strength of independence. Once, many feared that they would become simply a battleground of cold-war rivalry and fertile ground for Communist penetration. But this fear misjudged their pride in their national identities and their determination to preserve their newly won sovereignty.

Then, we were confronted by a monolithic Communist world. Today, the nature of that world has changed—the power of individual Communist nations has grown, but international Communist unity has been shattered. Once a unified bloc, its solidarity has been broken by the powerful forces of nationalism. The Soviet Union and Communist China, once bound by an alliance of friendship, had become bitter adversaries by the mid-1960's. The only times the Soviet Union has used the Red Army since World War II have been against its own allies—in East Germany in 1953, in Hungary in 1956, and in Czechoslovakia in 1968. The Marxist dream of international Communist unity has disintegrated.

Then, the United States had a monopoly or overwhelming superiority of nuclear weapons. Today, a revolution in the technology of war has altered the nature of the military balance of power. New types of weapons present new dangers. Communist China has acquired thermonuclear weapons. Both the Soviet Union and the United States have acquired the ability to inflict unacceptable damage on the other, no matter which strikes first. There can be no gain and certainly no victory for the power that provokes a thermonuclear exchange. Thus, both sides have recognized a vital mutual interest in halting the dangerous momentum of the nuclear arms race.

Then, the slogans formed in the past century were the ideological accessories of the intellectual debate. Today, the "isms" have lost their vitality—indeed the restlessness of youth on both sides of the dividing line testifies to the need for a new idealism and deeper purposes.

This is the challenge of the opportunity before America as it enters the 1970's.

THE FRAMEWORK FOR A DURABLE PEACE

In the first postwar decades, American energies were absorbed in coping with a cycle of recurrent crises, whose fundamental origins lay in the destruction of World War II and the tensions attending the emergence of scores of new nations. Our opportunity today—and challenge—is to get at the causes of crises, to take a longer view, and to help build the international relationships that will provide the framework of a durable peace.

I have often reflected on the meaning of "peace," and have reached one certain conclusion: Peace must be far more than the absence of war. Peace must provide a durable structure of international relationships which inhibits or removes the causes of war. Building a lasting peace requires a foreign policy guided by three basic principles:

- Peace requires *partnership*. Its obligations, like its benefits, must be shared. This concept of partnership guides our relations with all friendly nations.

- Peace requires *strength*. So long as there are those who would threaten our vital interests and those of our allies with military force, we must be strong. American weakness could tempt would-be aggressors to make dangerous miscalculations. At the same time, our own strength is important only in relation to the strength of others. We—like others—must place high priority on enhancing our security through cooperative arms control.

- Peace requires a *willingness to negotiate*. All nations—and we are no exception—have important national interests to protect. But the most fundamental interest of all nations lies in building the structure of peace. In partnership with our allies, secure in our own strength, we will seek those areas in which we can agree among ourselves and with others to accommodate conflicts and overcome rivalries. We are working toward the day when all nations will have a stake in peace, and will therefore be partners in its maintenance.

Within such a structure, international disputes can be settled and clashes contained. The insecurity of nations, out of which so much conflict arises, will be eased, and the habits of moderation and compromise will be nurtured. Most important, a durable peace will give full opportunity to the powerful forces driving toward economic change and social justice.

This vision of a peace built on partnership, strength and willingness to negotiate is the unifying theme of this report. In the sections that follow, the first steps we have taken during this past year—the policies we have devised and the programs we have initiated to realize this vision—are placed in the context of these three principles.

1. PEACE THROUGH PARTNERSHIP—
THE NIXON DOCTRINE

As I said in my address of November 3, "We Americans are a do-it-yourself people—an impatient people. Instead of teaching someone else to do a job, we like to do it ourselves. This trait has been carried over into our foreign policy."

The postwar era of American foreign policy began in this vein in 1947 with the proclamation of the Truman Doctrine and the Marshall Plan, offering American economic and military assistance to countries threatened by aggression. Our policy held that democracy and prosperity, buttressed by American military strength and organized in a worldwide network of American-led alliances, would insure stability and peace. In the formative years of the postwar period, this great effort of international political and economic reconstruction was a triumph of American leadership and imagination, especially in Europe.

For two decades after the end of the Second World War, our foreign policy was guided by such a vision and inspired by its success. The vision was based on the fact that the United States was the richest and most stable country, without whose initiative and resources little security or progress was possible.

This impulse carried us through into the 1960's. The United States conceived programs and ran them. We devised strategies, and proposed them to our allies. We discerned dangers, and acted directly to combat them.

The world has dramatically changed since the days of the Marshall Plan. We deal now with a world of stronger allies, a community of independent developing nations, and a Communist world still hostile but now divided.

Others now have the ability and responsibility to deal with local disputes which once might have required our intervention. Our contribution and success will depend not on the frequency of our involvement in the affairs of others, but on the stamina of our policies. This is the approach which will best encourage other nations to do their part, and will most genuinely enlist the support of the American people.

This is the message of the doctrine I announced at Guam—the "Nixon Doctrine." Its central thesis is that the United States will participate in the defense and development of allies and friends, but that America cannot—and will not—conceive all the plans, design all the programs, execute all the decisions and undertake all the defense of the free nations of the world. We will help where it makes a real difference and is considered in our interest.

America cannot live in isolation if it expects to live in peace. We have no intention of withdrawing from the world. The only issue before us is how we can be most effective in meeting our responsibilities, protecting our interests, and thereby building peace.

A more responsible participation by our foreign friends in their own defense and progress means a more effective common effort toward the goals we all seek. Peace in the world will continue to require us to maintain our commitments—and we will. As I said at the United Nations, "It is not my belief that the way to peace is by giving up our friends or letting down our allies." But a more balanced and realistic American role in the world is essential if American commitments are to be sustained over the long pull. In my State of the Union Address, I affirmed that "to insist that other nations play a role is not a retreat from responsibility; it is a sharing of responsibility." This is not a way for America to withdraw from its indispensable role in the world. It is a way—the only way—we can carry out our responsibilities.

It is misleading, moreover, to pose the fundamental question so largely in terms of commitments. Our objective, in the first instance, is to support our interests over the long run with a sound foreign policy. The more that policy is based on a realistic assessment of our and others' interests, the more effective our role in the world can be. We are not involved in the world because we have commitments; we have commitments because we are involved. Our interests must shape our commitments, rather than the other way around.

We will view new commitments in the light of a careful assessment of our own national interests and those of other countries, of the specific threats to those interests, and of our capacity to counter those threats at an acceptable risk and cost.

We have been guided by these concepts during the past year in our dealings with free nations throughout the world.

- In Europe, our policies embody precisely the three principles of a durable peace: partnership, continued strength to defend our common interests when challenged, and willingness to negotiate differences with adversaries.
- Here in the Western Hemisphere we seek to strengthen our special relationship with our sister republics through a new program of action for progress in which all voices are heard and none predominates.
- In Asia, here the Nixon Doctrine was enunciated, partnership will have special meaning for our policies—as evidenced by our strengthened ties with Japan. Our cooperation with Asian nations

will be enhanced as they cooperate with one another and develop regional institutions.

- In Vietnam, we seek a just settlement which all parties to the conflict, and all Americans, can support. We are working closely with the South Vietnamese to strengthen their ability to defend themselves. As South Vietnam grows stronger, the other side will, we hope, soon realize that it becomes ever more in their interest to negotiate a just peace.

- In the Middle East, we shall continue to work with others to establish a possible framework within which the parties to the Arab-Israeli conflict can negotiate the complicated and difficult questions at issue. Others must join us in recognizing that a settlement will require sacrifices and restraints by all concerned.

- Africa, with its historic ties to so many of our own citizens, must always retain a significant place in our partnership with the new nations. Africans will play the major role in fulfilling their just aspirations—an end to racialism, the building of new nations, freedom from outside interference, and cooperative economic development. But we will add our efforts to theirs to help realize Africa's great potential.

- In an ever more interdependent world economy, American foreign policy will emphasize the freer flow of capital and goods between nations. We are proud to have participated in the successful cooperative effort which created Special Drawing Rights, a form of international money which will help insure the stability of the monetary structure on which the continued expansion of trade depends.

- The great effort of economic development must engage the cooperation of all nations. We are carefully studying the specific goals of our economic assistance programs and how most effectively to reach them.

- Unprecedented scientific and technological advances as well as explosions in population, communications, and knowledge require new forms of international cooperation. The United Nations, the symbol of international partnership, will receive our continued strong support as it marks its 25th Anniversary.

2. AMERICA'S STRENGTH

The second element of a durable peace must be America's strength. Peace, we have learned, cannot be gained by good will alone.

In determining the strength of our defenses, we must make precise and crucial judgments. We should spend no more than is necessary. But there is an irreducible minimum of essential military security: for if we are less strong than necessary, and if the worst happens, there will be no domestic society to look after. The magnitude of such a catastrophe, and the reality of the opposing military power that could threaten it, present a risk which requires of any President the most searching and careful attention to the state of our defenses.

The changes in the world since 1945 have altered the context and requirements of our defense policy. In this area, perhaps more than in any other, the need to reexamine our approaches is urgent and constant.

The last 25 years have seen a revolution in the nature of military power. In fact, there has been a series of transformations—from the atomic to the thermonuclear weapon, from the strategic bomber to the intercontinental ballistic missile, from the surface missile to the hardened silo and the missile-carrying submarine, from the single to the multiple warhead, and from air defense to missile defense. We are now entering an era in which the sophistication and destructiveness of weapons present more formidable and complex issues affecting our strategic posture.

The last 25 years have also seen an important change in the relative balance of strategic power. From 1945 to 1949, we were the only nation in the world possessing an arsenal of atomic weapons. From 1950 to 1966, we possessed an overwhelming superiority in strategic weapons. From 1967 to 1969, we retained a significant superiority. Today, the Soviet Union possesses a powerful and sophisticated strategic force approaching our own. We must consider, too, that Communist China will deploy its own intercontinental missiles during the coming decade, introducing new and complicating factors for our strategic planning and diplomacy.

In the light of these fateful changes, the Administration undertook a comprehensive and far-reaching reconsideration of the premises and procedures for designing our forces. We sought—and I believe we have achieved—a rational and coherent formulation of our defense strategy and requirements for the 1970's.

The importance of comprehensive planning of policy and objective scrutiny of programs is clear:

- Because of the lead-time in building new strategic systems, the decisions we make today substantially determine our military posture—and thus our security—five years from now. This places a premium on foresight and planning.
- Because the allocation of national resources between defense programs and other national programs is itself an issue of policy, it must be considered on a systematic basis at the early stages of the national security planning process.
- Because we are a leader of the Atlantic Alliance, our doctrine and forces are crucial to the policy and planning of NATO. The mutual confidence that holds the allies together depends on understanding, agreement, and coordination among the 15 sovereign nations of the Treaty.

- Because our security depends not only on our own strategic strength, but also on cooperative efforts to provide greater security for everyone through arms control, planning weapons systems and planning for arms control negotiations must be closely integrated.

For these reasons, this Administration has established procedures for the intensive scrutiny of defense issues in the light of overall national priorities. We have re-examined our strategic forces; we have reassessed our general purpose forces; and we have engaged in the most painstaking preparation ever undertaken by the United States Government for arms control negotiations.

3. WILLINGNESS TO NEGOTIATE—AN ERA OF NEGOTIATION

Partnership and strength are two of the pillars of the structure of a durable peace. Negotiation is the third. For our commitment to peace is most convincingly demonstrated in our willingness to negotiate our points of difference in a fair and businesslike manner with the Communist countries.

We are under no illusions. We know that there are enduring ideological differences. We are aware of the difficulty in moderating tensions that arise from the clash of national interests. These differences will not be dissipated by changes of atmosphere or dissolved in cordial personal relations between statesmen. They involve strong convictions and contrary philosophies, necessities of national security, and the deep-seated differences of perspectives formed by geography and history.

The United States, like any other nation, has interests of its own, and will defend those interests. But any nation today must define its interests with special concern for the interests of others. If some nations define their security in a manner that means insecurity for other nations, then peace is threatened and the security of all is diminished. This obligation is particularly great for the nuclear superpowers on whose decisions the survival of mankind may well depend.

The United States is confident that tensions can be eased and the danger of war reduced by patient and precise efforts to reconcile conflicting interests on concrete issues. Coexistence demands more than a spirit of good will. It requires the definition of positive goals which can be sought and achieved cooperatively. It requires real progress toward resolution of specific differences. This is our objective.

As the Secretary of State said on December 6:

> We will continue to probe every available opening that offers a prospect for better East-West relations, for the resolution of problems large or small, for greater security for all.
>
> In this the United States will continue to play an active role in concert with our allies.

This is the spirit in which the United States ratified the Non-Proliferation Treaty and entered into negotiation with the Soviet Union on control of the military use of the seabeds, on the framework of a settlement in the Middle East, and on limitation of strategic arms. This is the basis on which we and our Atlantic allies have offered to negotiate on concrete issues affecting the security and future of Europe, and on which the United States took steps last year to improve our relations with nations of Eastern Europe. This is also the spirit in which we have resumed formal talks in Warsaw with Communist China. No nation need be our permanent enemy.

AMERICA'S PURPOSE

These policies were conceived as a result of change, and we know they will be tested by the change that lies ahead. The world of 1970 was not predicted a decade ago, and we can be certain that the world of 1980 will render many current views obsolete.

The source of America's historic greatness has been our ability to see what had to be done, and then to do it. I believe America now has the chance to move the world closer to a durable peace. And I know that Americans working with each other and with other nations can make our vision real.

SELECTED BIBLIOGRAPHY

ALLISON, GRAHAM T. *Essence of Decision.* Boston, Mass.: Little, Brown, 1971.

ALPEROVITZ, GAR. *Atomic Diplomacy: Hiroshima and Potsdam.* New York: Vintage, 1967.

ARMACOST, MICHAEL H. *The Foreign Relations of the United States.* Belmont, Calif.: Dickenson, 1969.

BRANDON, DONALD. *American Foreign Policy.* New York: Appleton, 1966.

BRZEZINSKI, ZBIGNIEW. *Between Two Ages: America's Role in the Technetronic Era.* New York: Viking, 1970.

CARLETON, WILLIAM G. *The Revolution in American Foreign Policy.* New York: Random House, 1957.

COHEN, BERNARD C., ed. *Foreign Policy in American Government.* Boston, Mass.: Little, Brown, 1965.

CRABB, CECIL V., JR. *American Foreign Policy in the Nuclear Age.* New York: Harper & Row, 1972.

DE RIVERA, JOSEPH H. *The Psychological Dimension of Foreign Policy.* Columbus, Ohio: Merrill, 1968.

DESTLER, I. M. *Presidents, Bureaucrats, and Foreign Policy.* Princeton, N.J.: Princeton University Press, 1974.

DOUGHERTY, JAMES E., and PFALTZGRAFF, ROBERT L., JR. *Contending Theories of International Relations.* Philadelphia, Pa.: Lippincott, 1971.

EKIRCH, AUTHUR A., JR. *Ideas, Ideals, and American Diplomacy.* New York: Appleton, 1966.

FEDDER, EDWIN H. *NATO: The Dynamics of Alliance in the Postwar World.* New York: Dodd, Mead, 1973.

FERRELL, ROBERT H. *American Diplomacy.* New York: Norton, 1969.

FRANKEL, JOSEPH. *The Making of Foreign Policy.* London: Oxford University Press, 1963.

FULBRIGHT, J. WILLIAM. *The Pentagon Propaganda Machine.* New York: Vintage, 1971.

FURNISS, EDGAR S., JR., and SNYDER, RICHARD C. *An Introduction to American Foreign Policy*. New York: Holt, Rinehart & Winston, 1959.

GLICK, EDWARD B. *Peaceful Conflict*. Harrisburg, Pa.: Stackpole Books, 1967.

HALPER, THOMAS. *Foreign Policy Crisis*. Columbus, Ohio: Merrill, 1971.

HALPERIN, MORTON H. *Defense Strategies for the Seventies*. Boston: Little, Brown, 1971.

HAMMOND, PAUL Y. *The Cold War Years: American Foreign Policy Since 1945*. New York: Harcourt Brace Jovanovich, 1969.

HERMANN, CHARLES F. *Crises in Foreign Policy*. Indianapolis, Ind.: Bobbs-Merrill, 1969.

HIRSCHFIELD, ROBERT W., ed. *The Power of the Presidency: Concepts and Controversy*. New York: Atherton, 1968.

HOFFMANN, STANLEY. *Gulliver's Troubles*. New York: McGraw-Hill, 1968.

HOOPES, TOWNSEND. *The Limits of Intervention*. New York: McKay, 1969.

HOWARD, MICHAEL. *Studies in War and Peace*. New York: Viking, 1970.

JACOBSON, HAROLD K., and ZIMMERMAN, WILLIAM, eds. *The Shaping of Foreign Policy*. New York: Atherton, 1969.

JANIS, IRVING L. *Victims of Groupthink*. Boston, Mass.: Houghton Mifflin, 1972.

JOHNSON, DONALD B., and WALKER, JACK, eds. *The Dynamics of the American Presidency*. New York: Wiley, 1964.

JOHNSON, RICHARD A. *The Administration of United States Foreign Policy*. Austin, Tex.: University of Texas Press, 1971.

KISSINGER, HENRY A. *American Foreign Policy*. New York: Norton, 1969.

KLARE, MICHAEL T. *War Without End*. New York: Vintage, 1972.

LEFEVER, ERNEST. *Ethics and United States Foreign Policy*. New York: Living Age Books, 1957.

LEGG, KEITH R., and MORRISON, JAMES F. *Politics and the International System*. New York: Harper & Row, 1971.

LERCHE, CHARLES O., JR. *America in World Affairs*. New York: McGraw-Hill, 1967.

LONDON, KURT. *The Making of Foreign Policy*. Philadelphia, Pa.: Lippincott, 1965.

LOVELL, JOHN P. *Foreign Policy in Perspective*. New York: Holt, Rinehart & Winston, 1970.

MCLELLAN, DAVID S. *The Cold War in Transition*. New York: Macmillan, 1966.

MORGENTHAU, HANS J. *A New Foreign Policy for the United States*. New York: Praeger, 1970.

MOSHER, FREDERICK C., and HARR, JOHN E. *Programming Systems and Foreign Affairs Leadership*. New York: Oxford University Press, 1970.

NELSON, JOAN M. *Aid, Influence, and Foreign Policy*. New York: Macmillan, 1968.

NUECHTERLEIN, DONALD E. *United States National Interests in a Changing World*. Lexington, Ky.: University of Kentucky Press, 1973.

PADOVER, SAUL K. *Understanding Foreign Policy*. New York: Public Affairs Committee, Inc., 1959.

RADWAY, LAURENCE I. *Foreign Policy and National Defense*. Glenview, Ill.: Scott, Foresman, 1969.

RAINEY, GENE E., ed. *Contemporary American Foreign Policy: The Official Voice*. Columbus, Ohio: Merrill, 1969.

RAPOPORT, ANATOL. *The Big Two*. New York: Pegasus, 1971.

ROBINSON, JAMES A. *Congress and Foreign Policy-Making.* Homewood, Ill.: Dorsey Press, 1967.

ROCHE, JOHN P., and LEVY, LEONARD W. *The Presidency.* Harcourt Brace Jovanovich, 1964.

ROSENAU, JAMES N., ed. *Domestic Sources of Foreign Policy.* New York: Free Press, 1967.

ROSENAU, JAMES N., ed. *Linkage Politics.* New York: Free Press, 1969.

ROURKE, FRANCIS E. *Bureaucracy, Politics and Public Policy.* Boston, Mass.: Little, Brown, 1969.

SAPIN, BURTON M. *The Making of United States Foreign Policy.* New York: Praeger, 1966.

SCOTT, ANDREW M. *The Revolution in Statecraft.* New York: Random House, 1965.

SEABURY, PAUL. *The United States in World Affairs.* New York: McGraw-Hill, 1973.

SPANIER, JOHN W. *American Foreign Policy Since World War II.* New York: Praeger, 1968.

SPANIER, JOHN W., and USLANDER, ERIC M. *How American Foreign Policy Is Made.* New York: Praeger, 1974.

SNYDER, RICHARD C.; BRUCK, H. W.; and SAPIN, BURTON. *Foreign Policy Decision-Making.* New York: Free Press, 1962.

STUPAK, RONALD J. *The Shaping of Foreign Policy: The Role of the Secretary of State as Seen by Dean Acheson.* New York: Bobbs-Merrill, Odyssey, 1969.

WILKINSON, DAVID O. *Comparative Foreign Relations.* Belmont, Calif.: Dickenson, 1969.

WOLF, CHARLES, JR. *United States Policy and the Third World.* Boston: Little, Brown, 1967.

YARMOLINSKY, ADAM. *The Military Establishment.* New York: Harper & Row, 1971.

INDEX